REEDS MARINA GUIDE 2018

The source directory for all sail & power boat owners

© Adlard Coles Nautical 2017

Adlard Coles Nautical,
50 Bedford Square, London W1B 3DP
Tel: 0207 631 5600
Fax: 0207 631 5800
e-mail: info@reedsalmanacs.co.uk
www.reedsalmanacs.co.uk

Cover photo: Lymington Yacht Haven
01590 677071
www.yachthavens.com

Section 1

The Marinas and Services Section has been fully updated for the 2018 season. These useful pages provide chartlets and facility details for some 200 marinas around the shores of the UK and Ireland, including the Channel Islands, the perfect complement to any Reeds Nautical Almanac.

Section 2

The Marine Supplies & Services section lists more than 1000 services at coastal and other locations around the British Isles. It provides a quick and easy reference to manufacturers and retailers of equipment, services and supplies both nationally and locally together with emergency services.

Advertisement Sales
Enquiries about advertising space should be addressed to:
adlardcoles@bloomsbury.com

Printed by Bell and Bain Ltd,
Glagow

Section 1
Marinas and Services Section .... -98

Area Guide Chart 2

Area 1 - SW England
Area 1 Marina Chart 3
Falmouth Marina 4
Falmouth Haven Marina 4
Port Pendennis Marina 4
Mylor Yacht Harbour 6
Mayflower Marina 7
Q Anne's Battery 7
Sutton Harbour 9
Plymouth Yacht Haven 9
Darthaven Marina 11
Dart Marina 11
Noss Marina 11
Dartside Quay 12
Brixham Marina 12
Torquay Marina 12
Portland Marina 13
Weymouth Marina 13
Weymouth Harbour 13

Area 2 - Central S England
Area 2 Marina Chart 15
Ridge Wharf 16
Lake Yard Marina 16
Cobb's Quay Marina 16
Poole Quay Boat Haven 16
Port of Poole Marina 17
Parkstone Yacht Haven 17
Salterns Marina 17
Yarmouth Harbour/H Hayles 17
Lymington Yacht Haven 19
Berthon Lymington Marina 19
Lymington Harbour 19
Bucklers Hard 20
Cowes Yacht Haven 20
Shepards Wharf Marina 21
E Cowes Marina 21
Island Harbour Marina 21
Hythe Marina Village 22
Town Quay 22
Ocean Village Marina 22
Shamrock Quay 22
Kemps Quay 23
Saxon Wharf 23
Hamble Point Marina 23
Port Hamble Marina 23
Mercury Yacht Harbour 24
Universal Marina 24
Swanwick Marina 24
Ryde Leisure Harbour 24
Bembridge Marina 25
Haslar Marina 25
Gosport Marina 25
Royal Clarence Marina 26
WicorMarine YH 26
Port Solent Marina 26
Southsea Marina 26
Sparkes Marina 27
Northney Marina 27
Emsworth Yacht Harbour 27
Chichester Marina 28
Birdham Pool 28

Area 3 - SE England
Area 3 Marina Chart 30
Littlehampton Marina 31
Lady Bee Marina 31
Brighton Marina 31
Newhaven Marina 32
Sovereign Hbr Marina 32
Harbour of Rye 32
Dover Marina 33
Ramsgate Royal Hbr 33

Area 4 - E England
Area 4 Marina Chart 35
Gillingham Marina 36
Port Werburgh 36
Chatham Maritime Marina 37

Limehouse Basin 37
Gallions Point Marina 37
South Dock Marina 38
St Katharine Haven 38
Chelsea Harbour 38
Brentford Dock Marina 39
Penton Hook Marina 39
Windsor Marina 39
Bray Marina 39
Burnham Yacht Harbour 40
Essex Marina 40
Bridgemarsh Marina 41
Heybridge Basin 41
Bradwell Marina 41
Fambridge Yacht Haven 42
Blackwater Marina 42
Tollesbury Marina 42
Titchmarsh Marina 43
Walton Yacht Basin 43
Suffolk Yacht Harbour 43
Shotley Marina 44
Royal Harwich YC 44
Woolverstone Marina 44
Fox's Marina 45
Ipswich Haven Marina 46
Neptune Marina 46
R Norfolk & Suffolk YC 46
Lowestoft Haven Marina 47
Lowestoft CC 47

Area 5 - NE England
Area 5 Marina Chart 49
Wisbech Yacht Harbour 50
Boston Gateway Marina 50
Meridian Quay Marina 50
Hull Marina 51
South Ferriby Marina 52
Whitby Marina 52
Hartlepool Marina 52
Sunderland Marina 52
N Shields Royal Quays 53
St Peters Marina 53
R Northumberland Marina 53
Amble Marina 53

Area 6 - SE Scotland
Area 6 Marina Chart 54
Port Edgar Marina.................... 55
Arbroath Harbour 55

Area 7 - NE Scotland
Area 7 Marina Chart 57
Peterhead Bay Marina 58
Banff Harbour Marina 58
Nairn Marina 58
Whitehills Marina 59
Lossiemouth Marina 59
Inverness Marina 60
Seaport Marina 60
Caley Marina 60
Wick Marina 60
Kirkwall Marina 61
Stromness Marina 61

Area 8 - NW Scotland
Area 8 Marina Chart 63
Stornoway 64
Mallaig Marina 64
Tobermory Marina 64
Dunstaffnage Marina 64
Oban Marina 65
Melfort Pier and Hbr 65
Craobh Haven Marina.............. 65
Ardfern Yacht Centre 65

Area 9 - SW Scotland
Area 9 Marina Chart 67
Port Ellen Marina 68
Crinan Boatyard 68
Tarbert Harbour 69
Port Bannatyne 69
Portavadie Marina 69

Campbeltown Marina 69
Holy Loch Marina 69
Rhu Marina 70
Sandpoint Marina 70
James Watt Dock Marina 71
Kip Marina 71
Largs Yacht Haven 72
Clyde Marina 72
Troon Yacht Haven 73
Stranraer Marina 73
Kirkcudbright Marina 73
Maryport Marina 73

Area 10 - NW England
Area 10 Marina Chart 74
Whitehaven Marina 75
Glasson Dock 75
Douglas Marina 76
Peel Marina 76
Fleetwood Harbour Marina 76
Preston Marina 77
Liverpool Marina 77
Conwy Marina 77
Deganwy Marina 78
Holyhead Marina 78
Pwllheli Marina 78

Area 11 - South Wales
Area 11 Marina Chart 79
Aberystwyth Marina 80
Milford Marina 80
Neyland Yacht Haven 81
Swansea Marina 82
Penarth Marina 82
Cardiff Marina 82
Sharpness Marina 82
Bristol Marina 83
Portishead Quays Marina 83
Padstow Harbour 83

Area 12 - S Ireland
Area 12 Marina Chart 84
Malahide Marina 85
Howth Marina 85
Dun Laoghaire Marina 86
Arklow Marina 86
Kilmore Quay 86
Waterford City Marina 87
Crosshaven BY Marina 87
Salve Marine 87
Cork Harbour Marina............... 87
Royal Cork YC Marina 88
Kinsale YC Marina 88
Castlepark Marina 88
Lawrence Cove Marina 88
Cahersiveen Marina 89
Dingle Marina 89
Fenit Harbour 89
Kilrush Creek Marina 89

Area 13 - N Ireland
Area 13 Marina Chart 91
Galway City Marina 92
Foyle Marina 92
Coleraine Marina 92
Seatons Marina 92
Coleraine Harbour Marina 93
Ballycastle Marina 93
Carrickfergus Marina 93
Bangor Marina 94
Carlingford Marina 94
Ardglass Marina 94
Portaferry Marina 94

Area 14 - Channel Islands
Area 14 Marina Chart 95
Beaucette Marina 96
St Peter Port 96
St Peter Port Victoria Marina ...96
St Helier Harbour 98

Section 2
Marine Supplies and Services Section 99–128

MARINA GUIDE 2018

Area Guide
Showing Coastal Divisions

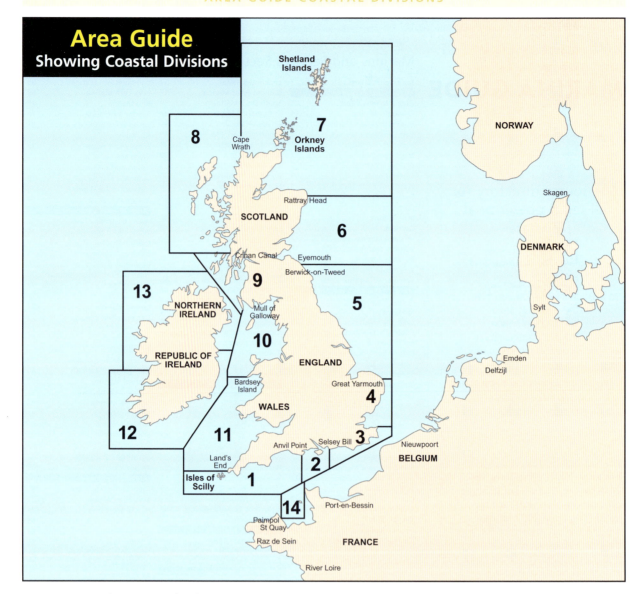

Area 1	South West England	Isles of Scilly to Anvil Point
Area 2	Central Southern England	Anvil Point to Selsey Bill
Area 3	South East England	Selsey Bill to North Foreland
Area 4	East England	North Foreland to Great Yarmouth
Area 5	North East England	Great Yarmouth to Berwick-upon-Tweed
Area 6	South East Scotland	Eyemouth to Rattray Head
Area 7	North East Scotland	Rattray Head to Cape Wrath including Orkney & Shetland Is
Area 8	North West Scotland	Cape Wrath to Crinan Canal
Area 9	South West Scotland	Crinan Canal to Mull of Galloway
Area 10	North West England	Isle of Man & N Wales, Mull of Galloway to Bardsey Is
Area 11	South Wales & Bristol Channel	Bardsey Island to Land's End
Area 12	South Ireland	Malahide, clockwise to Liscannor Bay
Area 13	North Ireland	Liscannor Bay, clockwise to Lambay Island
Area 14	Channel Islands	Guernsey and Jersey

AREA 1

SOUTH WEST ENGLAND – Isles of Scilly to Anvil Point

Reeds PDF ebooks

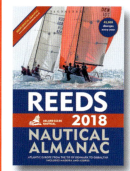

In response to popular demand, all the Reeds Almanacs are now available as searchable, highlightable PDF ebooks. (All ebooks incorporate the Marina Guide.)

Visit www.reedsnauticalalmanac.co.uk for further information

Key to Marina Plans symbols

	Bottled gas	P	Parking
	Chandler		Pub/Restaurant
	Disabled facilities		Pump out
	Electrical supply		Rigging service
	Electrical repairs		Sail repairs
	Engine repairs		Shipwright
	First Aid		Shop/Supermarket
	Fresh Water		Showers
D	Fuel - Diesel		Slipway
P	Fuel - Petrol	WC	Toilets
	Hardstanding/boatyard		Telephone
@	Internet Café		Trolleys
	Laundry facilities	V	Visitors berths
	Lift-out facilities		Wi-Fi

Area 1 - South West England

MARINAS
Telephone Numbers
VHF Channel
Access Times

Falmouth Marina
01326 316620 Ch 80 H24
Falmouth Haven Marina
01326 310991 Ch 12 H24
Port Pendennis Marina
01326 211211 Ch 80 H24
Mylor Yacht Harbour
01326 372121 Ch 80 H24

Dartside Quay
01803 845445 Ch 80 H24
Dart Marina
01803 832580 Ch 80 H24
Noss Marina
01803 839087 Ch 80 H24
Darthaven Marina
01803 752545 Ch 80 H24

Portland Marina
08454 302012
Ch 80 H24

Torquay Marina
01803 200210
Ch 80 H24

Brixham Marina
01803 882929
Ch 80 H24

Weymouth Harbour
01305 838423 Ch 12
Weymouth Marina
01305 767576
Ch 80 H24

Mayflower Marina 01752 556633 Ch 80 H24
Q Anne's Battery Marina 01752 671142 Ch 80 H24
Sutton Harbour 01752 204702 Ch 12 H24
Plymouth Yacht Haven 01752 404231 Ch 80 H24

St Mary's Isles of Scilly

Subscribe annually and receive the Almanac for just £32.50 (rrp £49.99)

Visit **www.reedsnauticalalmanac.co.uk/subscribetoreeds**

MARINAS & SERVICES

FALMOUTH MARINA

Falmouth Marina
North Parade, Falmouth, Cornwall, TR11 2TD
Tel: 01326 316620 Fax: 01326 313939
Email: falmouth@premiermarinas.com
www.premiermarinas.com

VHF Ch 80
ACCESS H24

Falmouth Marina lies tucked away in sheltered waters at the southern end of the Fal Estuary. Welcoming to both visiting and residential yachts, its comprehensive facilities include a restaurant, convenience store and hairdresser, while just a 20-minute walk away is Falmouth's town centre where you will find no shortage of shops and eating places. Comprising more than 70 sq miles of navigable water, the Fal Estuary is an intriguing cruising area full of hidden creeks and inlets.

FACILITIES AT A GLANCE

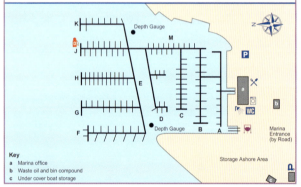

Key
a Marina office
b Waste oil and bin compound
c Under cover boat storage

FALMOUTH HAVEN MARINA

Falmouth Haven Marina
44 Arwenack Street
Tel: 01326 310991 Fax: 01326 211352
Email: welcome@falmouthhaven.co.uk

VHF Ch 12
ACCESS H24

Run by Falmouth Harbour Commissioners (FHC), Falmouth Haven Marina has become increasingly popular since its opening in 1982, enjoying close proximity to the amenities and entertainments of Falmouth town centre. Sheltered by a breakwater, the Haven caters for 100 boats and offers petrol and diesel supplies as well as good shower and laundry facilities.

Falmouth Harbour is considered by some to be the cruising capital of Cornwall and its deep water combined with easily navigable entrance – even in the severest conditions – makes it a favoured destination for visiting yachtsmen.

FACILITIES AT A GLANCE

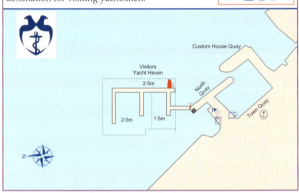

PORT PENDENNIS MARINA

Port Pendennis Marina
Challenger Quay, Falmouth, Cornwall, TR11 3YL
Tel: 01326 211211 Fax: 01326 311116
www.portpendennis.com

VHF Ch 80
ACCESS H24

Easily identified by the tower of the National Maritime Museum, Port Pendennis Marina is a convenient arrival or departure point for trans-Atlantic or Mediterranean voyages. Lying adjacent to the town centre, Port Pendennis is divided into an outer marina, with full tidal access, and inner marina, accessible three hours either side of HW. Among its impressive array of marine services is Pendennis Shipyard, one of Britain's most prestigious yacht builders, while other amenities on site include car hire, tennis courts and a yachtsman's lounge, from where you can send faxes or e-mails. Within walking distance of the marina are beautiful sandy beaches, an indoor swimming pool complex and castle.

FACILITIES AT A GLANCE

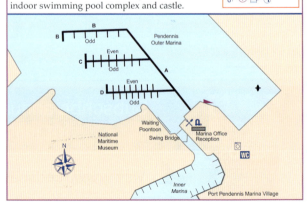

- **World class sails**
- **Local loft service ...**

MADE IN BRITAIN

Newlyn, Cornwall
+44 (0) 1736 366004
info@solosails.com
www.solosails.com

solosails

MARINA GUIDE 2018

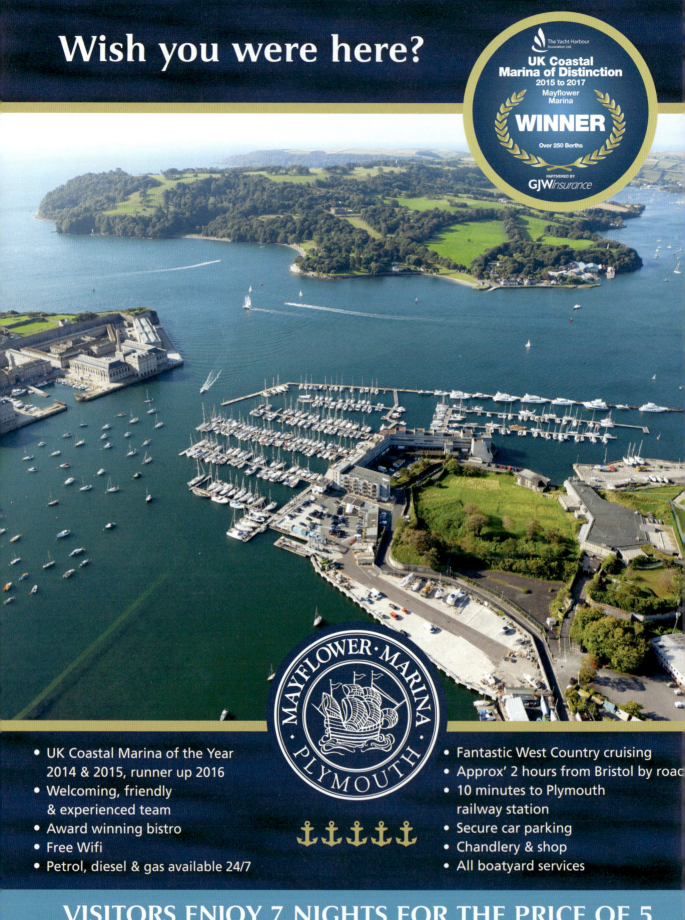

SOUTH WEST ENGLAND — AREA 1

MYLOR YACHT HARBOUR

Mylor Yacht Harbour Marina
Mylor, Falmouth, Cornwall, TR11 5UF
Tel: 01326 372121 Fax: 01326 372120
Email: enquiries@mylor.com

VHF: Ch M, 80
ACCESS: H24

Situated on the western shore of Carrick Roads in the beautiful Fal Estuary, Mylor Yacht Harbour has been improved and expanded in recent years, now comprising two substantial breakwaters, three inner pontoons and approximately 250 moorings. With 24 hour access, good shelter and excellent facilities, it ranks among the most popular marinas on the SW Coast of England.

Formerly the Navy's smallest dockyard, established in 1805, Mylor is today a thriving yachting centre as well as home to the world's only remaining sailing oyster fishing fleet. With Falmouth just 10 mins away, local attractions include the Eden Project in St Austell and the National Maritime Museum in Falmouth.

FACILITIES AT A GLANCE

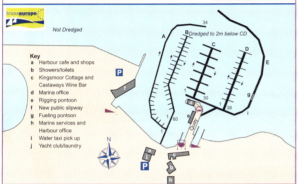

Key
a Harbour cafe and shops
b Showers/toilets
c Kingsmoor Cottage and Castaways Wine Bar
d Marina office
e Rigging pontoon
f New public slipway
g Fueling pontoon
h Marine services and Harbour office
i Water taxi pick up
j Yacht club/laundry

MAYFLOWER MARINA

Mayflower International Marina
Ocean Quay, Richmond Walk, Plymouth, PL1 4LS
Tel: 01752 556633 Fax: 01752 606896
Email: info@mayflowermarina.co.uk

VHF: Ch 80
ACCESS: H24

Sitting on the famous Plymouth Hoe, with the Devon coast to the left and the Cornish coast to the right, Mayflower Marina is a friendly, well-run marina. Facilities include 24 hour access to fuel, gas and a launderette, full repair and maintenance services as well as an on site bar and brasserie. The marina is located only a short distance from Plymouth's town centre, where there are regular train services to and from several major towns and cities.

FACILITIES AT A GLANCE

Key
a Marina office
b Brokerage, chandlery
c Cafe
d Bar
e Brasserie
f Berth holders toilets and showers
g Ocean Court Flats

QUEEN ANNE'S BATTERY

Queen Anne's Battery
Plymouth, Devon, PL4 0LP
Tel: 01752 671142
Email: qab@mdlmarinas.co.uk   www.queenannesbattery.co.uk

VHF: Ch 80
ACCESS: H24

Plymouth, a vibrant and fast growing city, is home to Queen Anne's Battery, a 235 resident berth marina with outstanding facilities for yachtsmen and motor cruisers alike. Located just south of Sutton Harbour, QAB promises a welcoming stay with alongside pontoon berthing protected by the surrounding breakwater. While on the city's doorstep, the marina is short walk away from the historical Barbican, providing peace and tranquility to visitors.

The marina is often frequented by crowds of people marveling the many prestigious international yacht and powerboat races Plymouth Sound facilitates.

QAB is an exposed treasure along a beautiful historic coastline, at times resembling a mini 'Cowes' with its vibrancy.

FACILITIES AT A GLANCE

Key
a Toilets and showers
b Royal Western Yacht Club
c Marina office and provisions shop
d Bar/restaurant
e Cafe

MARINA GUIDE 2018

SIMPLY SUPERIOR™

The new Axiom MFD from Raymarine is reinventing navigation. With faster performance, intuitive operation, and leading-edge technology, Axiom delivers unmatched awareness, above and below the water line.

AXIOM™

Images for illustrative purpose only

Raymarine®

SOUTH WEST ENGLAND — AREA 1

PLYMOUTH YACHT HAVEN

Plymouth Yacht Haven Ltd
Shaw Way, Mount Batten, Plymouth, PL9 9XH
Tel: 01752 404231 Fax: 01752 484177
Email: plymouth@yachthavens.com www.yachthavens.com

VHF Ch 80
ACCESS H24

Situated minutes from Plymouth sound, Plymouth Yacht Haven enjoys a tranquil setting, yet is just a five minute water taxi ride from the bustling barbican with all its restaurants and attractions. The Yacht Haven offers excellent protection from the prevailing SW winds and is within easy reach of some of the most fantastic cruising grounds.

This 450-berth marina can accommodate vessels up to 45m in length and 7m in draught. Members of staff are on site 24/7 to welcome you as a visitor and to serve diesel. With an on site 75T travel hoist and storage, a restaurant, chandlery, and extensive range of marine service, Plymouth Yacht Haven has plenty to offer both on and off the water.

FACILITIES AT A GLANCE

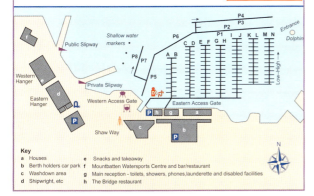

Key
a Houses
b Berth holders car park
c Washdown area
d Shipwright, etc
e Snacks and takeaway
f Mountbatten Watersports Centre and bar/restaurant
g Main reception - toilets, showers, phones,launderette and disabled facilities
h The Bridge restaurant

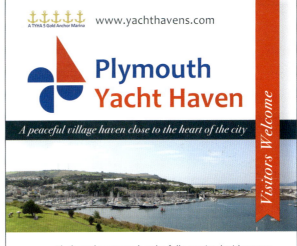

A TYHA 5 Gold Anchor Marina
www.yachthavens.com

Plymouth Yacht Haven

A peaceful village haven close to the heart of the city

Visitors Welcome

- Sheltered pontoon berths fully serviced with water, electricity & FREE Wi-Fi
- All new luxury showers, washrooms and laundry
- 24 hour access, fuel and service
- Boatyard facilities with a hoist up to 75 tonnes, plus indoor and outdoor boat storage
- Full marina services on-site including a chandlery and brokerage
- Fabulous food and stunning views at The Bridge Bar & Restaurant
- Water taxi to the Barbican

ALL NEW LUXURY FACILITIES

Plymouth Yacht Haven   Tel: 01752 404231   VHF Ch 80
Email: plymouth@yachthavens.com

SUTTON HARBOUR

Sutton Harbour
The Jetty, Sutton Harbour, Plymouth, PL4 0DW
Tel: 01752 204702 Fax: 01752 204693
Email: marina@sutton-harbour.co.uk
www.suttonharbourmarina.com

VHF Ch 12
ACCESS H24

Sutton Harbour Marina, located in the heart of Plymouth's historic Barbican area and a short stroll from the city centre, offers 5-star facilities in a sheltered location, surrounded by boutique waterfront bars and restau a minimum 3.5m depth, the harbour has 24hr lock access on request with free flow approx 3hrs either side of high tide. The marina of choice for international yacht races such as The Transat and Fastnet. Visitors are invited to come and enjoy the unrivalled shelter, facilities, atmosphere and location that Sutton harbour offers.

FACILITIES AT A GLANCE

Key
a Fish market
b National Marine Aquarium
c Customs House
d The Cove
e Marina office
f Lock tower

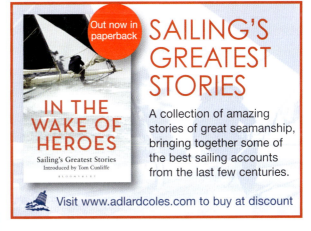

Out now in paperback

SAILING'S GREATEST STORIES

IN THE WAKE OF HEROES — Sailing's Greatest Stories, Introduced by Tom Cunliffe

A collection of amazing stories of great seamanship, bringing together some of the best sailing accounts from the last few centuries.

Visit www.adlardcoles.com to buy at discount

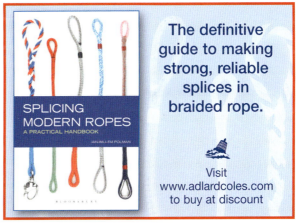

The definitive guide to making strong, reliable splices in braided rope.

SPLICING MODERN ROPES — A PRACTICAL HANDBOOK

Visit www.adlardcoles.com to buy at discount

MARINA GUIDE 2018

THIS SUMMER UPGRADE TO A PREMIER MARINA. YOU'LL LOVE THE DIFFERENCE.

The best thing about Premier Marinas is its welcoming staff and superb customer service. But we know you want it all, so we continue to invest in making your time with us perfect - from luxury facilities to new locations, new restaurants and more. But don't just take our word for it join us overnight, tour our marinas for a week with Great Escapes, or opt for monthly berthing and enjoy a lazy summer break in a Premier marina. Call now or visit premiermarinas.com

GREAT ESCAPES BUY 5 NIGHTS AND STAY 7
PREMIERMARINAS.COM

NEW LOCATION! NOSS ON DART

42 FREE VISITOR NIGHTS AT ANY PREMIER MARINA | FUEL AT COST | 8 WEEKS STORAGE ASHORE | BOATYARD DISCOUNTS | OPTION TO CHANGE MARINAS | QUALITY WIFI

EASTBOURNE 01323 470099 BRIGHTON 01273 819919 CHICHESTER 01243 512731 SOUTHSEA 023 9282 2719 PORT SOLENT 023 9221 0765 GOSPORT 023 9252 4811 SWANWICK 01489 884081 NOSS ON DART 01803 839087 FALMOUTH 01326 316620

SOUTH WEST ENGLAND

AREA 1

DARTHAVEN MARINA

Darthaven Marina
Brixham Road, Kingswear, Devon, TQ6 0SG
Tel: 01803 752242 Fax: 01803 752722
Email: admin@darthaven.co.uk
www.darthaven.co.uk

VHF Ch 80
ACCESS H24

Darthaven Marina is a family run business situated in the village of Kingswear on the east side of the River Dart. Within half a mile from Start Bay and the mouth of the river, it is the first marina you come to from seaward and is accessible at all states of the tide. Darthaven prides itself on being more than just a marina, offering a high standard of marine services with both electronic and engineering experts plus wood and GRP repairs on site. A shop, post office and three pubs are within a walking distance of the marina, while a frequent ferry service takes passengers across the river to Dartmouth.

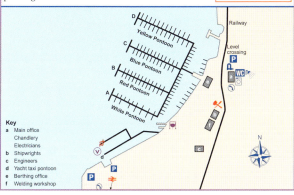

Key
a Main office
   Chandlery
   Electricians
b Shipwrights
c Engineers
d Yacht taxi pontoon
e Berthing office
f Welding workshop

DART MARINA

Dart Marina
Sandquay Road, Dartmouth, Devon, TQ6 9PH
Tel: 01803 837161 Fax: 01803 835040
Email: yachtharbour@dartmarina.com
www.dartmarinayachtharbour.com

VHF Ch 80
ACCESS H24

Dart Marina Yacht Harbour, in one of the most stunning locations on the UK coastline, is a peaceful spot for simply sitting on deck relaxing and perfectly positioned for day sailing or more ambitious cruising. With visitor berths, 110 annual berths, all accessible at any tide, the Yacht Harbour is sought after for its intimate atmosphere and stylish setting.

Professional, knowledgeable and helpful, the marina team is on-site all year round and there are impeccable facilities including showers, bathrooms and laundry.

In Dartmouth there are restaurants, bistros, cafes, delis, independent shops, galleries, a cinema, chandlers, antique and lifestyle shops in abundance.

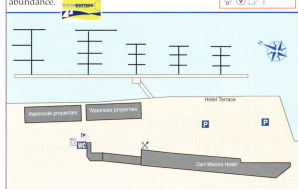

NOSS MARINA

Noss Marina
Bridge Road, Kingswear, Devon, TQ6 0EA
Tel: 01803 839087 Fax: 01803 835620
Email: info@nossmarina.co.uk
www.nossmarina.co.uk

VHF Ch 80
ACCESS H24

Upstream of Dartmouth on the east shore of the River Dart is Noss Marina. Enjoying a peaceful rural setting, this marina is well suited to those who prefer a quieter atmosphere. Besides 180 fully serviced berths, 50 fore-and-aft moorings in the middle reaches of the river are also run by the marina, with mooring holders entitled to use all the facilities available to berth holders. During summer, a passenger ferry service runs regularly between Noss-on-Dart and Dartmouth, while a grocery service to your boat can be provided on request.

Key
a Marina office
b Amenities

MARINA GUIDE 2018

MARINAS & SERVICES

DARTSIDE QUAY

Dartside Quay
Galmpton Creek, Brixham, Devon, TQ5 0EH
Tel: 01803 845445
Email: dartsidequay@mdlmarinas.co.uk
www.dartsidequay.co.uk

VHF Ch 80
ACCESS H24

Located at the head of Galmpton Creek, Dartside Quay lies three miles upriver from Dartmouth.

In a sheltered position and with beautiful views across to Dittisham, it offers extensive boatyard facilities. The seven-acre dry boat storage area has space for over 300 boats and is serviced by a 65-ton hoist operating from a purpose-built dock, plus a 16-ton trailer hoist operating on a slipway.

There are also a number of summer mud moorings available and a well stocked chandlery, in fact if the item you want is not in stock we can order it in for you.

FACILITIES AT A GLANCE

Key
a Commercial unit
b Lower main quarry
c Middle quarry
d Top quarry
e Upper main quarry
f Cottage
g Battery, hazardous waste and oil disposal
h Admin/yard office and chandlery

BRIXHAM MARINA

Brixham Marina
Berry Head Road, Brixham, Devon, TQ5 9BW
Tel: 01803 882929
Email: brixham@mdlmarinas.co.uk
www.brixhammarina.co.uk

VHF Ch 80
ACCESS H24

Home to one of Britain's largest fishing fleets, Brixham Harbour is located on the southern shore of Tor Bay, which is well sheltered from westerly winds and where tidal streams are weak. Brixham Marina, housed in a separate basin to the work boats, provides easy access in all weather conditions and at all states of the tide. Basic provisions and diesel are available and there is a bar and restaurant, ideal for when you've worked up an appetite out on the water.

Local attractions include a walk out to Berry Head Nature Reserve and a visit to the replica of Sir Francis Drake's *Golden Hind*.

FACILITIES AT A GLANCE

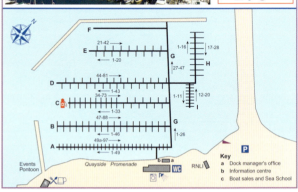

Key
a Dock manager's office
b Information centre
c Boat sales and Sea School

An essential boater's companion

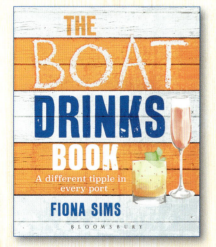

An expert look at enjoyable things to drink in key sailing spots around the world

Visit www.adlardcoles.com to buy at discount

TORQUAY MARINA

Torquay Marina
Torquay, Devon, TQ2 5EQ
Tel: 01803 200210
Email: torquaymarina@mdlmarinas.co.uk
www.torquaymarina.co.uk

VHF Ch 80
ACCESS H24

Tucked away in the north east corner of Torbay, Torquay Marina is well sheltered from the prevailing SW'ly winds, providing safe entry in all conditions and at any state of the tide. Located in the centre of Torquay, the marina enjoys easy access to the town's numerous shops, bars and restaurants.

Torquay is ideally situated for either exploring Tor Bay itself, with its many delightful anchorages, or else for heading further west to experience several other scenic harbours such as Dartmouth and Salcombe. It also provides a good starting point for crossing to Brittany, Normandy or the Channel Islands.

FACILITIES AT A GLANCE

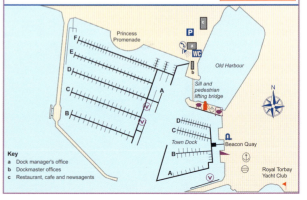

Key
a Dock manager's office
b Dockmaster offices
c Restaurant, cafe and newsagents

MARINA GUIDE 2018

SOUTH WEST ENGLAND — AREA 1

PORTLAND MARINA

Portland Marina
Osprey Quay, Portland, Dorset, DT5 1DX
Tel: 08345 430 2012
www.deanreddyhoff.co.uk
Email: berths@portlandmarina.co.uk

VHF Ch 80 ACCESS H24

Portland Marina is an ideal location for both annual berthing and weekend stopovers. The marina offers first class facilities including washrooms, on-site bar and restaurant, lift out and storage up to 50T, dry stacking up to 9m, 24-hour manned security, fuel berth, sewage pump out, extensive car parking and a full range of marine services including a chandlery.

The marina is within walking distance of local pubs and restaurants on Portland with Weymouth's bustling town centre and mainline railway station just a short bus or ferry ride away.

FACILITIES AT A GLANCE

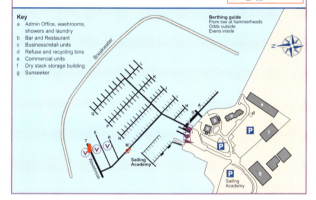

Key
a Admin Office, washrooms, showers and laundry
b Bar and Restaurant
c Business/retail units
d Refuse and recycling bins
e Commercial units
f Dry stack storage building
g Sunseeker

Berthing guide
From low at hammerheads
Odds outside
Evens inside

WEYMOUTH HARBOUR

Harbour Office
13 Custom House Quay, Weymouth, Dorset, DT4 8BG
Tel: 01305 838423 Fax: 01305 767927
Email: berthingoffice@weymouth-harbour.gov.uk
www.weymouth-harbour.co.uk

VHF Ch 12 ACCESS H24

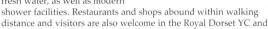

Weymouth Harbour, situated on the Jurassic Coast, lays NE of Portland in the protected waters of Weymouth Bay. Located in the heart of the old town and accessible at any state of tide, the Georgian harbour has numerous overnight berths. Pontoons on both quays have electricity and fresh water, as well as modern shower facilities. Restaurants and shops abound within walking distance and visitors are also welcome in the Royal Dorset YC and Weymouth SC, both situated on the quayside.

Vessels are advised to call *Weymouth Harbour* on Ch12 on approach, and vessels over 15m are recommended to give prior notification of intended arrival.

FACILITIES AT A GLANCE

Key
a Waiting pontoon for bridge
b Lifeboat
c Weymouth Sailing Club
d Royal Dorset Yacht Club

WEYMOUTH MARINA

Weymouth Marina
70 Commercial Road, Weymouth, Dorset, DT4 8NA
Tel: 01305 767576 Fax: 01305 767575
www.weymouth-marina.co.uk
Email: sales@weymouth-marina.co.uk

VHF Ch 80 ACCESS H24

With more than 280 permanent and visitors' berths, Weymouth is a modern, purpose-built marina ideally situated for yachtsmen cruising between the West Country and the Solent. It is also conveniently placed for sailing to France or the Channel Islands. Accessed via the town's historic lifting bridge, which opens every even hour 0800–2000 (plus 2100 Jun–Aug), the marina is dredged to 2.5m below chart datum. It provides easy access to the town centre, with its abundance of shops, pubs and restaurants, as well as to the traditional seafront where an impressive sandy beach is overlooked by an esplanade of hotels.

FACILITIES AT A GLANCE

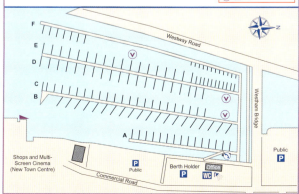

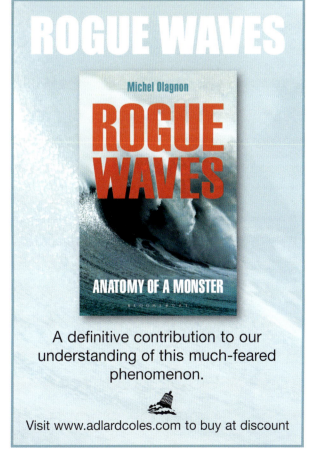

ROGUE WAVES

Michel Olagnon

ROGUE WAVES
ANATOMY OF A MONSTER

Bloomsbury

A definitive contribution to our understanding of this much-feared phenomenon.

Visit www.adlardcoles.com to buy at discount

MARINA GUIDE 2018   13

SWINGING MOORINGS   JET DOCKS   SUPER YACHT BERTHS   PERMANENT BERTHS   POOLE QUAY   VISITOR/PERMANENT BERTHS

Set sail for Poole
with your pride & joy

Marina of the Year 2017 UK Coastal Under 250 Berths WINNER
Marina of the Year 2016 UK Coastal Under 250 Berths WINNER

PERMANENT BERTHS
Whatever you love to do, you will enjoy our permanent berth marina. It's in a private position that makes the most of the views and gorgeous sunsets, yet it's still close to Poole's historic quay, old town and vibrant shopping centre.

- 75 permanent berths
- Superyacht berths
- Floating docks for jet skis and RIBs up to 6.1m
- 24 hour security
- Showers & toilets, laundry, electric & water
- Deep water: 2.5 - 6m
- Water taxi service, parking

VISITOR MARINA
Use your boat as a holiday home; entertain family, friends, colleagues or customers onboard; sail the stunning Jurassic Coast. Enjoy all the attractions of Poole, Bournemouth and beautiful Dorset. A warm welcome always awaits!

- 125 visitor berths all year for vessels up to 65m in length and up to 4.5m draft
- Swinging moorings
- Floating docks for jet skis and RIBs up to 6.1m
- Showers & toilets, laundry, electric & water

SWINGING MOORINGS
Relax with a glass of wine, on a sunny afternoon, on your own swinging mooring in Poole Harbour overlooking Brownsea Island. Away from the madding crowd, these offer you ultimate privacy, peace & tranquillity.

JET SKI OR RIBS
Keeping your craft on a Jet Ski or RIB Dock has the advantage of 'out-of-water' storage but still offers the convenience of marina berthing and more time for leisure.

Poole Town Quay, Poole, Dorset BH15 1HJ
t: 01202 649488
www.poolequayboathaven.co.uk
VHF Channel 80 call sign "Poole Quay Boat Haven"

HOME OF THE POOLE HARBOUR BOAT SHOW

AREA 2

CENTRAL SOUTHERN ENGLAND – Anvil Point to Selsey Bill

Reeds PDF ebooks

In response to popular demand, all the Reeds Almanacs are now available as searchable, highlightable PDF ebooks. (All ebooks incorporate the Marina Guide.)

Visit www.reedsnauticalalmanac.co.uk for further information

Key to Marina Plans symbols

- Bottled gas
- Chandler
- Disabled facilities
- Electrical supply
- Electrical repairs
- Engine repairs
- First Aid
- Fresh Water
- Fuel - Diesel
- Fuel - Petrol
- Hardstanding/boatyard
- Internet Café
- Laundry facilities
- Lift-out facilities
- Parking
- Pub/Restaurant
- Pump out
- Rigging service
- Sail repairs
- Shipwright
- Shop/Supermarket
- Showers
- Slipway
- Toilets
- Telephone
- Trolleys
- Visitors berths
- Wi-Fi

Area 2 - Central Southern England

MARINAS
Telephone Numbers
VHF Channel
Access Times

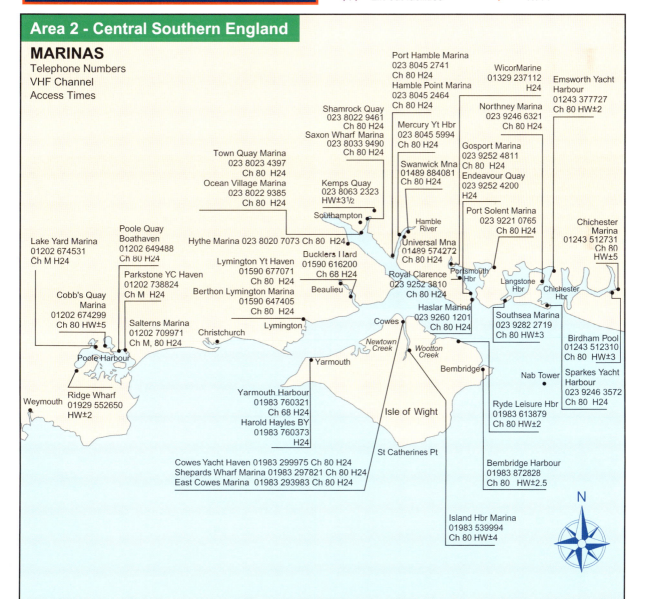

Port Hamble Marina 023 8045 2741 Ch 80 H24
Hamble Point Marina 023 8045 2464 Ch 80 H24
WicorMarine 01329 237112 H24
Emsworth Yacht Harbour 01243 377727 Ch 80 HW±2
Shamrock Quay 023 8022 9461 Ch 80 H24
Saxon Wharf Marina 023 8033 9490 Ch 80 H24
Mercury Yt Hbr 023 8045 5994 Ch 80 H24
Northney Marina 023 9246 6321 Ch 80 H24
Town Quay Marina 023 8023 4397 Ch 80 H24
Ocean Village Marina 023 8022 9385 Ch 80 H24
Kemps Quay 023 8063 2323 HW±3½
Swanwick Mna 01489 884081 Ch 80 H24
Gosport Marina 023 9252 4811 Ch 80 H24
Endeavour Quay 023 9252 4200 H24
Port Solent Marina 023 9221 0765 Ch 80 H24
Chichester Marina 01243 512731 Ch 80 HW±5
Lake Yard Marina 01202 674531 Ch M H24
Poole Quay Boathaven 01202 649488 Ch 80 H24
Hythe Marina 023 8020 7073 Ch 80 H24
Ducklers Hard 01590 616200 Ch 68 H24
Universal Mna 01489 574272 Ch 80 H24
Lymington Yt Haven 01590 677071 Ch 80 H24
Parkstone YC Haven 01202 738824 Ch M H24
Royal Clarence 023 9252 3810 Ch 80 H24
Cobb's Quay Marina 01202 674299 Ch 80 HW±5
Berthon Lymington Marina 01590 647405 Ch 80 H24
Southsea Marina 023 9282 2719 Ch 80 HW±3
Birdham Pool 01243 512310 Ch 80 HW±3
Salterns Marina 01202 709971 Ch M, 80 H24
Haslar Marina 023 9260 1201 Ch 80 H24
Sparkes Yacht Harbour 023 9246 3572 Ch 80 H24
Ridge Wharf 01929 552650 HW±2
Yarmouth Harbour 01983 760321 Ch 68 H24
Ryde Leisure Hbr 01983 613879 Ch 80 HW±2
Harold Hayles BY 01983 760373 H24
Cowes Yacht Haven 01983 299975 Ch 80 H24
Shepards Wharf Marina 01983 297821 Ch 80 H24
East Cowes Marina 01983 293983 Ch 80 H24
Bembridge Harbour 01983 872828 Ch 80 HW±2.5
Island Hbr Marina 01983 539994 Ch 80 HW±4

MARINA GUIDE 2018

MARINAS & SERVICES

RIDGE WHARF YACHT CENTRE

Ridge Wharf Yacht Centre
Ridge, Wareham, Dorset, BH20 5BG
Tel: 01929 552650 Fax: 01929 554434
Email: office@ridgewharf.co.uk www.ridgewharf.co.uk

VHF —
ACCESS HW±2

On the south bank of the River Frome, which acts as the boundary to the North of the Isle of Purbeck, is Ridge Wharf Yacht Centre. Access for a 1.5m draught is between one and two hours either side of HW, with berths drying out to soft mud. The Yacht Centre cannot be contacted on VHF, so it is best to phone up ahead of time to inquire about berthing availability.

A trip upstream to the ancient market town of Wareham is well worth while, although owners of deep-draughted yachts may prefer to go by dinghy. Tucked between the Rivers Frome and Trent, it is packed full of cafés, restaurants and shops.

LAKE YARD MARINA

Lake Yard Marina
Lake Drive, Hamworthy, Poole, Dorset BH15 4DT
Tel: 01202 674531 Fax: 01202 677518
Email: office@lakeyard.com www.lakeyard.com

VHF Ch M
ACCESS H24

Lake Yard is situated towards the NW end of Poole Harbour, just beyond the SHM No 73. The entrance can be easily identified by 2FR (vert) and 2FG (vert) lights. Enjoying 24 hour access, the marina has no designated visitors' berths, but will accommodate visiting yachtsmen if resident berth holders are away. Its on site facilities include full maintenance and repair services as well as hard standing and a 50 ton boat hoist, although for the nearest fuel go to Corralls (Tel 01202 674551), opposite the Town Quay. Lake Yard's Waterfront Club, offering spectacular views across the harbour, opens seven days a week for lunchtime and evening meals.

COBB'S QUAY MARINA

Cobb's Quay Marina
Hamworthy, Poole, Dorset, BH15 4EL
Tel: 01202 674299
Email: cobbsquay@mdlmarinas.co.uk
www.cobbsquaymarina.co.uk

⚓⚓⚓⚓
VHF Ch 80
ACCESS HW±5

Lying on the west side of Holes Bay in Poole Harbour, Cobb's Quay is accessed via two lifting bridges, which operate simultaneously. The hourly lifting schedule which runs from 0530 to 2330 (except for weekday rush hours) marks the entrance into Holes Bay accessible HW±5. With fully serviced pontoons for yachts up to 20m LOA, visitors can enjoy the facilities including the highly reputable Cobb's YC. The marina also offers a convenient 240-berth dry stack area for motorboats up to 10m. Offering increased security and lower maintenance costs, the service includes unlimited launching on demand 24/7. Poole Harbour is the second largest natural harbour in the world and is rich in wildlife, water sports and secret hideaways.

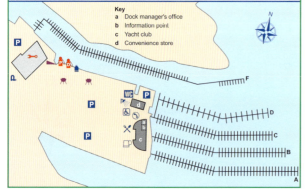

POOLE QUAY BOAT HAVEN

Poole Quay Boat Haven
Poole Town Quay, Poole, Dorset, BH15 1HJ
Tel: 01202 649488 Fax: 01202 785619
Email: info@poolequayboathaven.co.uk

⚓⚓⚓⚓
VHF Ch 80
ACCESS H24

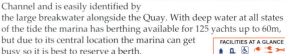

Once inside the Poole Harbour entrance small yachts heading for Poole Quay Boat Haven should use the Boat Channel running parallel south of the dredged Middle Ship Channel, which is primarily used by ferries sailing to and from the Hamworthy terminal. The marina can be accessed via the Little Channel and is easily identified by the large breakwater alongside the Quay. With deep water at all states of the tide the marina has berthing available for 125 yachts up to 60m, but due to its central location the marina can get busy so it is best to reserve a berth.

There is easy access to all of Poole Quay's facilities including restaurants, bars, Poole Pottery and the Waterfront Museum.

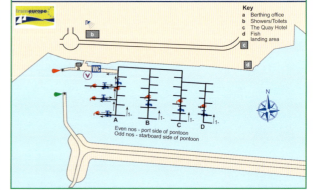

CENTRAL SOUTHERN ENGLAND

AREA 2

PORT OF POOLE MARINA

Port of Poole Marina
Poole Town Quay, Poole, Dorset, BH15 1HJ
Tel: 01202 649488 Fax: 01202 785619
Email: info@poolequayboathaven.co.uk

VHF Ch 80 | ACCESS H24

Beware of the chain ferry operating at the entrance to Poole harbour. Once inside small yachts heading for the marina should use the Boat Channel running parallel south of the Middle Ship Channel. The marina is to the east of the main ferry terminals and can be identified by a large floating breakwater at the entrance.

The marina has deep water at all tides and berthing for 60 permanent vessels. It is also used as an overflow for visitors from Poole Quay Boat Haven, subject to availability.

A water taxi is available during daylight hours to access the quay for restaurants and shops, also accessible with a 10–15min walk round the quays.

FACILITIES AT A GLANCE

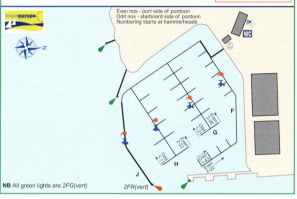

PARKSTONE YACHT HAVEN

Parkstone Yacht Club
Pearce Avenue, Parkstone, Poole, Dorset, BH14 8EH
Tel: 01202 738824 Fax: 01202 716394
Email: office@parkstoneyc.co.uk

VHF Ch M | ACCESS H24

Situated on the north side of Poole Harbour between Salterns Marina and Poole Quay Boat Haven, Parkstone Yacht Haven can be entered at all states of the tides. Its approach channel has been dredged to 2.0m and is clearly marked by buoys. Run by the Parkstone Yacht Club, the Haven provides 200 deep water berths for members and visitors' berths. Other services include a new office facility with laundry and WCs, bar, restaurant, shower/changing rooms and wi-fi. With a busy sailing programme for over 2,500 members, the Yacht Club plays host to a variety of events including Poole Week, which is held towards the end of August. Please phone for availability.

FACILITIES AT A GLANCE

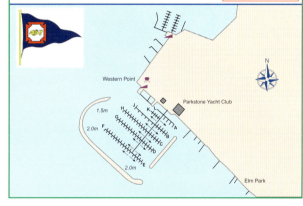

SALTERNS MARINA

Salterns Marina
40 Salterns Way, Lilliput, Poole
Dorset, BH14 8JR
Tel: 01202 709971 Fax: 01202 700398
Email: marina@salterns.co.uk www.salterns.co.uk

VHF Ch M, 80 | ACCESS H24

Holding the Five Gold Anchor award, Salterns Marina provides a service which is second to none. Located off the North Channel, it is approached from the No 31 SHM and benefits from deep water at all states of the tide. Facilities include 220 alongside pontoon berths as well as 75 swinging moorings with a free launch service. However, with very few designated visitors' berths, it is best to contact the marina ahead of time for availability.

Fuel, diesel and gas can all be obtained 24/7 and the well-stocked chandlery, incorporating a coffee shop, stays open seven days a week.

FACILITIES AT A GLANCE

YARMOUTH HBR/HAROLD HAYLES BY

Yarmouth Harbour
Yarmouth, Isle of Wight, PO41 0NT
Tel: 01983 760321 Fax: 01983 761192
info@yarmouth-harbour.co.uk
www.yarmouth-harbour.co.uk

VHF Ch 68 | ACCESS H24

Harold Hayles Ltd
The Quay, Yarmouth, Isle of Wight, PO41 0RS
Tel: 01983 760373 Fax: 01983 760666
Email: info@haroldhayles.co.uk
www.haroldhayles.co.uk

VHF | ACCESS H24

The most western harbour on the Isle of Wight, Yarmouth is not only a convenient passage stopover but a very desirable destination in its own right, with virtually all weather and tidal access, although strong N to NE'ly winds can produce a considerable swell. The HM launch patrols the harbour entrance and will direct visiting yachtsmen to a walkashore or standalone pontoon berths; call *Yarmouth Harbour* on Ch 68 prior to entering the harbour. The pretty harbour and town offer plenty of fine restaurants and amenities.

Walkashore pontoon moorings are also available from the Harold Hayles and River Yar BYs in the SW corner of the harbour, the latter S of the bridge. Pre-booking is preferred for both individuals or rallies.

FACILITIES AT A GLANCE

MARINA GUIDE 2018   17

'SUMMERTIME IS ALWAYS
THE BEST OF WHAT MIGHT BE'
CHARLES BOWDEN

VISIT OUR NEW
SHIPYARD FISHMARKET
BAR & KITCHEN

DESTINATION
BERTHON

BERTHON
SERVICE

MAINTENANCE
& REPAIRS

SUMMER
VALETING

OUR STAFF LOOK FORWARD TO WELCOMING YOU & YOUR CREW
TO THE SUPERB FACILITIES AT BERTHON LYMINGTON MARINA

Bookable Berths | Larger Turning Areas | Higher, More Stable Fingers | Friendly, Highly Rated Dockmasters
| Outstanding Washrooms | On-site Shipyard Fishmarket, Bar & Kitchen

Find out what Berthon and Lymington can offer...
www.berthon.co.uk/about-berthon

BERTHON

UK OPEN 7 DAYS A WEEK

Lymington, Hampshire SO41 3YL England
Tel: 44 (0) 1590 673312   Fax: 44 (0) 1590 647446

@BerthonGroup

enquiries@berthon.co.uk
www.berthon.co.uk

CENTRAL SOUTHERN ENGLAND

AREA 2

LYMINGTON YACHT HAVEN

Lymington Yacht Haven
King's Saltern Road, Lymington, SO41 3QD
Tel: 01590 677071
Email: lymington@yachthavens.com   www.yachthavens.com

VHF Ch 80   ACCESS H24

Lymington Yacht Haven has the enviable position of being the first marina that comes into sight on your port hand side as you make your way up the well-marked Lymington river channel. Nestled between the 500 acre Lymington to Keyhaven nature reserve and the famous Georgian market town of Lymington, there is something for everyone.

Lymington Yacht Haven is manned 24/7 for fuel and berthing and boasts the most modern luxury shore side facilities you will find in the UK. Bike and electric car hire are available through the marina office to explore the beautiful New Forest.

FACILITIES AT A GLANCE

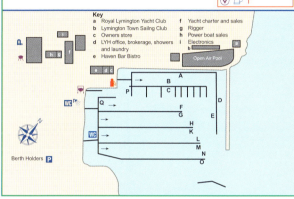

Key
a Royal Lymington Yacht Club
b Lymington Town Sailing Club
c Owners store
d LYH office, brokerage, showers and laundry
e Haven Bar Bistro
f Yacht charter and sales
g Rigger
h Power boat sales
i Electronics

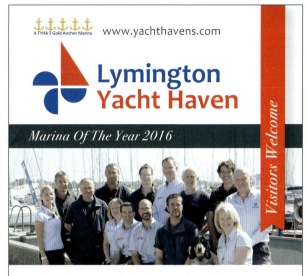

- Perfectly situated at the mouth of Lymington River
- Sheltered pontoon berths fully serviced with water, electricity and FREE Wi-Fi
- 24 hour access, service and fuel
- Luxury shoreside facilities and Haven Restaurant
- An easy 10 minute walk to Lymington High Street
- Special Winter Visitor Rates (Nov-Feb inclusive)

Lymington Yacht Haven   Tel: 01590 677071
VHF Ch 80   Email: lymington@yachthavens.com

BERTHON LYMINGTON MARINA

Berthon Lymington Marina Ltd
The Shipyard, Lymington, Hampshire, SO41 3YL
Tel: 01590 647405   Fax: 01590 647446
www.berthon.co.uk   Email: marina@berthon.co.uk

VHF Ch 80   ACCESS H24

Situated approximately half a mile up river of Lymington Yacht Haven, on the port hand side, is Lymington Marina. Easily accessible at all states of the tide, it offers between 60 to 70 visitors' berths, with probably the best washrooms in the Solent. Its close proximity to the town centre and first rate services mean that booking is essential on busy weekends. Lymington Marina's parent, Berthon Boat Co, has state of the art facilities and a highly skilled work force of 100+ to deal with any repair, maintenance or refit.

Lymington benefits from having the New Forest on its doorstep and the Solent Way footpath provides an invigorating walk to and from Hurst Castle.

FACILITIES AT A GLANCE

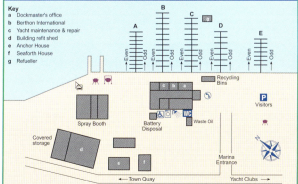

Key
a Dockmaster's office
b Berthon International
c Yacht maintenance & repair
d Building refit shed
e Anchor House
f Seaforth House
g Refueller

LYMINGTON HARBOUR

Lymington Harbour Commisioner
Bath Road, Lymington, SO41 3SE
Tel: 01590 672014   Fax: 01590 671823
Email: onfo@lymingtonharbour.co.uk

VHF Ch 66   ACCESS H24

Lymington Harbour Commission provides berths at Dan Bran Pontoon and Lymington Town Quay in addition to the river moorings. Dan Bran is accessible at all states of the tide inside the wave screen. Power is available along its 650' length with use of the facilities at Lymington Town SC and walk ashore access to the town. It is sited between the marinas a short walk from Town Quay, and ideal for club rallies or events as it can accommodate up to 50 boats together.

Town Quay provides shelter up river at the foot of the cobbles, which lead directly to the town centre. 20 boats (up to 2m draft) raft up to 4 deep on a walk ashore pontoon. 50 fore and aft moorings lie just off the quay.

FACILITIES AT A GLANCE

Key
a Royal Lymington Yacht Club
b Lymington Town Sailing Club
c Yacht charter and sales
d Power boat sales

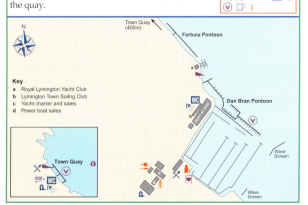

MARINA GUIDE 2018

MARINAS & SERVICES

BUCKLERS HARD MARINA

Bucklers Hard
Beaulieu, Brockenhurst, Hampshire, SO42 7XB
Tel: 01590 616200
www.beaulieuriver.co.uk Email: river@beaulieu.co.uk

VHF	Ch 68
ACCESS	H24

Meandering through the New Forest, the Beaulieu River is considered by many to be one of the most attractive harbours on the mainland side of the Solent. Two miles upstream from the mouth of the river lies Bucklers Hard, an historic 18th century village where shipwrights skilfully constructed warships for Nelson's fleet. The Maritime Museum, showing the history of boat-building in the village, is open throughout the year.

The marina, which provides overnight security, offers deep water to visitors at all states of the tide, although the bar at the river's entrance should be avoided two hours either side of LW.

FACILITIES AT A GLANCE

COWES YACHT HAVEN

Cowes Yacht Haven
Vectis Yard, Cowes, Isle of Wight, PO31 7BD
Tel: 01983 299975 Fax: 01983 200332
www.cowesyachthaven.com
Email: info@cowesyachthaven.com

VHF	Ch 80
ACCESS	H24

Situated virtually at the centre of the Solent, Cowes is best known as Britain's premier yachting centre and offers all types of facilities to yachtsmen. Cowes Yacht Haven, operating 24 hours a day, has very few permanent moorings and is dedicated to catering for visitors and events. At peak times it can become very crowded and for occasions such as Aberdeen Asset Management Cowes Week you need to book up in advance.

FACILITIES AT A GLANCE

VISITING COWES ON YOUR OWN BOAT?
Why not visit one of the most popular yacht clubs on the island, the famous
ISLAND SAILING CLUB
Home of the Round the Island Race.
Bar & dining room open every day all year.
Check website for opening times & full details of club activities.
70 High Street, Cowes PO31 7RE   Tel: 01983 296621
Email: admin@islandsc.org.uk   www.islandsc.org.uk

Richardsons YACHT SERVICES LTD

Island Harbour Marina
Mill Lane, Newport IoW PO30 2LA
• TRAVELIFT • REPAIRS • REFITS
• ENGINEERING • INSTALLATIONS
• PAINTING • ELECTRICAL
AGENTS FOR BETA, VETUS, MERMAID & LOMBARDINI INBOARD ENGINES AND TOHATSU OUTBOARDS
Extensive Chandlery and Equipment Sales
OPEN 7 DAYS A WEEK
01983 821095 • info@richardsonsyacht.co.uk
www.richardsonsyacht.co.uk

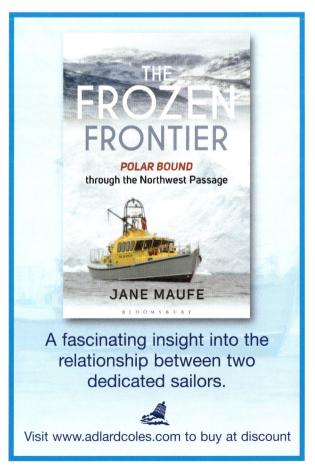

A fascinating insight into the relationship between two dedicated sailors.

Visit www.adlardcoles.com to buy at discount

CENTRAL SOUTHERN ENGLAND — **AREA 2**

SHEPARDS WHARF MARINA

Shepards Wharf Marina & Dry Sailing Centre
Medina Road, Cowes, Isle of Wight, PO31 7HT
Tel: 01983 297821
www.shepardswharfmarina.co.uk

VHF Ch 80
ACCESS H24

Two minutes walk from Cowes town centre, Shepards Wharf has capacity for 130 visiting boats, 40 residents, and a dry sailing basin. A family-friendly marina offering cruising and racing yachtsmen affordable berthing in a welcoming atmosphere.

Visitor berths can be booked in advance. All berths benefit from water, electricity, free wi-fi, inclusive showers, and site-wide CCTV. Discounted rates for rallies of six or more boats, sailing schools, and winter berthing. Onsite are the Amabi Restaurant, Girls for Sail, Island Divers, and Solent Sails.

The Sugar Store Events Centre has a prime waterside location overlooking the Solent, with decking and marina pier, and nearby transport links.

Competitively priced fuel is available from Cowes Harbour Fuels 200m south of the chain ferry.

SHEPARDS WHARF MARINA

The marina for cruising & racing yachtsmen

FAMILY FRIENDLY
FIRST CLASS FACILITIES
COWES HIGH STREET 2 MINS

Marina Berthing
Booking for visitor berths
Full marina facilities
Free WiFi, onsite restaurant

Dry Sailing Centre
For RIBs & day boats
Launch capacity 6 tonnes
Annual & seasonal packages

Rallies & Regattas
The rally friendly marina
Discounts for 6+ boats
Waterside Sugar Store Events Centre

Great location, great staff - you are guaranteed a smile on arrival!

Tel: **01983 297821**
Email: shepards.chc@cowes.co.uk
www.shepardswharfmarina.co.uk
Shepards Wharf Marina, Medina Road
Cowes, Isle of Wight, PO31 7HT

www.cowesharbourcommission.co.uk RYA /shepardswharfmarina @shepardswharf

EAST COWES MARINA

East Cowes Marina
Britannia Way, East Cowes, Isle of Wight, PO32 6UB
Tel: 01983 293983   Fax: 01983 299276
www.eastcowesmarina.co.uk
Email: berths@eastcowesmarina.co.uk

VHF Ch 80
ACCESS H24

Accommodating around 235 residential yachts and 150 visiting boats at all states of the tide, East Cowes Marina is situated on the quiet and protected east bank of the Medina River, about a quarter mile above the chain ferry. A small convenience store is just five minutes walk away. The new centrally heated shower and toilet facilities ensure the visitor a warm welcome at any time of the year, as does the on-site pub and restaurant.

Several water taxis provide a return service to Cowes, ensuring a quick and easy way of getting to West Cowes.

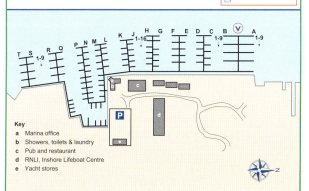

Key
a Marina office
b Showers, toilets & laundry
c Pub and restaurant
d RNLI, Inshore Lifeboat Centre
e Yacht stores

ISLAND HARBOUR MARINA

Island Harbour Marina
Mill Lane, Binfield, Newport, Isle of Wight, PO30 2LA
Tel: 01983 539994   Fax: 01983 523401
Email: info@island-harbour.co.uk

VHF Ch 80
ACCESS HW±4

Situated in beautiful rolling farmland about half a mile south of Folly Inn, Island Harbour Marina provides around 200 visitors' berths. Protected by a lock that is operated daily from 0800 – 2100 during the summer and from 0800 – 1730 during the winter, the marina is accessible for about three hours either side of HW for draughts of 1.5m.

Due to its secluded setting, the marina's on site chandlery also sells essential provisions and newspapers. A half hour walk along the river brings you to Newport, the capital and county town of the Isle of Wight.

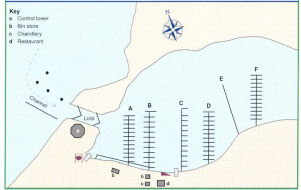

Key
a Control tower
b Bin store
c Chandlery
d Restaurant

MARINA GUIDE 2018   21

MARINAS & SERVICES

HYTHE MARINA VILLAGE

Hythe Marina Village
Shamrock Way, Hythe, Southampton, SO45 6DY
Tel: 023 8020 7073
Email: hythe@mdlmarinas.co.uk
www.hythemarinavillage.co.uk

VHF Ch 80
ACCESS H24

Situated on the western shores of Southampton Water, Hythe Marina Village is approached by a dredged channel leading to a lock basin. The lock gates are controlled H24 throughout the year with a waiting pontoon south of the approach basin.

Hythe Marina Village incorporates full marine services as well as on-site restaurants and a selection of shops can be found in the town centre, a 5 minute walk away. Forming an integral part of the New Forest Waterside, Hythe is the perfect base from which to explore Hampshire's pretty inland villages and towns, or alternatively you can catch the ferry to Southampton's Town Quay.

Key
a Restaurants and bars
b Lock building
c Boat storage and Trailer park

TOWN QUAY

Associated British Ports
Town Quay, Southampton, SO14 2AQ
Tel: 02380 234397   Mobile: 07764 293588
Email: info@townquay.com   www.townquay.com

VHF Ch 80
ACCESS H24

In the heart of Southampton, Town Quay is walking distance from the City's cultural quarter, West Quay Shopping Centre and a variety of restaurants, bars and theatres making the marina a vibrant place to stay all year round.

The marina is accessible at all states of the tide and the reception is open 24 hours a day with free drinks and wi-fi. Free cycle hire and use of a gas BBQ on the 'chill out' deck is available.

Located on the eastern shores of Southampton Water, Town Quay offers unrivalled views of Southampton's busy maritime activity and direct access to the world famous cruising and racing waters of the Solent.

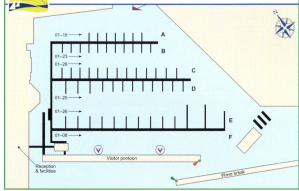

OCEAN VILLAGE MARINA

Ocean Village Marina
2 Channel Way, Southampton, SO14 3TG
Tel: 023 8022 9385
Email: oceanvillage@mdlmarinas.co.uk
www.oceanvillagemarina.co.uk

VHF Ch 80
ACCESS H24

The entrance to Ocean Village Marina lies on the port side of the River Itchen, just before the Itchen Bridge. With the capacity to accommodate large yachts and tall ships, the marina, accessible 24 hours a day, is a renowned home for international yacht races.

Situated at the heart of an exciting new waterside development incorporating shops, cinemas, restaurants and a £50m luxury spa hotel complex, as well as the Royal Southampton Yacht Club, Ocean Village offers a vibrant atmosphere for all visitors.

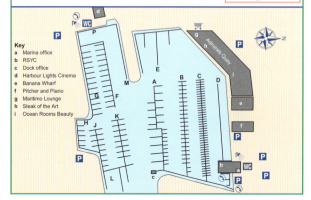

Key
a Marina office
b RSYC
c Dock office
d Harbour Lights Cinema
e Banana Wharf
f Pitcher and Piano
g Maritimo Lounge
h Steak of the Art
i Ocean Rooms Beauty

SHAMROCK QUAY

Shamrock Quay
William Street, Northam, Southampton, Hants, SO14 5QL
Tel: 023 8022 9461
Email: shamrockquay@mdlmarinas.co.uk
www.shamrockquay.co.uk

VHF Ch 80
ACCESS H24

Shamrock Quay, lying upstream of the Itchen Bridge on the port hand side, offers excellent facilities to yachtsmen. It also benefits from being accessible and manned 24 hours a day. On-site there is a 75-ton travel hoist and a 47-ton boat mover, and for dining out there is a choice of restaurants and bars.

The city centre is about two miles away, where among the numerous attractions are the Medieval Merchant's House in French Street, the Southampton City Art Gallery and the SeaCity Museum in the Civic Centre.

Key
a Offices, bars and restaurants
b Marina office
c Café

CENTRAL SOUTHERN ENGLAND

AREA 2

KEMPS QUAY

Kemp's Shipyard Ltd
Quayside Road, Southampton, SO18 1BZ
Tel: 023 8063 2323   Fax: 023 8022 6002
Email: enquiries@kempsquay.com

VHF
ACCESS HW±3.5

At the head of the River Itchen on the starboard side is Kemps Quay, a family-run marina with a friendly, old-fashioned feel. Accessible only 3½ hrs either side of HW, it has a limited number of deep water berths, the rest being half tide, drying out to soft mud. Its restricted access is, however, reflected in the lower prices.

Although situated on the outskirts of Southampton, a short bus or taxi ride will soon get you to the city centre. Besides a nearby BP Garage selling bread and milk, the closest supermarkets can be found in Bitterne Shopping Centre, which is five minutes away by bus.

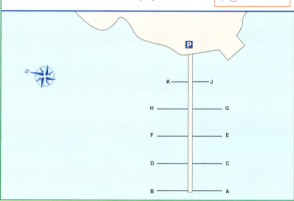

SAXON WHARF

Saxon Wharf
Lower York Street, Northam, Southampton, SO14 5QF
Tel: 023 8033 9490
Email: saxonwharf@mdlmarinas.co.uk
www.saxonwharfmarina.co.uk

VHF Ch 80
ACCESS H24

Placed on the River Itchen in Southampton, Saxon Wharf is a marine service centre specifically designed for the superyacht market. With a 200-ton boat hoist and heavy duty pontoons, Saxon Wharf is the ideal location for large vessels in need of secure, quick turnaround lift-outs, repair work or even full-scale refits.

With a Dry Stack facility boasting the largest capacity forklift truck in the UK, Saxon Wharf can now dry stack boats of up to 13m LOA. There is also ample storage ashore and 24-hour security. Shamrock Quay, where there are bars and restaurants, is within 300 metres of this location.

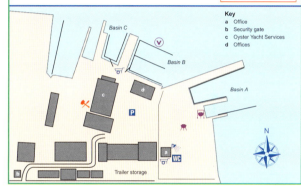

Key
a Office
b Security gate
c Oyster Yacht Services
d Offices

HAMBLE POINT MARINA

Hamble Point Marina
School Lane, Hamble, Southampton, SO31 4NB
Tel: 023 8045 2464
Email: hamblepoint@mdlmarinas.co.uk
www.hamblepointmarina.co.uk

VHF Ch 80
ACCESS H24

Situated virtually opposite Warsash, this is the first marina you will come to on the western bank of the Hamble. Accommodating yachts and power boats up to 30m in length, it offers easy access to the Solent.

The marina boasts extensive facilities including 121 Dry Stack berths for motorboats up to 10 metres and over 50 tenants who provide boat-owners with a wide range of marine services from boat repairs to electrical work. Hamble Point is within a 20-minute walk of Hamble Village, where there are a plethora of pubs and restaurants on offer.

Key
a Information
b First aid point
c Marina office
d Administration office
e Chandlery
f Ketch Rigger Bar and Restaurant
g Sailmakers

PORT HAMBLE MARINA

Port Hamble Marina
Satchell Lane, Hamble, Southampton, SO31 4QD
Tel: 023 8045 2741
Email: porthamble@mdlmarinas.co.uk
www.porthamblemarina.co.uk

VHF Ch 80
ACCESS H24

Port Hamble Marina is situated on the River Hamble right in the heart of the South Coast's sailing scene. With thousands of visitors every year, this busy marina is popular with racing enthusiasts and cruising vessels looking for a vibrant atmosphere. The picturesque Hamble village, with its inviting pubs and restaurants, is only a few minutes walk away.

On site, Port Hamble also offers excellent amenities including luxurious all-new male and female facilities, alongside boutique style extension shower rooms. Banana Wharf bar and restaurant provides the perfect spot to meet, eat and drink by the water whilst petrol and diesel is available seven days a week. Locally there are several companies on hand who cater for every boating need.

Key
a Dock manager's office
b Boat sales
c Royal Air Force YC
d Banana Wharf Bar & Restaurant

MARINA GUIDE 2018

MARINAS & SERVICES

MERCURY YACHT HARBOUR

Mercury Yacht Harbour
Satchell Lane, Hamble, Southampton, SO31 4HQ
Tel: 023 8045 5994
Email: mercury@mdlmarinas.co.uk
www.mercuryyachtharbour.co.uk

VHF Ch 80
ACCESS H24

Mercury Yacht Harbour is the third marina from seaward on the western bank of the River Hamble, tucked away in a picturesque, wooded site adjacent to Badnam Creek. Enjoying deep water at all states of the tide, it accommodates yachts up to 24m LOA and boasts an extensive array of facilities.

The on-site chandlery stocks a plethora of essential items, and for a good meal look no further than The Waters Edge Bar and Restaurant whose balcony offers striking views over the water. Hamble Village is only a 20-minute walk away.

FACILITIES AT A GLANCE

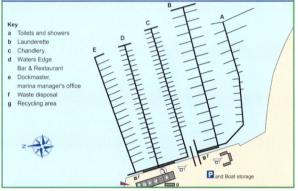

Key
a Toilets and showers
b Launderette
c Chandlery
d Waters Edge Bar & Restaurant
e Dockmaster, marina manager's office
f Waste disposal
g Recycling area

UNIVERSAL MARINA

Universal Marina
Crableck Lane, Sarisbury Green, Southampton, SO31 7ZN
Tel: 01489 574272 Fax: 01489 574273
Email: info@universalmarina.co.uk

VHF Ch 80
ACCESS H24

Universal Marina is one of the few remaining independent marinas offering south coast moorings. Universal Marina's unique location is unbeatable, tucked in between the oak trees on the East Bank of the Hamble where 68 acres of natural wildlife and marshlands surrounds the busy and friendly marina. Positioned only minutes off the M27, it is one of the most accessible marinas on the south coast. The 250 berth complex, features all the latest facilities required by the modern day boat owner, recently upgraded pontoons, power, water and wifi available to each berth. Visitors are welcome & although there are no dedicated visitor berths these are available by prior arrangement.

FACILITIES AT A GLANCE

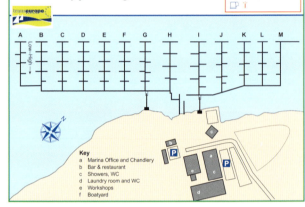

Key
a Marina Office and Chandlery
b Bar & restaurant
c Showers, WC
d Laundry room and WC
e Workshops
f Boatyard

SWANWICK MARINA

Swanwick Marina
Swanwick, Southampton, Hampshire, SO31 1ZL
Tel: 01489 884081 Fax: 01489 579073
Email: swanwick@premiermarinas.com
www.premiermarinas.com

VHF Ch 80
ACCESS H24

Situated on the east bank of the River Hamble next to Bursledon Bridge, Swanwick Marina is accessible at all states of the tide and can accommodate yachts up to 20m LOA.

The marina's fully-licensed bar and bistro, The Boat House, overlooking the river, is open for breakfast, lunch and dinner all year round. Alternatively, just a short row or walk away is the celebrated Jolly Sailor pub in Bursledon on the west bank, made famous for being the local watering hole in the British television series *Howard's Way*.

FACILITIES AT A GLANCE

Key
a Marina office
b Pub/restaurant
c Chandlery
d Boat sales offices

RYDE LEISURE HARBOUR

Ryde Harbour
The Esplanade, Ryde, Isle of Wight, PO33 1JA
Tel: 01983 613879 Fax: 01983 613903
www.rydeharbour.com Email: ryde.harbour@iow.gov.uk

VHF Ch 80
ACCESS HW±2

Known as the 'gateway to the Island', Ryde, with its elegant houses and abundant shops, is among the Isle of Wight's most popular resorts. Its well-protected harbour is conveniently close to the exceptional beaches as well as to the town's restaurants and amusements.

Drying to 2.5m and therefore only accessible to yachts that can take the ground, the harbour accommodates 90 resident boats as well as up to 75 visiting yachts. Fin keel yachts may dry out on the harbour wall.

Ideal for family cruising, Ryde offers a wealth of activities, ranging from ten pin bowling and ice skating to crazy golf and tennis.

FACILITIES AT A GLANCE

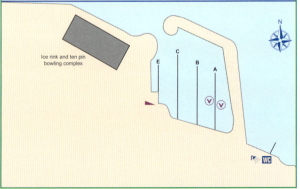

CENTRAL SOUTHERN ENGLAND   AREA 2

BEMBRIDGE HARBOUR

Bembridge Harbour
Harbour Office, The Duver, St Helens, Ryde
Isle of Wight, PO33 1YB
Tel: 01983 872828 Fax: 01983 872922
Email: chris@bembridgeharbour.co.uk
www.bembridgeharbour.co.uk

VHF Ch 80
ACCESS HW±2.5

Bembridge is a compact, pretty harbour whose entrance, although restricted by the tides (recommended entry for a 1.5m draught is 2½hrs before HW), is well sheltered in all but north north easterly gales. Offering excellent sailing clubs, beautiful beaches and fine restaurants, this Isle of Wight port is a first class haven with plenty of charm. With approximately 120 new visitors' berths on the Duver Marina pontoons, which can now be booked online, the marina at St Helen's Quay at the western end of the harbour is now allocated to annual berth holders only.

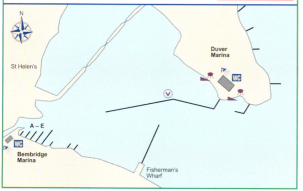

HASLAR MARINA

Haslar Marina
Haslar Road, Gosport, Hampshire, PO12 1NU
Tel: 023 9260 1201 Fax: 023 9260 2201
www.haslarmarina.co.uk Email: sales@haslarmarina.co.uk

VHF Ch 80
ACCESS H24

This modern, purpose-built marina lies to port on the western side of Portsmouth Harbour entrance and is easily recognised by its prominent lightship incorporating a bar and restaurant. Accessible at all states of the tide, Haslar's extensive facilities do not however include fuel, the nearest being at the Gosport Marina only a few cables north.

Within close proximity is the Royal Navy Submarine Museum and the Museum of Naval Firepower 'Explosion' both worth a visit.

GOSPORT MARINA

Premier Gosport Marina
Mumby Road, Gosport, Hampshire, PO12 1AH
Tel: 023 9252 4811 Fax: 023 9258 9541
Email: gosport@premiermarinas.com
www.premiermarinas.com

VHF Ch 80
ACCESS H24

A few cables north of Haslar Marina, again on the port hand side, lies Gosport Marina. Boasting 519 fully-serviced, visitors' and 80 dry stack berths, its extensive range of facilities incorporates a fuel barge on its southern breakwater as well as shower and laundry amenities. Numerous boatyard and engineering specialists are also located in and around the premises.

Within easy reach of the marina is Gosport town centre, offering a cosmopolitan selection of restaurants along with several supermarkets and shops.

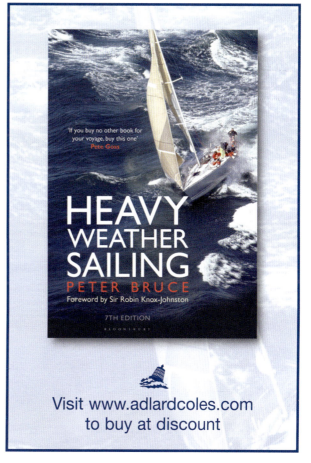

MARINA GUIDE 2018

MARINAS & SERVICES

ROYAL CLARENCE MARINA

Royal Clarence Marina, Royal Clarence Yard
Weevil Lane, Gosport, Hampshire PO12 1AX
Tel: 02392 523523 Fax: 02392 523523
Email: mikebraidley@castlemarinas.co.uk
www.royalclarencemarina.org

VHF Ch 80
ACCESS H24

Royal Clarence Marina enjoys a unique setting, with the former Royal Navy victualling yard as its backdrop and views across to Gunwharf Quays on the opposite side of the harbour. The remarkably peaceful and calm marina lies within a deep water basin with 5.25m draught and offers berths up to 18m in length. RCM also has over 150m of alongside berthing making it the ideal location for rallies and other maritime events. Only five minutes from the entrance to Portsmouth Harbour, the marina is ideally located for cruising and racing in the Solent and beyond.

FACILITIES AT A GLANCE

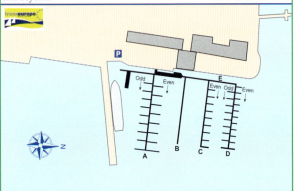

WICORMARINE YACHT HAVEN

WicorMarine Yacht Haven
Cranleigh Road, Portchester, Hampshire, PO16 9DR
Tel: 01329 237112 Fax: 01329 248595
Email: inbox@wicormarine.co.uk

VHF
ACCESS H24

WicorMarine Yacht Haven is situated in the picturesque upper reaches of Portsmouth Harbour away from the hustle and bustle. Their deepwater pontoons offer an affordable alternative to busy marinas and are only 30 mins from the harbour entrance.

An excellent range of boatyard facilities including a 12T boat hoist, undercover storage, H24 showers and toilets, diesel, fresh water, on site repair services and a well-stocked chandlery complete with Calor Gas and Camping Gaz exchange. A water taxi operates at peak times during the sailing season but they also offer dinghy storage and owners' store. The popular, licensed Salt Café is open to visitors all year round where you can take in the stunning views of the harbour from the waterfront deck.

FACILITIES AT A GLANCE

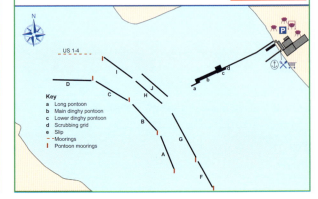

PORT SOLENT MARINA

Port Solent Marina
South Lockside, Portsmouth, PO6 4TJ
Tel: 023 9221 0765 Fax: 023 9232 4241
www.premiermarinas.com
Email: portsolent@premiermarinas.com

VHF Ch 80
ACCESS H24

Port Solent Marina is located to the north east of Portsmouth Harbour, not far from the historic Portchester Castle. Accessible via a 24-hour lock, this purpose built marina offers a full range of facilities. The Boardwalk comprises an array of shops and restaurants, while close by is a David Lloyd Health Centre and a large Odeon cinema.

No visit to Portsmouth Harbour is complete without a trip to the Historic Dockyard, home to Henry VIII's *Mary Rose*, Nelson's HMS *Victory* and the first iron battleship, HMS *Warrior*, built in 1860.

FACILITIES AT A GLANCE

SOUTHSEA MARINA

Southsea Marina
Fort Cumberland Road, PO4 9RJ
Tel: 02392 822719 Fax: 02392 822220
Email: southsea@premiermarinas.com
www.premiermarinas.com

VHF Ch 80
ACCESS HW±3

Southsea Marina is a small and friendly marina located on the western shore of Langstone Harbour, an expansive tidal bay situated between Hayling Island and Portsmouth. The channel is clearly marked by seven starboard and nine port hand markers. A tidal gate allows unrestricted movement in and out of the marina up to 3 hours either side of HW operates the entrance. The minimum depth in the marina entrance during this period is 1.6m and a waiting pontoon is available. There are excellent on site facilities including a bar, restaurant and chandlery.

FACILITIES AT A GLANCE

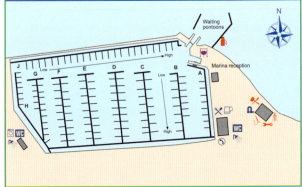

MARINA GUIDE 2018

CENTRAL SOUTHERN ENGLAND

AREA 2

SPARKES MARINA

Sparkes Marina
38 Wittering Road, Hayling Island, Hampshire, PO11 9SR
Tel: 023 9246 3572
Email: sparkes@mdlmarinas.co.uk www.sparkesmarina.co.uk

VHF Ch 80 ACCESS H24

Just inside the entrance to Chichester Harbour, on the eastern shores of Hayling Island, lies Sparkes Marina. One of two marinas in Chichester to have full tidal access, its facilities include 24-hour showers and toilets, a laundry room, an office/reception, and the Piranha Bar & Restaurant.

In addition to its berthing and marina services, Sparkes has many skilled professionals on site, including specialists in engineering, outboard engines, glass fibre repairs, rigging, sails and covers, marine carpentry, electrical, boat management and valeting. There is storage ashore for over 200 boats and a 40 ton mobile crane (lifting capacity 15 tons).

FACILITIES AT A GLANCE

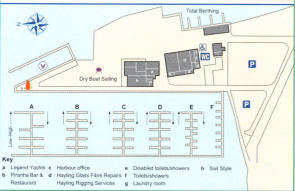

Key
a Legend Yachts
b Piranha Bar & Restaurant
c Harbour office
d Hayling Glass Fibre Repairs
  Hayling Rigging Services
e Disabled toilets/showers
f Toilets/showers
g Laundry room
h Sail Style

NORTHNEY MARINA

Northney Marina
Northney Road, Hayling Island, Hampshire, PO11 0NH
Tel: 023 9246 6321
Email: northney@mdlmarinas.co.uk
www.northneymarina.co.uk

VHF Ch 80 ACCESS H24

Situated in Chichester Harbour, Northney Marina and its slipway are accessible at all states of the tide. The 228-berth marina is set on the northern shore of Hayling Island in the well marked Sweare Deep Channel, which branches off to port almost at the end of Emsworth Channel.

Offering excellent boatyard facilities, the marina incorporates a provisions store and laundry area as well as fantastic ablution facilities plus wi-fi and 24/7 staff cover. There is also an events area for rallies.

FACILITIES AT A GLANCE

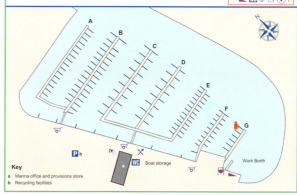

Key
a Marina office and provisions store
b Recycling facilities

EMSWORTH YACHT HARBOUR

Emsworth Yacht Harbour Ltd
Thorney Road, Emsworth, Hants, PO10 8BP
Tel: 01243 377727 Fax: 01243 373432
Email: info@emsworth-marina.co.uk
www.emsworth-marina.co.uk

VHF ACCESS HW±2

Accessible about one and a half to two hours either side of high water, Emsworth Yacht Harbour is a sheltered site, offering good facilities to yachtsmen.

Created in 1964 from a log pond, the marina is within easy walking distance of the pretty little town of Emsworth, which boasts at least 10 pubs, several high quality restaurants and two well-stocked convenience stores.

FACILITIES AT A GLANCE

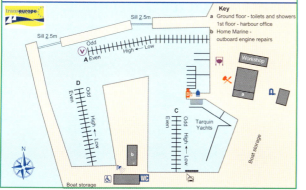

Key
a Ground floor - toilets and showers
  1st floor - harbour office
b Home Marine - outboard engine repairs

CHICHESTER MARINA

Chichester Marina
Birdham, Chichester, West Sussex, PO20 7EJ
Tel: 01243 512731 Fax: 01243 513472
Email: chichester@premiermarinas.com
www.premiermarinas.com

VHF Ch 80 ACCESS HW±5

Chichester Marina, nestling in an enormous natural harbour, has more than 1,000 berths, making it one of the largest in the UK. Its approach channel can be easily identified by the CM SHM pile. The channel was dredged to 0.5m below CD in 2004, giving access of around five hours either side of HW at springs. Besides the wide ranging marine facilities, there are also a restaurant and small convenience store on site. Chichester, which is only about a five minute bus or taxi ride away, has several places of interest, the most notable being the cathedral.

FACILITIES AT A GLANCE

Key
a Brush washing facility
b Toilets, showers, baby change, telephone
c Trailer sailer storage
d BA Peters offices
e Launderette
f Toilets, showers, baby change, telephone, disabled facilities
g Restaurant/bar, chandlery, shop
h Reception car park
i CYC boat park
j Marina control building
k Security checkpoint

MARINA GUIDE 2018

MARINAS & SERVICES

BIRDHAM POOL MARINA

Birdham Pool Marina
Birdham Pool, Chichester, Sussex
Tel: 01243 512310 Fax: 01243 513163
Email: mikebraidley@castlemarinas.co.uk

VHF Ch 80
ACCESS HW±3

Birdham Pool must be among Britain's most charming and rustic marinas. Its recently dredged channel allows access for up to four hours either side of HW via a lock. Any visiting yachtsman will not be disappointed by its unique and picturesque setting. The marina boasts a boatyard with skilled craftsmen offering a wide range of services as well as fuel. The channel is marked by green piles that should be left no more than 3m to starboard.

FACILITIES AT A GLANCE

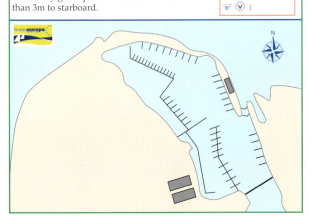

NAVIGATORS
MARINE SERVICE CENTRE

One-stop Yacht Care in Chichester Harbour

**Marine Engineering
Marine Electrics
Plumbing and Heating
Yacht Valeting
Gelcoat and GRP Repairs
Painting and Varnishing
Yacht Care Services**

Unit C2 Chichester Marina, Birdham, Chichester, PO20 7EJ
t: 01243 513336   e: info@navigatorsmarine.co.uk
www.navigatorsmarine.co.uk

VELOX PLUS Propeller Antifouling

COPPER COAT MULTI-SEASON ANTI-FOULING

Jet Thrusters Power, Sail and Catamarans

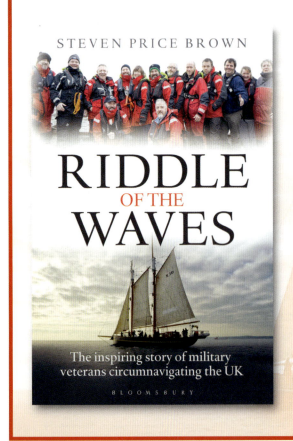

STEVEN PRICE BROWN

RIDDLE OF THE WAVES

The inspiring story of military veterans circumnavigating the UK

BLOOMSBURY

This unique and inspiring account follows the *Spirit of Falmouth's* voyage around the country that the men onboard had sworn to protect.

Visit www.adlardcoles.com
to buy at discount

28 MARINA GUIDE 2018

If you love the freedom of being afloat, Haslar Marina is perfectly located for escaping to sea or enjoying lazy days onboard.

TALK TO US

about a new home for your boat and the benefits of being a Dean & Reddyhoff berth holder

With marinas in **Hampshire**, **Dorset** and the **Isle of Wight**, we're only a short sail away.

02392 601201

haslar marina

deanreddyhoff.co.uk

MARINAS & SERVICES

SOUTH EAST ENGLAND – Selsey Bill to North Foreland

Reeds PDF ebooks

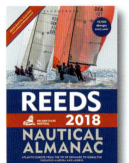

In response to popular demand, all the Reeds Almanacs are now available as searchable, highlightable PDF ebooks. (All ebooks incorporate the Marina Guide.)

Visit www.reedsnauticalalmanac.co.uk for further information

Key to Marina Plans symbols

- Bottled gas
- Chandler
- Disabled facilities
- Electrical supply
- Electrical repairs
- Engine repairs
- First Aid
- Fresh Water
- Fuel - Diesel
- Fuel - Petrol
- Hardstanding/boatyard
- Internet Café
- Laundry facilities
- Lift-out facilities
- Parking
- Pub/Restaurant
- Pump out
- Rigging service
- Sail repairs
- Shipwright
- Shop/Supermarket
- Showers
- Slipway
- Toilets
- Telephone
- Trolleys
- Visitors berths
- Wi-Fi

Area 3 - South East England

MARINAS
Telephone Numbers
VHF Channel
Access Times

- **Ramsgate Royal Harbour Marina** 01843 572100 Ch 14, 80 H24
- **Dover Marina** 01304 241663 Ch 80 H24
- **Harbour of Rye** 01797 225225 Ch 14 HW±2
- **Sovereign Harbour Marina** 01323 470099 Ch 17 H24
- **Newhaven Marina** 01273 513881 Ch 80 H24
- **Brighton Marina** 01273 819919 Ch M, 80 H24
- **Lady Bee Marina** 01273 593801 Ch 14 H24
- **Littlehampton Marina** 01903 713553 Ch 80 HW-3 to +2.5
- **Hillyards** 01903 713327 HW-3 to +2.5

Locations: N. Foreland, Margate, Ramsgate, S. Foreland, Dover, Folkestone, Rye, Eastbourne, Newhaven, Brighton, Shoreham, Littlehampton

Now available as an app!

A selection of Adlard Coles Nautical titles are now available as apps. Download these titles direct to your smart phone or tablet and take our expert authors with you wherever you go: www.adlardcoles.com

SOUTH EAST ENGLAND

AREA 3

LITTLEHAMPTON MARINA

Littlehampton Marina
Ferry Road, Littlehampton, W Sussex
Tel: 01903 713553 Fax: 01903 732264
Email: sales@littlehamptonmarina.co.uk

VHF Ch 80
ACCESS HW-3 to +2.5

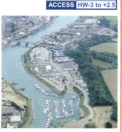

A typical English seaside town with funfair, promenade and fine sandy beaches, Littlehampton lies roughly midway between Brighton and Chichester at the mouth of the River Arun. It affords a convenient stopover for yachts either east or west bound, providing you have the right tidal conditions to cross the entrance bar with its charted depth of 0.7m. The marina lies about three cables above Town Quay and Fisherman's Quay, both of which are on the starboard side of the River Arun, and is accessed via a retractable footbridge that opens on request to the HM (note that you should contact him by 1630 the day before you require entry).

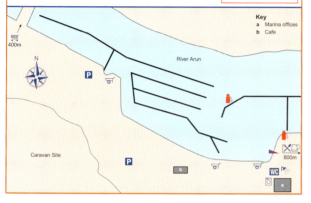

Key
a Marina offices
b Cafe

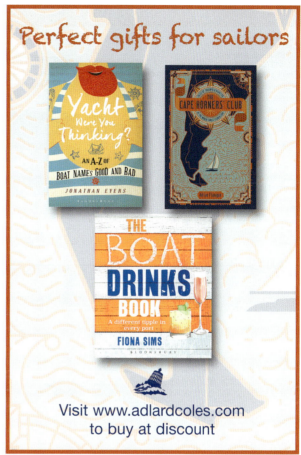

Perfect gifts for sailors

Visit www.adlardcoles.com to buy at discount

LADY BEE MARINA

Lady Bee Marina
138-140 Albion Street, Southwick
West Sussex, BN42 4EG
Tel: 01273 593801 Fax: 01273 870349

VHF Ch 14
ACCESS H24

Shoreham, only five miles west of Brighton, is one of the South Coast's major commercial ports handling, among other products, steel, grain, tarmac and timber. On first impressions it may seem that Shoreham has little to offer the visiting yachtsman, but once through the lock and into the eastern arm of the River Adur, the quiet Lady Bee Marina, with its Spanish waterside restaurant, can make this harbour an interesting alternative to the lively atmosphere of Brighton Marina. Run by the Harbour Office, the marina meets all the usual requirements, although fuel is available in cans from Southwick garage or from Corral's diesel pump situated in the western arm.

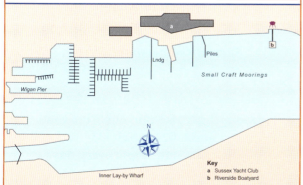

Key
a Sussex Yacht Club
b Riverside Boatyard

BRIGHTON MARINA

Brighton Marina
West Jetty, Brighton, East Sussex, BN2 5UP
Tel: 01273 819919 Fax: 01273 675082
Email: brighton@premiermarinas.com
www.premiermarinas.com

VHF Ch M, 80
ACCESS H24

Brighton Marina is the largest marina in the country and with its extensive range of shops, restaurants and facilities, is a popular and convenient stopover for east and west-going passagemakers. Note, however, that it is not advisable to attempt entry in strong S to SE winds.

Only half a mile from the marina is the historic city of Brighton itself, renowned for being a cultural centre with a cosmopolitan atmosphere. Among its numerous attractions are the exotic Royal Pavilion, built for King George IV in the 1800s, and the Lanes, with its multitude of antiques shops.

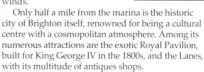

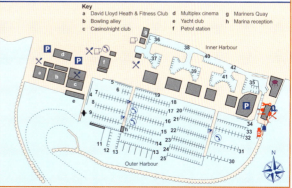

Key
a David Lloyd Heath & Fitness Club   d Multiplex cinema   g Mariners Quay
b Bowling alley   e Yacht club   h Marina reception
c Casino/night club   f Petrol station

MARINA GUIDE 2018

MARINAS & SERVICES

NEWHAVEN MARINA

Newhaven Marina
The Yacht Harbour, Fort Road, Newhaven
East Sussex, BN9 9BY
Tel: 01273 513881
Email: john.stirling@newhavenmarina.co.uk

VHF Ch 80
ACCESS H24

Some seven miles from Brighton, Newhaven lies at the mouth of the River Ouse. With its large fishing fleet and regular ferry services to Dieppe, the harbour has over the years become progressively commercial, therefore care is needed to keep clear of large vessels under manoeuvre.

The marina lies approximately quarter of a mile from the harbour entrance on the west bank and was recently dredged to allow full tidal access except on LWS.

FACILITIES AT A GLANCE

SOVEREIGN HARBOUR MARINA

Sovereign Harbour Marina
Pacific Drive, Eastbourne, East Sussex, BN23 5BJ
Tel: 01323 470099   Fax: 01323 470077
Email: sovereignharbour@premiermarinas.com
www.premiermarinas.com

VHF Ch 17
ACCESS H24

Opened in 1993 and taken over by Premier Marinas in 2007, Sovereign Harbour is accessible at all states of the tide and weather except for in strong NE to SE'ly winds. Entered via a lock H24, the Five Gold Anchor Award marina is part of one of the largest waterfront complexes in the UK, enjoying close proximity to shops, restaurants and a multiplex cinema. The Sovereign Harbour YC is on site and welcomes visitors to its bar and galley.

A short bus or taxi ride takes you to Eastbourne, where you will find shops and eating places to suit all tastes and budgets.

FACILITIES AT A GLANCE

Key
a The Waterfront, shops, restaurants, pubs and offices
b Harbour office - weather information and visitor's information
c Cinema
d Retail park - supermarket and post office
e Restaurant
f Toilets, showers, launderette and disabled facilities
g 24 hr fuel pontoon (diesel, petrol and holding tank pump out)
h Recycling centre
i Boatyard, boatpark, marine engineers, riggers and electricians
NB Berth numbering runs from low outer to high inner

HARBOUR OF RYE

Harbour of Rye
New Lydd Road, Camber, E Sussex, TN31 7QS
Tel: 01797 225225
Email: rye.harbour@environment-agency.gov.uk
www.environment-agency.gov.uk/harbourofrye

VHF Ch 14
ACCESS HW±2

The Strand Quay moorings are located in the centre of the historic town of Rye with all of its amenities a short walk away. The town caters for a wide variety of interests with the nearby Rye Harbour Nature Reserve, a museum, numerous antique shops and plentiful pubs, bars and restaurants. Vessels, up to a length of 15 metres, wishing to berth in the soft mud in or near the town of Rye should time their arrival at the entrance for not later than one hour after high water. Larger vessels should make prior arrangements with the Harbour Master. Fresh water, electricity, shower and toilet facilities are available.

FACILITIES AT A GLANCE

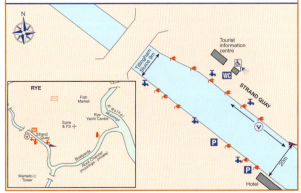

BOAT TRANSPORT BY SQUIRREL MARINE...
WITH JIM BRETT'S EXPERTISE

**Based in Kent
moving boats throughout the UK**

Specialised personal service

www.squirrelmarine.com
Jason.lengden@squirrelmarine.com
Jason 07446 821 333
Calls taken until 10pm every day

SOUTH EAST ENGLAND — AREA 3

DOVER MARINA

Dover Harbour Board
Harbour House, Dover, Kent, CT17 9TF
Tel: 01304 241663 Fax: 01304 242549
Email: marina@doverport.co.uk www.doverport.co.uk/marina

VHF Ch 80
ACCESS H24

Nestling under the famous White Cliffs, Dover sits between South Foreland to the NE and Folkestone to the SW. Boasting a maritime history stretching back as far as the Bronze Age, Dover is today one of Britain's busiest commercial ports, with a continuous stream of ferries and cruise liners plying to and from their European destinations. However, over the past years the harbour has made itself more attractive to the cruising yachtsman, with the marina, set well away from the busy ferry terminal, offering three sheltered berthing options in the Tidal Harbour, Granville Dock and Wellington Dock.

FACILITIES AT A GLANCE

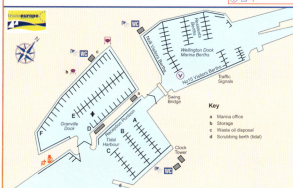

Key
a Marina office
b Storage
c Waste oil disposal
d Scrubbing berth (tidal)

ROYAL HARBOUR MARINA

Royal Harbour Marina, Ramsgate
Harbour Office, Military Road, Ramsgate, Kent, CT11 9LQ
Tel: 01843 572100 Fax: 01843 590941
Email: portoframsgate@thanet.gov.uk
www.portoframsgate.co.uk

VHF Ch 14, 80
ACCESS H24

Steeped in maritime history, Ramsgate was awarded 'Royal' status in 1821 by George IV in recognition of the warm welcome he received when sailing from Ramsgate. Offering good shelter and modern facilities, including both red and white diesel, the Royal Harbour comprises an outer marina accessible H24 and an inner marina, entered approximately HW±2. Permission to enter or leave the Royal Harbour must be obtained from Port Control on channel 14 and berthing instructions can be obtained from the Dockmaster on channel 80. Full information may be found on the website.

FACILITIES AT A GLANCE

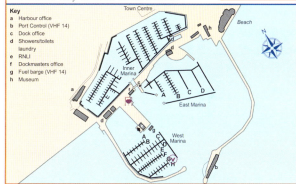

Key
a Harbour office
b Port Control (VHF 14)
c Dock office
d Showers/toilets laundry
e RNLI
f Dockmasters office
g Fuel barge (VHF 14)
h Museum

Gripping true life adventures

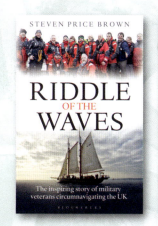
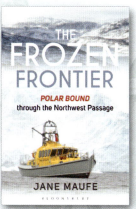

Visit www.adlardcoles.com to buy at discount

MARINA GUIDE 2018   33

Royal Harbour Marina

SAIL IN & SEE US

Have you considered a permanent mooring at the Royal Harbour Marina, Ramsgate?

- Kent's premier marina offering safe mooring 365 days a year with superb facilities
- 24 hour security, CCTV and foot patrols
- 40 tonne boat hoist
- Good road access

Please visit our website at www.portoframsgate.co.uk for our fees and charges

Contact us on: 01843 572100 or email portoframsgate@thanet.gov.uk

AREA 4

EAST ENGLAND – North Foreland to Great Yarmouth

Reeds PDF ebooks

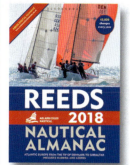

In response to popular demand, all the Reeds Almanacs are now available as searchable, highlightable PDF ebooks. (All ebooks incorporate the Marina Guide.)

Visit www.reedsnauticalalmanac.co.uk for further information

Key to Marina Plans symbols

	Symbol		Symbol
	Bottled gas	P	Parking
	Chandler		Pub/Restaurant
	Disabled facilities		Pump out
	Electrical supply		Rigging service
	Electrical repairs		Sail repairs
	Engine repairs		Shipwright
	First Aid		Shop/Supermarket
	Fresh Water		Showers
D	Fuel - Diesel		Slipway
P	Fuel - Petrol	WC	Toilets
	Hardstanding/boatyard		Telephone
@	Internet Café		Trolleys
	Laundry facilities	V	Visitors berths
	Lift-out facilities		Wi-Fi

Area 4 - East England

MARINAS
Telephone Numbers, VHF Channel, Access Times

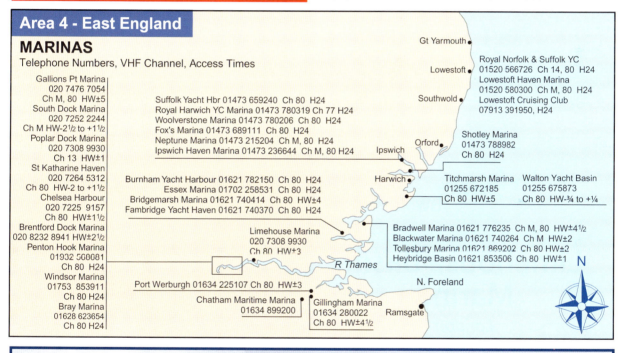

Gallions Pt Marina 020 7476 7054 Ch M, 80 HW±5
South Dock Marina 020 7252 2244 Ch M HW-2½ to +1½
Poplar Dock Marina 020 7308 9930 Ch 13 HW±1
St Katharine Haven 020 7264 5312 Ch 80 HW-2 to +1½
Chelsea Harbour 020 7225 9157 Ch 80 HW±1½
Brentford Dock Marina 020 8232 8941 Ch M HW±2½
Penton Hook Marina 01932 500081 Ch 80 H24
Windsor Marina 01753 853911 Ch 80 H24
Bray Marina 01628 623654 Ch 80 H24

Suffolk Yacht Hbr 01473 659240 Ch 80 H24
Royal Harwich YC Marina 01473 780319 Ch 77 H24
Woolverstone Marina 01473 780206 Ch 80 H24
Fox's Marina 01473 689111 Ch 80 H24
Neptune Marina 01473 215204 Ch M, 80 H24
Ipswich Haven Marina 01473 236644 Ch M, 80 H24

Burnham Yacht Harbour 01621 782150 Ch 80 H24
Essex Marina 01702 258531 Ch 80 H24
Bridgemarsh Marina 01621 740414 Ch 80 HW+4
Fambridge Yacht Haven 01621 740370 Ch 80 H24

Limehouse Marina 020 7308 9930 Ch 80 HW+3

Port Werburgh 01634 225107 Ch 80 HW±3
Chatham Maritime Marina 01634 899200
Gillingham Marina 01634 280022 Ch 80 HW±4½

Royal Norfolk & Suffolk YC 01520 566726 Ch 14, 80 H24
Lowestoft Haven Marina 01520 580300 Ch M, 80 H24
Lowestoft Cruising Club 07913 391950, H24

Shotley Marina 01473 788982 Ch 80 H24

Titchmarsh Marina 01255 672185 Ch 80 HW±5
Walton Yacht Basin 01255 675873 Ch 80 HW-¾ to +¼

Bradwell Marina 01621 776235 Ch M, 80 HW±4½
Blackwater Marina 01621 740264 Ch M HW±2
Tollesbury Marina 01621 869202 Ch 80 HW±2
Heybridge Basin 01621 853506 Ch 80 HW±1

Instant Weather Forecasting

You can predict the weather! With this unique little book, you can read the sky, pick up the clues and predict what the weather will do.

Visit www.adlardcoles.com to buy at discount

MARINAS & SERVICES

GILLINGHAM MARINA

Gillingham Marina
173 Pier Road, Gillingham, Kent, ME7 1UB
Tel: 01634 280022 Fax: 01634 280164
Email: berthing@gillingham-marina.co.uk
www.gillingham-marina.co.uk

VHF Ch 80
ACCESS HW±4.5

Gillingham Marina comprises a locked basin, accessible four and a half hours either side of high water, and a tidal basin upstream which can be entered approximately two hours either side of high water. Deep water moorings in the river cater for yachts arriving at other times.

Visiting yachts are usually accommodated in the locked basin, although it is best to contact the marina ahead of time. Lying on the south bank of the River Medway, the marina is approximately eight miles from Sheerness, at the mouth of the river, and five miles downstream of Rochester Bridge. Facilities include a well-stocked chandlery, brokerage and an extensive workshop.

PORT WERBURGH

Port Werburgh
Vicarage Lane, Hoo, Rochester, Kent, ME3 9TW
Tel: 01634 252107 Fax: 01634 253477
Email: jillswann@wanttoliveafloat.com

VHF Ch 80
ACCESS HW±3

Hoo Marina has been purchased by Residential Marine Ltd and is now incorporated into Port Werburgh. The port, some eight miles upriver from Sheerness, can be approached either straight across the mud flats at HW or via the creek, which has access HW±3 for shallow draught boats. The path of the creek is marked by withies, which must be kept to port.

The port accommodates residential and leisure boats from 20–200ft and has a lifting service available for craft up to 17 tons; a dry dock is available for larger boats. There are no workshop facilities but boat owners are encouraged to work on their own boats. Security is provided by H24 CCTV coverage.

All berths are supplied with water and electricity and the onsite amenity block has showers, toilets and a laundry room. There is a grocery store adjacent and shops in Hoo village approximately half a mile distant. There is a frequent bus service to nearby Rochester.

Limehouse Basin Marina
London

An oasis of calm in the heart of London

Fully serviced pontoons
Visitors welcome

020 7308 9930   bwml.co.uk   phil.cotman@bwml.co.uk

EAST ENGLAND — AREA 4

CHATHAM MARITIME MARINA

Chatham Maritime Marina, The Lock Building,
Leviathan Way, Chatham Maritime, Chatham, Medway, ME4 4LP
Tel: 01634 899200
Email: chatham@mdlmarinas.co.uk
www.chathammaritimemarina.co.uk

VHF Ch 80
ACCESS H24

Chatham Maritime Marina is situated on the banks of the River Medway in Kent, providing an ideal location from which to explore the surrounding area. There are plenty of secluded anchorages in the lower reaches of the Medway Estuary, while the river is navigable for some 13 miles from its mouth at Sheerness right up to Rochester, and even beyond for those yachts drawing less than 2m. Only 45 minutes from London by road, the marina is part of a multi-million pound leisure and retail development, accommodating 412 boats following a recent expansion.

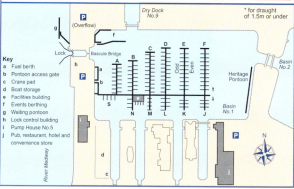

LIMEHOUSE MARINA

BWML Limehouse Marina
46 Goodhart Place, London, E14 8EG
Tel: 020 7308 9930 Fax: 020 7363 0428
Email: limehouse.marina@bwml.co.uk www.bwml.co.uk

VHF Ch 80
ACCESS HW±3

Limehouse Marina, situated where the canal system meets the Thames, is now considered the 'Jewel in the Crown' of the British inland waterways network. With complete access to 2,000 miles of inland waterway systems and with access to the Thames at most stages of the tide except around low water, the marina provides a superb location for river, canal and sea-going pleasure craft alike. Boasting a wide range of facilities and up to 90 berths, Limehouse Marina is housed in the old Regent's Canal Dock.

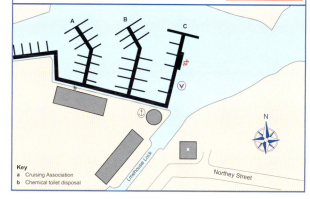

GALLIONS POINT MARINA

Gallions Point Marina, Gate 14, Royal Albert Basin
Woolwich Manor Way, North Woolwich
London, E16 2QY. Tel: 020 7476 7054 Fax: 020 7474 7056
Email: info@gallionspointmarina.co.uk
www.gallionspointmarina.co.uk

VHF Ch M, 80
ACCESS HW±5

Gallions Point Marina lies about 500 metres down-stream of the Woolwich Ferry on the north side of Gallions Reach. Accessed via a lock at the entrance to the Royal Albert Basin, the marina offers deep water pontoon berths as well as hard standing. Future plans to improve facilities include the development of a bar/restaurant, a chandlery and an RYA tuition school.

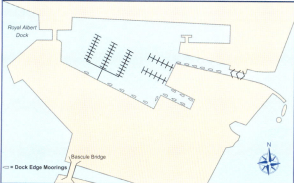

MARINA GUIDE 2018

MARINAS & SERVICES

SOUTH DOCK MARINA

South Dock Marina
Rope Street, Off Plough Way
London, SE16 7SZ
Tel: 020 7252 2244 Fax: 020 7237 3806
Email: christopher.magro@southwark.gov.uk

VHF	Ch M
ACCESS	HW-2.5 to +1.5

South Dock Marina is housed in part of the old Surrey Dock complex on the south bank of the River Thames. Its locked entrance is immediately downstream of Greenland Pier, just a few miles down river of Tower Bridge. For yachts with a 2m draught, the lock can be entered HW-2½ to HW+1½ London Bridge, although if you arrive early there is a holding pontoon on the pier. The marina can be easily identified by the conspicuous arched rooftops of Baltic Quay, a luxury waterside apartment block. Once inside this secure, 200-berth marina, you can take full advantage of all its facilities as well as enjoy a range of restaurants and bars close by or visit historic maritime Greenwich.

FACILITIES AT A GLANCE

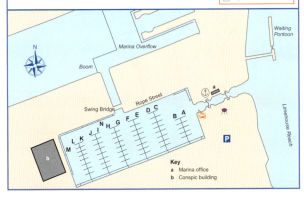

CHELSEA HARBOUR MARINA

Chelsea Harbour Marina
Estate Managements Office
C2-3 The Chambers, London, SW10 0XF
Tel: 07770 542783 Fax: 020 7352 7868
Email: harbourmaster@chelsea-harbour.co.uk

VHF	
ACCESS	HW±1.5

Chelsea Harbour is widely thought of as one of London's most significant maritime sites. It is located in the heart of SW London, therefore enjoying easy access to the amenities of Chelsea and the West End. On site is the Chelsea Harbour Design Centre, where 80 showrooms exhibit the best in British and International interior design, offering superb waterside views along with excellent cuisine in the Wyndham Grand.

The harbour lies approximately 48 miles up river from Sea Reach No 1 buoy in the Thames Estuary and is accessed via the Thames Flood Barrier in Woolwich Reach. With its basin gate operating one and a half hours either side of HW (+ 20 minutes at London Bridge), the marina welcomes visiting yachtsmen.

FACILITIES AT A GLANCE

ST KATHARINE DOCKS

St Katharine's Marina Ltd
50 St Katharine's Way, London, E1W 1LA
Tel: 020 7264 5312 Fax: 020 7702 2252
Email: marina.reception@skdocks.co.uk
www.skdocks.co.uk

VHF	Ch 80
ACCESS	HW -2 to +1.5

St Katharine's Marina is a 160 berth full service marina located in central London next to Tower Bridge.

St Katharine Docks is a unique marina benefiting from waterside dining, boutique shops and excellent transport links to the West End. Visitors are welcomed all year round and the marina provides its own calendar of events details of which can be found on the website and social media pages.

The marina is ideally situated for visiting the Tower of London, Tower Bridge, *HMS Belfast* and the City of London all of which can be reached on foot. A short river bus service away is Greenwich and the Cutty Sark and to the west the Shard and London Eye.

FACILITIES AT A GLANCE

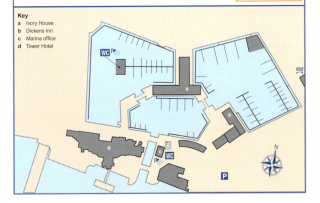

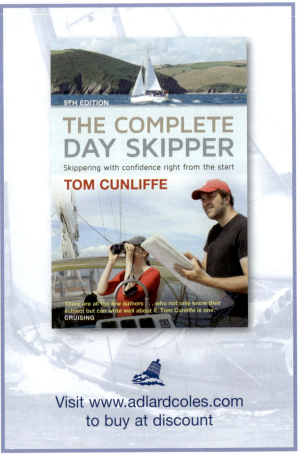

Visit www.adlardcoles.com
to buy at discount

MARINA GUIDE 2018

BRENTFORD DOCK MARINA

Brentford Dock Marina
2 Justin Close, Brentford, Middlesex, TW8 8QE
Tel: 020 8232 8941 Mob: 07970 143 987
E-mail: brentforddockmarina@gmail.com

VHF
ACCESS HW±2.5

Brentford Dock Marina is situated on the River Thames at the junction with the Grand Union Canal. Its hydraulic lock is accessible for up to two and a half hours either side of high water, although boats over 9.5m LOA enter on high water by prior arrangement. There is a grocery store on site. The main attractions within the area are the Royal Botanic Gardens at Kew and the Kew Bridge Steam Museum at Brentford.

FACILITIES AT A GLANCE

Key
a Shop
b Rubbish disposal
c Recycling bins
d Marina office and first aid
e Toilets, showers and slop out facilities

PENTON HOOK MARINA

Penton Hook Marina
Staines Road, Chertsey, Surrey, KT16 8PY
Tel: 01932 568681
Email: pentonhook@mdlmarinas.co.uk
www.pentonhookmarina.co.uk

VHF Ch 80
ACCESS H24

Penton Hook, the largest inland marina in Europe, is situated on what is considered to be one of the most attractive reaches of the River Thames; close to the vibrant town of Staines-on-Thames and about a mile downstream from Runnymede.

Providing unrestricted access to the River Thames through a deep water channel below Penton Hook Lock, the marina can accommodate ocean-going craft of up to 30m LOA and is ideally placed for a visit to Thorpe Park, reputedly one of the country's most popular family leisure attractions.

FACILITIES AT A GLANCE

Key
a Information point
b Dock manager's office
c Yacht club
d Repairs and under cover storage

WINDSOR MARINA

Windsor Marina
Maidenhead Road, Windsor
Berkshire, SL4 5TZ
Tel: 01753 853911
Email: windsor@mdlmarinas.co.uk www.windsormarina.co.uk

VHF Ch 80
ACCESS H24

Situated on the outskirts of Windsor town on the south bank of the River Thames, Windsor Marina enjoys a peaceful garden setting. On site is the Windsor Yacht Club and fuel (diesel and petrol), enabling you to fill up as and when you need.

A trip to the town of Windsor, comprising beautiful Georgian and Victorian buildings, would not be complete without a visit to Windsor Castle. With its construction inaugurated over 900 years ago by William the Conqueror, it is the oldest inhabited castle in the world and accommodates a priceless art and furniture collection.

FACILITIES AT A GLANCE

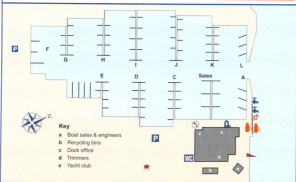

Key
a Boat sales & engineers
b Recycling bins
c Dock office
d Trimmers
e Yacht club

BRAY MARINA

Bray Marina
Monkey Island Lane, Bray
Berkshire, SL6 2EB
Tel: 01628 623654
Email: bray@mdlmarinas.co.uk www.braymarina.co.uk

VHF Ch 80
ACCESS H24

Bray Marina is situated in a country park setting among shady trees, providing berth holders with a tranquil mooring. From the marina there is direct access to the Thames and there are extensive well-maintained facilities available for all boat owners. The 400-berth marina boasts an active club, which holds social functions as well as boat training lessons and handling competitions, a small chandlery and engineering services.

Upstream is the National Trust property, Cliveden House, with its extensive gardens and woodlands. Cookham is home of the Queen's Swan Keeper, who can sometimes be seen in his traditional costume. Further on still is Hambledon Mill; from here the river is navigable as far as Lechlade.

FACILITIES AT A GLANCE

Key
a Boat storage
b Boat sales office
c Marina office, small chandlery, toilets, showers, repairs and engineering
d Battery, hazardous waste, oil and fuel disposal

MARINAS & SERVICES

BURNHAM YACHT HARBOUR MARINA

Burnham Yacht Harbour Marina Ltd
Burnham-on-Crouch, Essex, CM0 8BL
Tel: 01621 782150   Fax: 01621 785848
Email: admin@burnhamyachtharbour.co.uk

VHF Ch 80
ACCESS H24

Boasting four major yacht clubs, each with comprehensive racing programmes, Burnham-on-Crouch has come to be regarded by some as 'the Cowes of the East Coast'. At the western end of the town lies Burnham Yacht Harbour, dredged 2.2m below datum. Offering a variety of on site facilities, its entrance can be easily identified by a yellow pillar buoy with an 'X' topmark.

The historic town, with its 'weatherboard' and early brick buildings, elegant quayside and scenic riverside walks, exudes plenty of charm. Among its attractions are a sports centre, a railway museum and a two-screen cinema.

FACILITIES AT A GLANCE

Key
a Workshop
b Yacht sales
c Marina office
d Shower block
e The Swallowtail
f RNLI shore station
g Country park

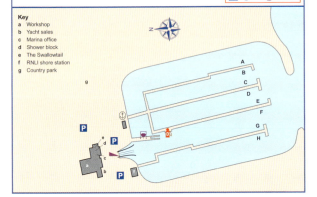

Burnham Yacht Harbour Marina Limited

Fully serviced modern Marina with 350 berths and storage facilities

- Shipwrights, riggers and engineers
- 11,000 square feet of repair buildings
- 30 tonne travel hoist useable at all states of the tide
- 100 tonne slipway
- Free wireless internet
- Visitors' berths with full access to showers, toilets and laundry facilities.
- On site chandlery, brokerage & The Swallowtail bar restaurant & function suite

Telephone 01621 782150
Harbour Master 01621 786832
VHF Channel 80
Email admin@burnhamyachtharbour.co.uk
www.burnhamyachtharbour.co.uk

ESSEX MARINA

Essex Marina
Wallasea Island, Essex, SS4 2HF
Tel: 01702 258531   Fax: 01702 258227
Email: info@essexmarina.co.uk
www.essexmarina.co.uk

VHF Ch 80
ACCESS H24

Surrounded by beautiful countryside, Essex Marina is situated in Wallasea Bay, about half a mile up river of Burnham on Crouch. Boasting 500 deep water berths, including 50 swinging moorings, the marina can be accessed at all states of the tide. On site are a 70 ton boat hoist, a chandlery and brokerage service as well as the Essex Marina Yacht Club.

Essex Marina is the home of Boats.co.uk. There is a ferry service which runs from Easter until the end of September, taking passengers across the river 6 days a week to Burnham, where you will find numerous shops and restaurants.

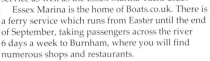

FACILITIES AT A GLANCE

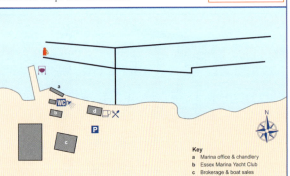

Key
a Marina office & chandlery
b Essex Marina Yacht Club
c Brokerage & boat sales
d Licenced bar & restaurant

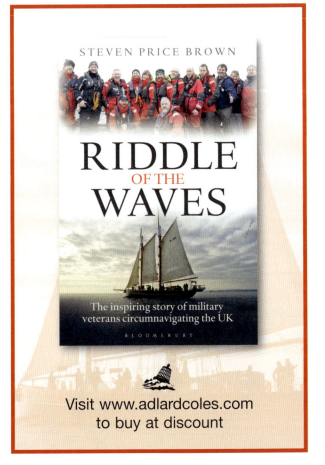

STEVEN PRICE BROWN

RIDDLE OF THE WAVES

The inspiring story of military veterans circumnavigating the UK

BLOOMSBURY

Visit www.adlardcoles.com to buy at discount

EAST ENGLAND AREA 4

BRIDGEMARSH MARINA

Bridgemarsh Marine
Fairholme, Bridge Marsh Lane, Althorne, Essex
Tel: 01621 740414   Mobile: 07968 696815   Fax: 01621 742216

VHF Ch 80
ACCESS HW±4

On the north side of Bridgemarsh Island, just beyond Essex Marina on the River Crouch, lies Althorne Creek. Here Bridgemarsh Marine accommodates over 100 boats berthed alongside pontoons supplied with water and electricity. A red beacon marks the entrance to the creek, with red can buoys identifying the approach channel into the marina. Accessible four hours either side of high water, the marina has an on site yard with two docks, a slipway and crane. The village of Althorne is just a short walk away, from where there are direct train services (taking approximately one hour) to London.

FACILITIES AT A GLANCE

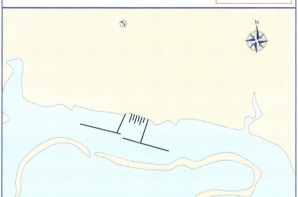

HEYBRIDGE BASIN

Heybridge Basin
Lock Hill, Heybridge Basin, Maldon, Essex, CM9 4RY
Tel: 07712 079764
Email: grant.everiss@waterways.org.uk
www.essexwaterways.com

VHF Ch 80
ACCESS HW±1

Towards the head of the River Blackwater and not far from Maldon, lies Heybridge Basin sea lock. It is situated at the lower end of the 14M Chelmer and Blackwater Navigation Canal and can be entered approximately 1-1.5hrs before HW for vessels drawing up to 2m. There is good holding ground in the river just outside the lock. There are in excess of 300 permanent moorings along the navigation and room for up to 20 rafting visiting vessels in the Basin, which has a range of facilities, including shower and laundry amenities. Please book at least 24hrs in advance especially during the summer months. The manned lock is operational for tides between 0600 and 2000.

FACILITIES AT A GLANCE

BRADWELL MARINA

Bradwell Marina, Port Flair Ltd, Waterside
Bradwell-on-Sea, Essex, CM0 7RB
Tel: 01621 776235   Fax: 01621 776393
Email: info@bradwellmarina.com
www.bradwellmarina.com

VHF Ch M, 80
ACCESS HW±4.5

Opened in 1984, Bradwell is a privately-owned marina situated in the mouth of the River Blackwater, serving as a convenient base from which to explore the Essex coastline or as a departure point for cruising further afield to Holland and Belgium.

The yacht basin can be accessed four and a half hours either side of HW and offers plenty of protection from all wind directions. With a total of 300 fully serviced berths, generous space has been allocated for manoeuvring between pontoons. Overlooking the marina is Bradwell Club House, incorporating a bar, restaurant, launderette and ablution facilities.

FACILITIES AT A GLANCE

Key
a Clubhouse
b Tower office

Bradwell Marina

- 350 Pontoon Berths in Rural Setting
- Access 4hrs either side H.W.
- VHF monitoring (CH.M, P1, 37 + 80)
- Water/electricity to all Pontoons
- Fuel jetty - petrol & diesel
- Bottled Calor gas
- Hot Showers
- 1st class workshop/repairs
- Day Launch Slipway
- Boat Hoistage to 45 tons
- Winter Storage
- Licensed Club (membership free)
- Free Wireless Internet

Port Flair Ltd., Waterside, Bradwell-on-Sea, Essex CM0 7RB
01621 776235/776391
www.bradwellmarina.com

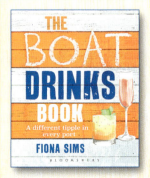

An essential boater's companion

An expert look at the drinking culture in key sailing spots around the world

 Visit www.adlardcoles.com to buy at discount

MARINA GUIDE 2018

MARINAS & SERVICES

FAMBRIDGE YACHT HAVEN

Fambridge Yacht Haven
Church Road, North Fambridge, Essex, CM3 6LU
Tel: 01621 740370   www.yachthavens.com
Email: fambridge@yachthavens.com

VHF Ch 80
ACCESS H24

Just under a mile upstream of North Fambridge, Stow Creek branches off to the north of the River Crouch. The creek, marked with occasional starboard hand buoys and leading lights, leads to the entrance to Fambridge Yacht Haven, which enjoys an unspoilt, tranquil setting between saltings and farmland. Home to West Wick Yacht Club, the marina has 220 berths and can accommodate vessels up to 17m LOA.

The nearby village of North Fambridge features the Ferryboat Inn, a favourite haunt with the boating fraternity. Only six miles down river lies Burnham-on-Crouch, while the Essex and Kent coasts are within easy sailing distance.

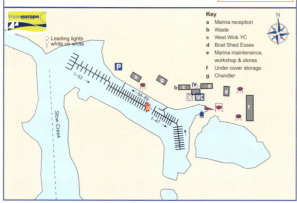

Key
a Marina reception
b Waste
c West Wick YC
d Boat Shed Essex
e Marina maintenance, workshop & stores
f Under cover storage
g Chandler

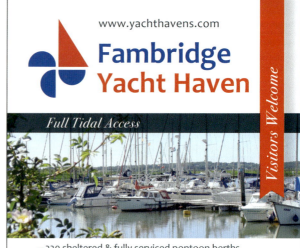

www.yachthavens.com

Fambridge Yacht Haven

Full Tidal Access

Visitors Welcome

— 220 sheltered & fully serviced pontoon berths
— 120 deepwater swinging moorings
— 120m visitor pontoon with full tidal access
— A TransEurope Marina
— FREE Wi-Fi for berth holders & visitors
— Walking distance from the famous Ferry Boat Inn
— Hassle-free Park & Ride Service
— Modern 25t & 18t slipway hoists & 30t mobile crane
— Extensive hard standing & undercover boat storage

Fambridge Yacht Haven Tel: 01621 740370   VHF Ch 80
Email: fambridge@yachthavens.com

BLACKWATER MARINA

Blackwater Marina
Marine Parade, Maylandsea, Essex
Tel: 01621 740264
Email: info@blackwater-marina.co.uk

VHF Ch M
ACCESS HW±2

Blackwater Marina is a place where families in day boats mix with Smack owners and yacht crews; here seals, avocets and porpoises roam beneath the big, sheltering East Coast skies and here the area's rich heritage of working Thames Barges and Smacks remains part of daily life today.
But it isn't just classic sailing boats that thrive on the Blackwater. An eclectic mix of motor cruisers, open boats and modern yachts enjoy the advantages of a marina sheltered by its natural habitat, where the absence of harbour walls allows uninterrupted views of some of Britain's rarest wildlife and where the 21st century shoreside facilities are looked after by experienced professionals, who are often found sailing on their days off.

Key
a Maylandsea Bay YC
b Harlow (Blackwater) Sailing Club
c Marina office

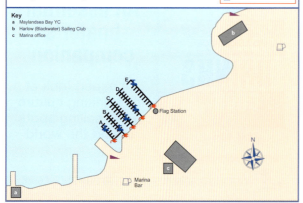

TOLLESBURY MARINA

Tollesbury Marina
The Yacht Harbour, Tollesbury, Essex, CM9 8SE
Tel: 01621 869202 Fax: 01621 868489
email: harbourmaster@tollesburymarina.com

VHF Ch 80
ACCESS HW±2

Tollesbury Marina lies at the mouth of the River Blackwater in the heart of the Essex countryside. Within easy access from London and the Home Counties, it has been designed as a leisure centre for the whole family, with on-site activities comprising tennis courts and a covered heated swimming pool as well as a convivial bar and restaurant. Accommodating over 240 boats, the marina can be accessed two hours either side of HW and is ideally situated for those wishing to explore the River Crouch to the south and the Rivers Colne, Orwell and Deben to the north.

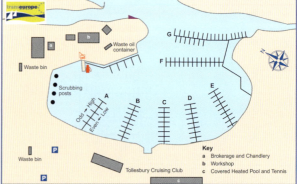

Key
a Brokerage and Chandlery
b Workshop
c Covered Heated Pool and Tennis

42 MARINA GUIDE 2018

EAST ENGLAND

AREA 4

TITCHMARSH MARINA

Titchmarsh Marina Ltd
Coles Lane, Walton on the Naze, Essex, CO14 8SL
Tel: 01255 672185 Fax: 01255 851901
Email: info@titchmarshmarina.co.uk
www.titchmarshmarina.co.uk

VHF	Ch 80
ACCESS	HW±5

Titchmarsh Marina sits on the south side of The Twizzle in the heart of the Walton Backwaters. As the area is designated a 'wetland of international importance', the marina has been designed and developed to function as a natural harbour. The 420 berths are well-sheltered by the high-grassed clay banks, offering good protection in all conditions. The marina entrance has a depth of 1.3m at LWS but once inside the basin this increases to around 2m; there is a tide gauge at the fuel berth. Among the excellent facilities onsite are the well-stocked chandlery and the Harbour Lights restaurant and bar serving food daily.

FACILITIES AT A GLANCE

Key
a Harbour master, chandlery (+ cycle hire) marine engineers, marine electronics
b Hardstanding
c Harbour Lights - restaurant and bar

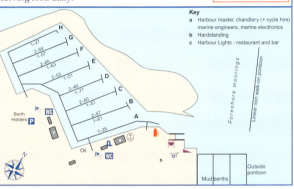

Friendly service in the beautiful Walton Backwaters
www.titchmarshmarina.co.uk
Tel: 01255 672 185   VHF: Channel 80
Email: info@titchmarshmarina.co.uk
Berthing Available - Various Options & Rates
Winter - Special Rates Ashore or Afloat
Storage Ashore - Long/ Short Term
Full Marina Facilities
Walton-on-the-Naze, Essex CO14 8SL

Gordon Bennett

The exhilarating true story of the first yacht race across the Atlantic, and the notorious New York playboy who won it.

Visit www.adlardcoles.com to buy at discount

WALTON YACHT BASIN

Walton and Frinton Yacht Trust
Mill Lane, Walton on the Naze, CO14 8PF
Managed by Bedwell & Co Tel: 01255 675873
After hours Tel: 07514 492815

VHF	Ch 80
ACCESS	HW-0.75,HW+0.25

Walton Yacht Basin lies at the head of Walton Creek, an area made famous in Arthur Ransome's *Swallows & Amazons* and *Secret Waters*. The creek can only be navigated HW±2, although yachts heading for the Yacht Basin should arrive on a rising tide as the entrance gate is kept shut once the tide turns in order to retain the water inside. Before entering the gate, moor up against the Club Quay to enquire about berthing availability.

A short walk away is the popular seaside town of Walton, full of shops, pubs and restaurants. Its focal point is the pier which, overlooking superb sandy beaches, offers various attractions. Slightly further out of town, the Naze affords pleasant coastal walks with striking panoramic views.

FACILITIES AT A GLANCE

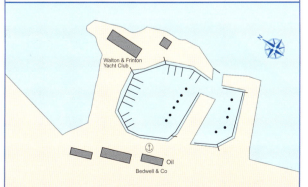

SUFFOLK YACHT HARBOUR

Suffolk Yacht Harbour Ltd
Levington, Ipswich, Suffolk, IP10 0LN
Tel: 01473 659240 Fax: 01473 659632
Email: info@syharbour.co.uk
www.syharbour.co.uk

VHF	Ch 80
ACCESS	H24

A friendly, independently-run marina on the East Coast of England, Suffolk Yacht Harbour enjoys a beautiful rural setting on the River Orwell, yet is within easy access of Ipswich, Woodbridge and Felixstowe. With approximately 550 berths, the marina offers extensive facilities while the Haven Ports Yacht Club provides a bar and restaurant.

FACILITIES AT A GLANCE

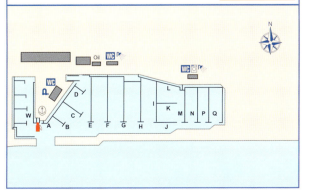

MARINA GUIDE 2018

MARINAS & SERVICES

SHOTLEY MARINA

Shotley Marina Ltd
Shotley Gate, Ipswich, Suffolk, IP9 1QJ
Tel: 01473 788982 Fax: 01473 788868
Email: sales@shotleymarina.co.uk
www.shotleymarina.co.uk   www.shotleymarina.com

VHF Ch 80
ACCESS H24

Based in the well protected Harwich Harbour where the River Stour joins the River Orwell, Shotley Marina is only eight miles from the county town of Ipswich. Entered via a lock at all states of the tide, its first class facilities include extensive boat repair and maintenance services as well as a well-stocked chandlery and on site bar and restaurant. The marina is strategically placed for sailing up the Stour to Manningtree, up the Orwell to Pin Mill or exploring the Rivers Deben, Crouch and Blackwater as well as the Walton Backwaters.

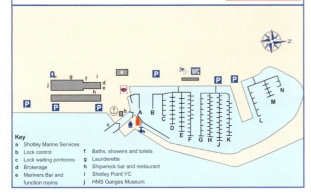

Key
- a Shotley Marine Services
- b Lock control
- c Lock waiting pontoons
- d Brokerage
- e Mariners Bar and function rooms
- f Baths, showers and toilets
- g Launderette
- h Shipwreck bar and restaurant
- i Shotley Point YC
- j HMS Ganges Museum

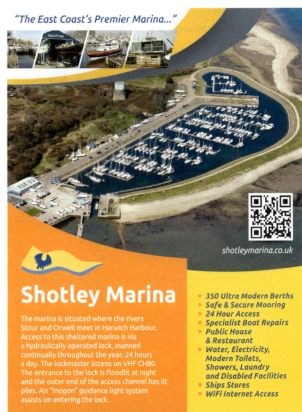

ROYAL HARWICH YACHT CLUB MARINA

Royal Harwich Yacht Club Marina
Marina Road, Woolverstone, Suffolk, IP9 1AT
Tel: 01473 780319 Fax: 01473 780919 Berths: 07742 145994
www.royalharwichyachtclub.co.uk
Email: office.manager@royalharwich.co.uk

VHF Ch 77
ACCESS H24

This 54 berth marina is ideally situated at a mid point on the Orwell between Levington and Ipswich. The facility is owned and run by the Royal Harwich Yacht Club and enjoys a full catering and bar service in the Clubhouse. The marina benefits from full tidal access, and can accommodate yachts up to 14.5m on the hammerhead. Within the immediate surrounds, there are boat repair services, and a well stocked chandlery. The marina is situated a mile's walk from the world famous Pin Mill and is a favoured destination with visitors from Holland, Belgium and Germany. The marina welcomes racing yachts and cruisers, and is able to accommodate multiple bookings.

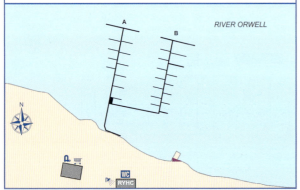

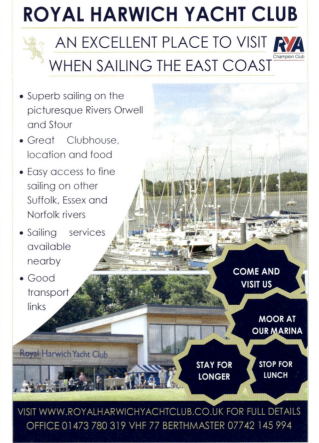

44   MARINA GUIDE 2018

EAST ENGLAND — AREA 4

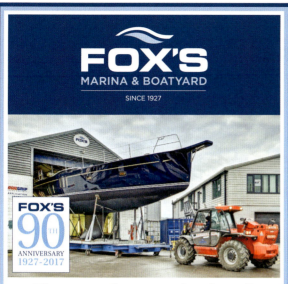

The complete service for all sailing and motor yachts

At **Fox's Marina & Boatyard,** our team is a great mix of experienced cruising/racing sailors and time served engineers and craftsmen. Whether you own a dinghy or a superyacht, we understand our customer's problems and how to resolve them quickly and cost effectively.

Fox's Marina Ipswich LimitedIpswich, Suffolk, IP2 8SA
+44 (0) 1473 689111   foxs@foxsmarina.com

foxsmarina.com

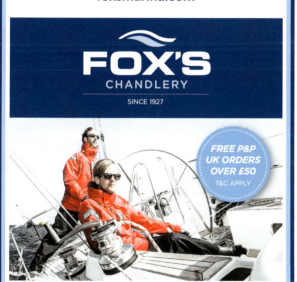

FREE P&P UK ORDERS OVER £50 T&C APPLY

Great choice, fantastic value and expert advice online and in store

Fox's Chandlery opened its doors over 45 years ago, making it one of the oldest and largest chandlery and marine stores of it's kind in the UK. Whether you're shopping in our store or from our website, we work hard to offer you great choice, fantastic value, expert advice and an after sales service that is second to none.

Fox's Chandlery, Fox's Marina Ipswich, Suffolk, IP2 8NJ
+44 (0) 1473 688431   sales@foxschandlery.com

foxschandlery.com

FOX'S MARINA

Fox's Marina & Boatyard
The Strand, Ipswich, Suffolk, IP2 8SA
Tel: 01473 689111
Email: foxs@foxsmarina.com   www.foxsmarina.com

VHF Ch 80   ACCESS H24

Located on the picturesque River Orwell, Fox's provides good shelter in all conditions and access at all states of tide with 100 pontoon berths and ashore storage for 200 vessels. A 70T hoist is able to handle boats up to 80ft in length.

Fox's Marina & Boatyard offers a full range of in-house services and, with 10,000 sq ft of heated workshop space, are specialists in repairs and refits of sailing/motor yachts and commercial craft. Specific services include coppercoat and osmosis treatment, specialist GRP and gelcoat repairs, spray painting and varnishing, and custom stainless fabrication.

Also on-site, Fox's Marine & Country store, is the largest stockist of marine chandlery and equipment, sailing, leisure and country clothing in East Anglia.

FACILITIES AT A GLANCE

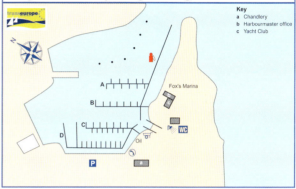

Key
a Chandlery
b Harbourmaster office
c Yacht Club

WOOLVERSTONE MARINA

Woolverstone Marina
Woolverstone, Ipswich, Suffolk, IP9 1AS
Tel: 01473 780206
Email: woolverstone@mdlmarinas.co.uk
www.woolverstonemarina.co.uk

VHF Ch 80   ACCESS H24

Woolverstone Marina is set in 22 acres of glorious parkland on the picturesque River Orwell. Within easy reach of the sea and a multitude of scenic destinations, this is a great base to start cruising. Walton Backwaters and the River Deben are only a short distance away. If you prefer longer distance cruising then Belgium and Holland are directly across the North Sea.

Besides boat repair services, an on-site chandlery and brand new ablution facilities, the marina also incorporates a yacht brokerage and the Riverside Restaurant and Bar, which overlooks the river.

FACILITIES AT A GLANCE

Key
a Marina office, toilets, showers, and launderette
b Riverside Restaurant and Bar

MARINA GUIDE 2018   45

MARINAS & SERVICES

NEPTUNE MARINA

Neptune Marina Ltd
Neptune Quay, Ipswich, IP4 1QJ
Tel: 01473 215204
Email: enquiries@neptune-marina.com

VHF Ch M, 80
ACCESS H±2.5

Neptune Marina is situated at Neptune Quay on the historic waterfront, and ever-increasing shoreside developments. This 26-acre dock is accessible through a H24 lock gate, with a waiting pontoon outside. Onsite facilities include boatyard and lift-out facilities plus superfast wifi for boat owners.

The Neptune Marina building occupies an imposing position in the NE corner of the dock with quality coffee shop and associated retail units. There are a number of excellent restaurants along the quayside and adjacent to the marina.

The modern town centre catering for all needs is just a 10-minute walk away.

FACILITIES AT A GLANCE

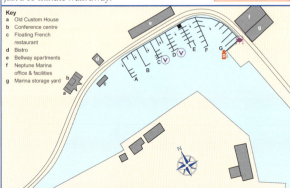

Key
a Old Custom House
b Conference centre
c Floating French restaurant
d Bistro
e Bellway apartments
f Neptune Marina office & facilities
g Marina storage yard

IPSWICH HAVEN MARINA

Ipswich Haven Marina
Associated British Ports
New Cut East, Ipswich, Suffolk, IP3 0EA
Tel: 01473 236644 Fax: 01473 236645
Email: ipswichhaven@abports.co.uk

VHF Ch M, 80
ACCESS H24

Lying at the heart of Ipswich, the Haven Marina enjoys close proximity to all the bustling shopping centres, restaurants, cinemas and museums that this County Town of Suffolk has to offer. The main railway station is only a 10-minute walk away, where there are regular connections to London, Cambridge and Norwich, all taking just over an hour to get to.

Within easy reach of Holland, Belgium and Germany, East Anglia is proving an increasingly popular cruising ground. The River Orwell, displaying breathtaking scenery, was voted one of the most beautiful rivers in Britain by the RYA.

FACILITIES AT A GLANCE

Key
a Toilets, showers, laundry, office
b Licensed bistro
c R&J Marine Electronics
d Boat sales
e Fairline PDI Shed
f Future restaurant retail
g Burton Waters Repair Shop

EAST ENGLAND

AREA 4

LOWESTOFT HAVEN MARINA

Lowestoft Haven Marina
School Road, Lowestoft, Suffolk, NR33 9NB
Tel: 01502 580300
Email: lowestofhaven@abports.co.uk
www.lowestofthavenmarina.co.uk

VHF Ch M, 80
ACCESS H24

Lowestoft Haven Marina is based on Lake Lothing with easy access to both the open sea and the Norfolk Broads. The town centres of both Lowestoft and Oulton Broad are within a short distance of the marina.

The marina's 140 berths can accommodate vessels from 7–20m. Offering a full range of modern facilities the marina welcomes all visitors.

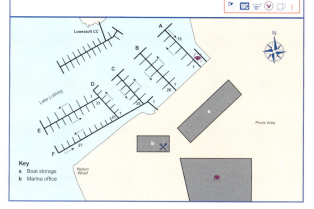

Key
a Boat storage
b Marina office

Pratt Naval Architecture Limited

Naval Architecture, Design & Consultancy
Yachts & Megayachts - Motor & Sail - Small Commercial Craft
Overseeing newbuildings, refits and restorations
Condition and damage surveys
MCA SCV Codes Compliance - all Categories
Specification and Overseeing of Repairs
Stability Information, Structural & Powering Analysis
Laser scanning & measurements

Tel. +44 (0)1473 788 077   info@prattnavalarchitecture.com
Mob. +44 (0)7765 788 077   www.prattnavalarchitecture.com

MRINA

The Studio, 4 Frogs Lane, Church End, Shotley,
Ipswich, Suffolk IP9 1EP, England

YDSA
FULL MEMBER

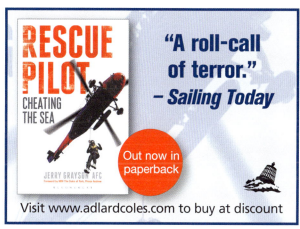

"A roll-call of terror."
– Sailing Today

RESCUE PILOT: CHEATING THE SEA
JERRY GRAYSON AFC

Out now in paperback

Visit www.adlardcoles.com to buy at discount

ROYAL NORFOLK & SUFFOLK YACHT CLUB

Royal Norfolk and Suffolk Yacht Club
Royal Plain, Lowestoft, Suffolk, NR33 0AQ
Tel: 01502 566726
Email: admin@rnsyc.org.uk   www.rnsyc.net

VHF Ch 14, 80
ACCESS H24

With its entrance at the inner end of the South Pier, opposite the Trawl Basin on the north bank, the Royal Norfolk and Suffolk Yacht Club marina occupies a sheltered position in Lowestoft Harbour. Lowestoft has always been an appealing destination to yachtsmen due to the fact that it can be accessed at any state of the tide, 24 hours a day. Note, however, that conditions just outside the entrance can get pretty lively when the wind is against tide. The clubhouse is enclosed in an impressive Grade 2 listed building overlooking the marina and its facilities include a bar and restaurant as well as a formal dining room.

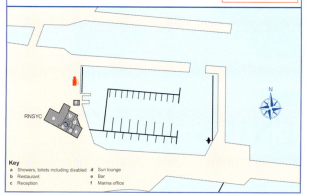

Key
a Showers, toilets including disabled   d Sun lounge
b Restaurant   e Bar
c Reception   f Marina office

LOWESTOFT CRUISING CLUB

Lowestoft Cruising Club
Off Harbour Road, Oulton Broad, Lowestoft, Suffolk, NR32 3LY
Tel: 07810 522515
www.lowestoftcruisingclub.co.uk

VHF
ACCESS H24

Lowestoft Cruising Club welcomes visitors and can offer a friendly atmosphere, some of the finest moorings and at very competitive rates. Whatever the weather, these moorings provide a calm, safe haven for visiting yachts and with the Mutford lock only 250 metres away, easy access onto the Norfolk and Suffolk Broads. Facilities include electricity and water, plus excellent showers, toilets and secure car parking. These moorings are the nearest ones to the railway stations (to Norwich and Ipswich), bus routes, shops, banks, pubs and restaurants in Oulton Broad.

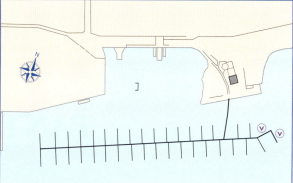

MARINA GUIDE 2018

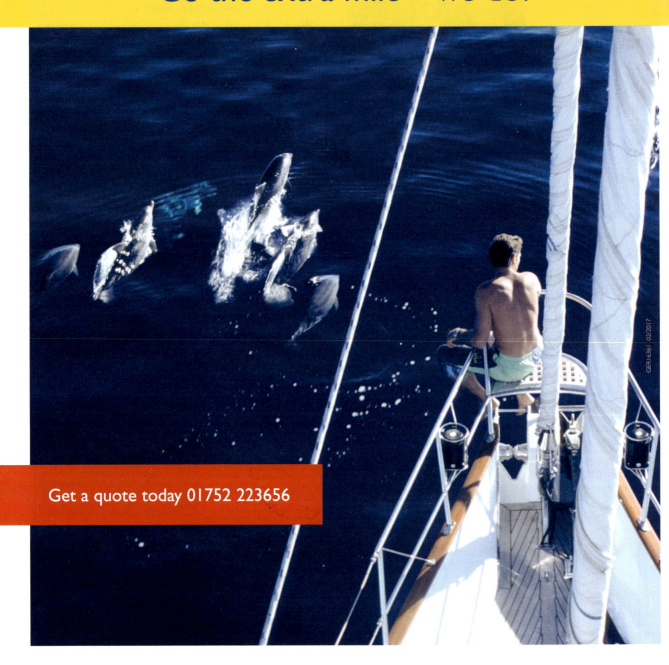

NORTH EAST ENGLAND - Great Yarmouth to Berwick-upon-Tweed

Reeds PDF ebooks

In response to popular demand, all the Reeds Almanacs are now available as searchable, highlightable PDF ebooks. (All ebooks incorporate the Marina Guide.)

Visit www.reedsnauticalalmanac.co.uk for further information

Key to Marina Plans symbols

	Bottled gas	P	Parking
	Chandler		Pub/Restaurant
	Disabled facilities		Pump out
	Electrical supply		Rigging service
	Electrical repairs		Sail repairs
	Engine repairs		Shipwright
	First Aid		Shop/Supermarket
	Fresh Water		Showers
D	Fuel - Diesel		Slipway
P	Fuel - Petrol	WC	Toilets
	Hardstanding/boatyard		Telephone
@	Internet Café		Trolleys
	Laundry facilities	V	Visitors berths
	Lift-out facilities		Wi-Fi

Area 5 - North East England

MARINAS
Telephone Numbers
VHF Channel
Access Times

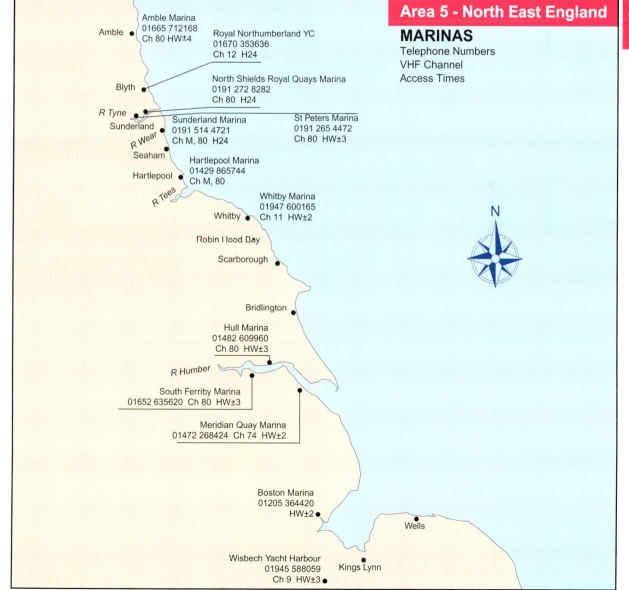

Amble — Amble Marina 01665 712168 Ch 80 HW±4

Royal Northumberland YC 01670 353636 Ch 12 H24

Blyth

North Shields Royal Quays Marina 0191 272 8282 Ch 80 H24

R Tyne

Sunderland — Sunderland Marina 0191 514 4721 Ch M, 80 H24

St Peters Marina 0191 265 4472 Ch 80 HW±3

R Wear

Seaham

Hartlepool — Hartlepool Marina 01429 865744 Ch M, 80

R Tees

Whitby — Whitby Marina 01947 600165 Ch 11 HW±2

Robin Hood Bay

Scarborough

Bridlington

Hull Marina 01482 609960 Ch 80 HW±3

R Humber

South Ferriby Marina 01652 635620 Ch 80 HW±3

Meridian Quay Marina 01472 268424 Ch 74 HW±2

Boston Marina 01205 364420 HW±2

Wells

Wisbech Yacht Harbour 01945 588059 Ch 9 HW±3

Kings Lynn

WISBECH YACHT HARBOUR

Wisbech Yacht Harbour
Harbour Master, Harbour Office, The Boathouse,
Harbour Square, Wisbech, Cambridgeshire PE13 3BH
Tel: 01945 588059   Fax: 01945 580589
Email: afoster@fenland.gov.uk   www.fenland.gov.uk

VHF Ch 9
ACCESS HW±3

Regarded as the capital of the English Fens, Wisbech is situated about 25 miles north east of Peterborough and is a market town of considerable character and historical significance. Rows of elegant houses line the banks of the River Nene, with the North and South Brink still deemed two of the finest Georgian streets in England.

Wisbech Yacht Harbour, linking Cambridgeshire with the sea, is proving increasingly popular as a haven for small craft, despite the busy commercial shipping. In recent years the facilities have been developed and improved upon and the HM is always on hand to help with passage planning both up or downstream.

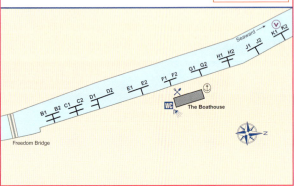

BOSTON GATEWAY MARINA

Boston Gateway Marina
Witham Bank East, Boston, Lincs, PE21 9JU
Tel: 07480 525230
Email: enquiries@bostongatewaymarina.co.uk

VHF
ACCESS H±2

Located near Boston Grand Sluice Lock on the sunny side of the River Witham, the marina is ideally situated for easy access to The Wash and is suitable for both sea-going and river boats. It is a short walk to the centre of the historic town of Boston, Lincolnshire, but retains a tranquil feel. The marina offers visitor, short-term and longer-term moorings to suit each individual customer. Power and water are available for all boats.

The town centre offers the normal variety of facilities within easy walking distance. Local tourist attractions include the 14th century St Botolph's Church – 'The Stump' – the 1390s Boston Guildhall Musuem and a 450-year old market to name but a few.

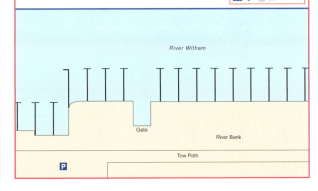

WISBECH YACHT HARBOUR

Providing safe, secure pontoon berths on the tidal River Nene in the centre of Wisbech, 'Capital of the Fens'.

- Fully serviced marina berths with modern Toilets, Showers and Laundry Room.
- Berths up to 20m LOA, 2.5m draft.
- 8 miles from The Wash, 15 miles to the inland waterways.
- Perfect for long stay, just passing through or a base for exploring the East Coast.
- 75t boat travel hoist: handling vessels up to 27m within its secure compound both have CCTV coverage.
- Winter storage afloat or ashore.
- Good transport links and shops.

**The Boathouse, Harbour Square
WISBECH, Cambridgeshire, PE13 3BH
Tel: 01945 588059 • Fax: 01945 580589.
www.fenland.gov.uk/wisbechyachtharbour**

MERIDIAN QUAY MARINA

**Humber Cruising Assn
Meridian Quay Marina**
Fish Docks, Grimsby, DN31 3SD
Tel: 01472 268424   Fax: 01472 269832
www.hcagrimsby.co.uk
Email: berthmaster@hcagrimsby.co.uk

VHF Ch 74
ACCESS HW±2

Situated in the locked fish dock of Grimsby, at the mouth of the River Humber, Meridian Quay Marina is run by the Humber Cruising Association and comprises approximately 200 alongside berths plus 30 more for visitors. Accessed two hours either side of high water via lock gates, the lock should be contacted on VHF Ch 74 (call sign 'Fish Dock Island') as you make your final approach. The pontoon berths are equipped with water and electricity; there is a fully licensed clubhouse. Also available are internet access and laundry facilities.

NORTH EAST ENGLAND

AREA 5

HULL MARINA

Hull Marina
W 13, Kingston Street, Hull, HU1 2DQ
Tel: 01482 609960 Fax: 01482 224148
Email: david.parkinson@bwml.co.uk
www.bwml.co.uk

VHF Ch 80
ACCESS HW±3

Situated on the River Humber, Hull Marina is literally a stone's throw from the bustling city centre with its array of arts and entertainments. Besides the numerous historic bars and cafés surrounding the marina, there are plenty of traditional taverns to be sampled in the Old Town, while also found here is the Street Life Museum, vividly depicting the history of the city.

Yachtsmen enter the marina via a tidal lock, operating HW±3, and should try to give 15 minutes' notice of arrival via VHF Ch 80. Hull is perfectly positioned for exploring the Trent, Ouse and the Yorkshire coast as well as across the North Sea to Holland or Belgium.

FACILITIES AT A GLANCE

THE NORTH'S LARGEST CHANDLERY

KILDALE MARINE

The largest stock in the region.
Great technical knowledge.
Full rigging service.

Supplying everything for:
- Yachts
- Cruisers
- Dinghies
- Books & Charts
- Clothing & Footwear

MUSTO   Gill   HENRI LLOYD   HARKEN   LOWRANCE
spinlock   Raymarine   ICOM   International yachtpaint.com

Kildalemarine.co.uk
01482 227464

Kildale Marine Ltd,
Hull Marina, Hull HU1 2DQ
Opening hours
6-days a week, closed Tuesday.

Hull Marina
Yorkshire

Fully serviced pontoons

Visitors welcome

Fully serviced boatyard and workshops with 50 tonne hoist

Hull Marina is a proud member of the TransEurope Marinas group

01482 609960   bwml.co.uk   david.parkinson@bwml.co.uk

MARINA GUIDE 2018

MARINAS & SERVICES

SOUTH FERRIBY MARINA

South Ferriby Marina
Red Lane, South Ferriby, Barton on Humber, Lincs, DN18 6JH
Tel: 01652 635620 (Lock 635219) Mobile: 07828 312071
Email: enquiries@southferribymarina.com

VHF Ch 74
ACCESS HW±3

Situated at the entrance to the non-tidal River Ancholme the existing marina has been established since 1966 and is well placed to provide easy access to the River Humber and North Sea. This is a family run business providing a range of services including a boatyard and chandlery. Access is by way of lock at HW±3.

The marina has excellent road and rail services within easy reach, while South Ferriby village has two pubs and a Post Office/Spar Shop just a short walk away.

The picturesque River Ancholme is navigable for about 17 miles; the maximum headroom under bridges is 4.42 metres (14ft 6ins).

Key
a Chandlery
b Shipwrights workshop

WHITBY MARINA

Whitby Marina
Whitby Harbour Office, Endeavour Wharf
Whitby, North Yorkshire YO21 1DN
Harbour Office: 01947 602354 Marina: 01947 600165
Email: port.services@scarborough.gov.uk

VHF Ch 11
ACCESS HW±2

The only natural harbour between the Tees and the Humber, Whitby lies some 20 miles north of Scarborough on the River Esk. The historic town is said to date back as far as the Roman times, although it is better known for its abbey, which was founded over 1,300 years ago by King Oswy of Northumberland. Another place of interest is the Captain Cook Memorial Museum, a tribute to Whitby's greatest seaman.

A swing bridge divides the harbour into upper and lower sections, with the marina being in the Upper Harbour. The bridge opens on request (VHF Ch 11) each half hour for two hours either side of high water.

Key
a Marina office
b Waste oil bin

HARTLEPOOL MARINA

Hartlepool Marina
Lock Office, Slake Terrace, Hartlepool, TS24 0RU
Tel: 01429 865744 www.hartlepool-marina.com
Email: enquiries@hartlepool-marina.com

VHF Ch M, 80
ACCESS

Hartlepool Marina is a modern boating facility on the NE coast now boasting an extensively refurbished North amenity block. Nestling on the Tees Valley the multi award winning marina promotes up to 500 pontoon berths alongside a variety of reputable services all surrounded by an exciting array of on water activities, a cosmopolitan mix of bistros, bars, restaurants, shopping, hotels and entertainment options.

Beautiful cruising waters and golden sands to the North and South of the marina approach which is channel dredged to CD and accessible via a lock: vessels wishing to enter should contact the Marina Lock Office on VHF Ch M/80 before arrival.

Key
a Brittania House - amenity/cafe
b Neptune House - restaurant & bar
c Lock office and marina reception
d 220m complex with retail, restaurants and cafes
e Hartlepool Diving Club and HMS Abdiel sea cadet unit
f Fisherman's stores & landing area
g Office units
h Old West Quay Pub, restaurant and travel inn

SUNDERLAND MARINA

The Marine Activities Centre
Sunderland Marina, Sunderland, SR6 0PW
Tel: 0191 514 4721 Fax: 0191 514 1847
Email: mac.info@marineactivitiescentre.co.uk

VHF Ch M
ACCESS H24

Sunderland Marina sits on the the River Wear and is easily accessible through the outer breakwater at all states of tide. A short walk away from the city centre and beautiful beaches, facilities on site include the Snowgoose café and the Marina Vista Italian restaurant. Other pubs, restaurants, hotels and cafes are located nearby on the waterfront.

Sunderland Yacht Club is also located nearby and welcomes visiting yachtsman to its clubhouse.

Key
a. Marina Reception
b. Aroma Essence - beautican
c. Snow Goose - Café
d. Hairdresser
e. Trattoria Due - Italian Restaurant
f. RNLI Lifeboat station
g. Hard stand compound
h. Refuse Compound

MARINA GUIDE 2018

NORTH EAST ENGLAND — AREA 5

NORTH SHIELDS ROYAL QUAYS MARINA

North Shields Royal Quays Marina
Coble Dene Road, North Shields, NE29 6DU
Tel: 0191 272 8282 Fax: 0191 272 8288
www.quaymarinas.com
Email: royalquaysmarina@quaymarinas.com

VHF Ch 80
ACCESS H24

North Shields Royal Quays Marina enjoys close proximity to the entrance to the River Tyne, allowing easy access to and from the open sea as well as being ideally placed for cruising further up the Tyne. Just over an hour's motoring upstream brings you to the heart of the city of Newcastle, where you can tie up on a security controlled visitors' pontoon right outside the Pitcher and Piano Bar.

With a reputation for a high standard of service, the marina accommodates 300 pontoon berths, all of which are fully serviced. It is accessed via double sector lock gates which operate at all states of the tide and 24 hours a day.

FACILITIES AT A GLANCE

ST PETERS MARINA

St Peters Marina, St Peters Basin
Newcastle upon Tyne, NE6 1HX
Tel: 0191 2654472 Fax: 0191 2762618
Email: info@stpetersmarina.co.uk
www.stpetersmarina.co.uk

VHF Ch 80
ACCESS HW±3

Nestling on the north bank of the River Tyne, some eight miles upstream of the river entrance, St Peters Marina is a fully serviced, 150-berth marina with the capacity to accommodate large vessels of up to 37m LOA. Situated on site is the Bascule Bar and Bistro, while a few minutes away is the centre of Newcastle. This city, along with its surrounding area, offers an array of interesting sites, among which are Hadrian's Wall, the award winning Gateshead Millennium Bridge and the Baltic Art Centre.

FACILITIES AT A GLANCE

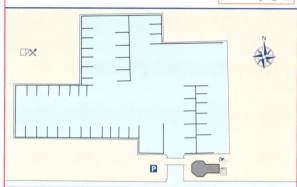

ROYAL NORTHUMBERLAND YACHT CLUB

Royal Northumberland Yacht Club
South Harbour, Blyth, Northumberland, NE24 3PB
Tel: 01670 353636

VHF Ch 12
ACCESS H24

The Royal Northumberland Yacht Club is based at Blyth, a well-sheltered port that is accessible at all states of the tide and in all weathers except for when there is a combination of low water and strong south-easterly winds. The yacht club is a private club with some 75 pontoon berths and a further 20 fore and aft moorings.

Visitors usually berth on the north side of the most northerly pontoon and are welcome to use the clubship, HY *Tyne* – a wooden lightship built in 1880 which incorporates a bar, showers and toilet facilities. The club also controls its own boatyard, providing under cover and outside storage space plus a 20 ton boat hoist.

FACILITIES AT A GLANCE

AMBLE MARINA

Amble Marina Ltd
Amble, Northumberland, NE65 0YP
Tel: 01665 712168
Email: marina@amble.co.uk   www.amble.co.uk

VHF Ch 80
ACCESS HW±4

Amble Marina is a small family run business offering peace, security and a countryside setting at the heart of the small town of Amble. It is located on the banks of the beautiful River Coquet and at the start of the Northumberland coast's area of outstanding natural beauty. Amble Marina has 250 fully serviced berths for residential and visiting yachts. Cafés, bars, restaurants and shops are all within a short walk.

From your berth watch the sun rise at the harbour entrance and set behind Warkworth Castle or walk on wide, empty beaches. There is so much to do or if you prefer simply enjoy the peace, tranquillity and friendliness at Amble Marina.

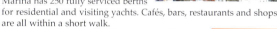

FACILITIES AT A GLANCE

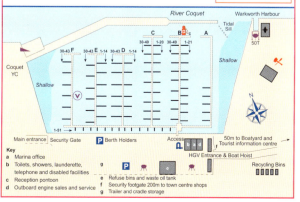

MARINA GUIDE 2018

MARINAS & SERVICES

SOUTH EAST SCOTLAND – Eyemouth to Rattray Head

Reeds PDF ebooks

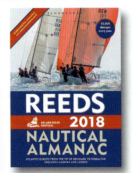

In response to popular demand, all the Reeds Almanacs are now available as searchable, highlightable PDF ebooks. (All ebooks incorporate the Marina Guide.)

Visit www.reedsnauticalalmanac.co.uk for further information

Key to Marina Plans symbols

	Bottled gas	P	Parking
	Chandler		Pub/Restaurant
	Disabled facilities		Pump out
	Electrical supply		Rigging service
	Electrical repairs		Sail repairs
	Engine repairs		Shipwright
	First Aid		Shop/Supermarket
	Fresh Water		Showers
D	Fuel - Diesel		Slipway
P	Fuel - Petrol	WC	Toilets
	Hardstanding/boatyard		Telephone
@	Internet Café		Trolleys
	Laundry facilities	V	Visitors berths
	Lift-out facilities		Wi-Fi

Area 6 - South East Scotland

MARINAS
Telephone Numbers
VHF Channel
Access Times

- Aberdeen
- Stonehaven
- Montrose
- Arbroath Harbour 01241 872166 Ch 11, 16 HW±3
- Arbroath
- Tayport
- Port Edgar Marina 0131 3313330 Ch 80 H24
- Port Edgar
- Granton
- Dunbar
- Berwick-upon-Tweed

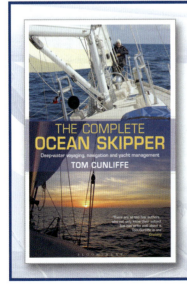

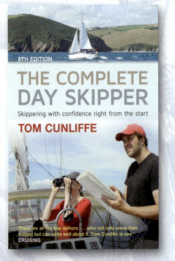

Be confident on the water with Adlard Coles Nautical

Visit www.adlardcoles.com to buy at discount

MARINA GUIDE 2018

SOUTH EAST SCOTLAND — AREA 6

PORT EDGAR MARINA

Port Edgar Marina
Shore Road, South Queensferry
West Lothian, EH30 9SQ
Tel: 0131 331 3330 Fax: 0131 331 4878
Email: info@portedgar.co.uk

VHF Ch 80
ACCESS H24

Nestled between the iconic Forth Bridges, Edinburgh's 300 berth marina is the ideal base for exploring the Capital and the Forth coastline.

A short walk away is the historic High Street of Queensferry with a great selection of bars and restaurants. Situated 15 minutes away from Edinburgh Airport with easy road access, the secure site provides full boatyard facilities including a 25T slipway hoist, chandlery and café.

FACILITIES AT A GLANCE

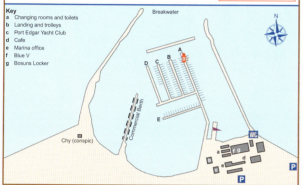

Key
a Changing rooms and toilets
b Landing and trolleys
c Port Edgar Yacht Club
d Cafe
e Marina office
f Blue V
g Bosuns Locker

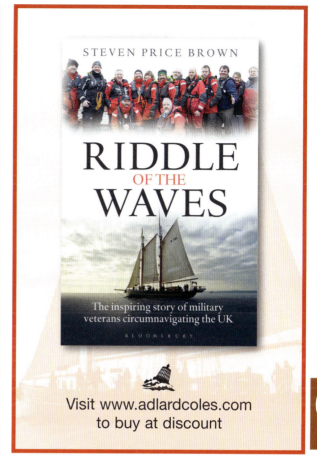

STEVEN PRICE BROWN

RIDDLE OF THE WAVES

The inspiring story of military veterans circumnavigating the UK

BLOOMSBURY

Visit www.adlardcoles.com
to buy at discount

ARBROATH HARBOUR

Arbroath Harbour
Harbour Office, Arbroath, DD11 1PD
Tel: 01241 872166 Fax: 01241 878472
Email: harbourmaster@angus.gov.uk

VHF Ch 11
ACCESS HW±3

Arbroath harbour has 59 floating pontoon berths with security entrance which are serviced with electricity and fresh water to accommodate all types of leisure craft. Half height dock gates with walkway are located between the inner and outer harbours, which open and close at half tide, maintaining a minimum of 2.5m of water in the inner harbour.

The town of Arbroath offers a variety of social and sporting amenities to visiting crews and a number of quality pubs, restaurants, the famous twelfth century Abbey and Signal Tower Museum are located close to the harbour. Railway and bus stations are only 1km from the harbour with direct north and south connections.

FACILITIES AT A GLANCE

Key
a Signal Tower Museum
b Tourist Information
c RNLI
d Harbourmaster
e Harbour gates & walkway

"Arbroath Harbour has 59 floating pontoon berths with security entrance which are serviced with electricity and fresh water to accommodate all types of leisure craft. Half height dock gates with a walkway are located between the inner and outer harbours, which open and close at half tide, maintaining a minimum of 2.5m of water in the inner harbour.

Other facilities in the harbour include free partking, toilets and showers, a crew room, fueling facilities, on site laundry facilities and boat builders' yard.

The town of Arbroath also offers a variety of social and sporting amenities to visiting crews and a number of quality pubs, restaurants, the famous twelfth century Abbey and Signal Tower Museum are located close to the harbour. The railway and bus stations are only 1km from the harbour with direct north and south connections."

Arbroath Harbour
Harbour Office . Arbroath . DD11 1PD

Harbour Master: Bruce Fleming
Tel: 01241 872166
Fax: 01241 878472
Email: harbourmaster@angus.gov.uk

Angus Council

WORLD CLASS SKIPPERS WANTED

NO PRESSURE

Sir Robin Knox-Johnston
Founder of the Clipper Round the World Yacht Race

Twelve extraordinary Skippers wanted. Six ocean crossings, 40,000 miles, 18 month contract and a competitive tax-free salary.

Join the elite and take on the world's longest yacht race, crewed exclusively by novice crew embarking on the race of their lives.

Clipper Race Skippers are exceptional. They have the fortitude to take on the toughest of mental challenges, and the physical endurance to successfully lead a team through Mother Nature's extreme environments on a 40,000 mile lap around the globe.

Now we're recruiting for the next edition of the Clipper Race. To qualify you must hold a Yachtmaster Ocean certificate [commercial endorsed] or International Yacht Training Master of Yachts.

⬇ APPLY NOW

clipperroundtheworld.com/careers
+44 (0) 2392 526000

CLIPPER ROUND THE WORLD

AREA 7

NORTH EAST SCOTLAND – Peterhead to Cape Wrath & Orkney & Shetland Is

Reeds PDF ebooks

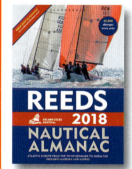

In response to popular demand, all the Reeds Almanacs are now available as searchable, highlightable PDF ebooks. (All ebooks incorporate the Marina Guide.)

Visit www.reedsnauticalalmanac.co.uk for further information

Key to Marina Plans symbols

	Bottled gas	P	Parking
	Chandler		Pub/Restaurant
	Disabled facilities		Pump out
	Electrical supply		Rigging service
	Electrical repairs		Sail repairs
	Engine repairs		Shipwright
	First Aid		Shop/Supermarket
	Fresh Water		Showers
D	Fuel - Diesel		Slipway
P	Fuel - Petrol	WC	Toilets
	Hardstanding/boatyard		Telephone
@	Internet Café		Trolleys
	Laundry facilities	V	Visitors berths
	Lift-out facilities		Wi-Fi

Area 7 - North East Scotland

MARINAS
Telephone Numbers
VHF Channel
Access Times

Shetland Islands

Kirkwall Marina
07810 465835
Ch 14 H24

Stromness Marina
07810 465825
Ch 14 H24

Orkney Islands

Scrabster

Wick • Wick Marina
01955 602030
Ch 14 H24

Helmsdale

Ullapool

Whitehills Marina
01261 861291
Ch 14 H4

Banff Harbour Marina
01261 815544
Ch 12 HW±4

Buckie Banff Macduff

Inverness Marina
07526 446348
Ch 12   Inverness

Peterhead Peterhead Bay Marina
01779 477868
Ch 14 H24

Caley Marina
01463 236539
Ch 74 H24

Findhorn
Burghead

Lossiemouth 01343 813066
Ch 12 HW±4

Seaport Marina
01463 725500
Ch 74 HW±4

Nairn Marina
01667 456008
Ch 10 HW±2

Hopeman

Mallaig

Aberdeen

MARINA GUIDE 2018

MARINAS & SERVICES

PETERHEAD BAY MARINA

Peterhead Port Authority
Harbour Office, West Pier, Peterhead, AB42 1DW
Tel: 01779 477868/483280
Email: marina@peterheadport.co.uk
www.peterheadport.co.uk

VHF Ch 14
ACCESS H24

Based in the south west corner of Peterhead Bay Harbour, the marina provides one of the finest marine leisure facilities in the east of Scotland. In addition to the services on site, there are plenty of nautical businesses in the vicinity, ranging from ship chandlers and electrical servicing to boat repairs and surveying.

Due to its easterly location, Peterhead affords an ideal stopover for those yachts heading to or from Scandinavia as well as for vessels making for the Caledonian Canal.

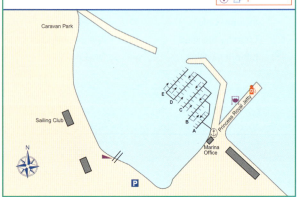

SET SAIL FOR PETERHEAD BAY MARINA
North East Scotland's Finest Marina

- Fully serviced pontoons
- Shower, toilet & laundry facilities
- Access at all states of the tide
- Visiting yachtsmen welcome
- Daily berths from £13 / weekly £65

Ideally located for vessels heading to or from the Caledonian Canal or making for Scandinavia

Harbour Office, West Pier, Peterhead, Aberdeenshire AB42 1DW
Tel: 01779 483600   Fax: 01779 475715   Web: www.peterheadport.co.uk

Winning Isn't Luck
Secrets for success from an Olympic and world champion racing yachtsman.

Visit **www.adlardcoles.com** to buy at discount

BANFF HARBOUR MARINA

Banff Harbour Marina
Harbour Office, Quayside, Banff, Aberdeenshire, AB45 1HQ
Tel: 01261 815544   Fax: 01261 815544
Email: james.henderson@aberdeenshire.gov.uk

VHF Ch 12
ACCESS HW±4

A former fishing and cargo port now used as a recreational harbour. Banff offers excellent facilities to both regular and visiting users. The marina now provides 92 berths, of which 76 are serviced pontoon berths and 16 unserviced, traditional moorings, in one of the safest harbours on the NE coast of Scotland.

The outer basin offers adequate berthing for visitors and a tidal area for regulars.

The harbour is tidal with a sandy bottom. Movement during low water neaps is no problem for the shallow drafted boat.

NAIRN MARINA

Nairn Marina
Nairn Harbour, Nairnshire, Scotland
Tel: 01667 456008   Fax: 01667 452877
Email: nairn.harbourmaster@virgin.net

VHF Ch 10
ACCESS HW±2

Nairn is a small town on the coast of the Moray Firth. Formerly renowned both as a fishing port and as a holiday resort dating back to Victorian times, it boasts miles of award-winning, sandy beaches, famous castles such as Cawdor, Brodie and Castle Stuart, and two championship golf courses. Other recreational activities include horse riding or walking through spectacular countryside.

The marina lies at the mouth of the River Nairn, entry to which should be avoided in strong N to NE winds. The approach is made from the NW at or around high water as the entrance is badly silted and dries out.

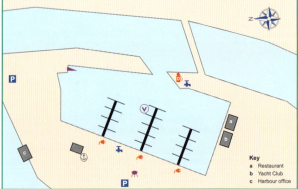

58   MARINA GUIDE 2018

NORTH EAST SCOTLAND — AREA 7

WHITEHILLS MARINA

Whitehills Harbour Commissioners
Whitehills, Banffshire AB45 2NQ
Tel: 01261 861291
www.whitehillsharbour.co.uk
Email: harbourmaster@whitehillsharbour.co.uk

VHF Ch 14
ACCESS H24

Built in 1900, Whitehills is a Trust Harbour fully maintained and run by nine commissioners elected from the village. It was a thriving fishing port up until 1999, but due to changes in the fishing industry, was converted into a marina during 2000.

Photo by Colin Heggie

Three miles west of Banff Harbour the marina benefits from good tidal access – although there is just 1.5m at springs – comprising 38 serviced berths, with electricity, as well as eight non-serviced berths.

Whitehills village has a wide range of facilities including a convenience store, a cafe/fish & chip shop, two pubs, a fresh fish shop as well as two good restaurants. It is also a great base for families, with an excellent playpark at Blackpots, just a short walk from the harbour.

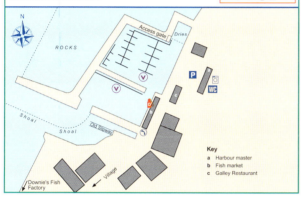

Whitehills Marina
An award-winning marina on the Moray Firth coast

- Secure inner basin
- Gas
- Diesel berth
- Secure winter storage
- WiFi
- Plenty of free parking
- Extensive range of shoreside facilities

Harbour Office, Harbour Place,
Whitehills, Banff AB45 2NQ
T: 01261 861 291   M: 07906 135 786
E: harbourmaster@whitehillsharbour.co.uk
www.whitehillsharbour.co.uk

LOSSIEMOUTH MARINA

Marina Office
Lossiemouth, Moray, IV31 6PB
Tel: 01343 813066
Email: info@lossiemouthmarina.com

VHF Ch 12
ACCESS HW±4

Situated on the southern shore of the Moray Firth, Lossiemouth provides 95 serviced finger berths, 5 serviced dedicated visitor berths and 25 small boat berths. The Marina has full lift out facilities and a boat repair shed capable of handling 4 vessels at any one time with a marine engineer based on site.

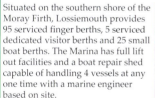

The Marina is close to the town centre with a good range of shops and restaurants and also two championship golf courses. A regular bus service provides easy access to Elgin railway station (6 miles) and Inverness airport (35miles). Lossiemouth has miles of sandy beaches and is the ideal starting point for the Speyside Whisky trail.

Elgin & Lossiemouth Harbour Company

Lossiemouth Marina lies approximately halfway between Inverness and Peterhead, providing 115 berths. Dedicated visitor pontoons with free service facilities (water and electricity) lie just inside the East basin. Complimentary wi-fi is also available in the East and West basins. Visitor packs can be collected from the Marina Office (Monday to Friday 9am-4pm) or from the Steamboat Inn, opposite the East basin, if arriving out of office hours. Modern toilet and shower blocks with laundry facilities can be located in both basins. Diesel, local shops, restaurants and ATM are all within short walking distance. Buses to Elgin (the nearest large town) are approximately every half hour. Lossiemouth Marina has excellent undercover workshop facilities, a 25 tonne sublift and crane for masting/demasting.

Lossiemouth Marina, Shore Street, Lossiemouth IV31 6PB
T: 01343 813066   M: 07969 213521/07583 985 706
Email: info@lossiemouthmarina.com
www.lossiemouthmarina.com
Location: Latitude 57°43'N, Longitude 03°17'W
Admiralty Chart: No.1462

MARINAS & SERVICES

INVERNESS MARINA

Inverness Marina
Longman Drive, Inverness, IV1 1SU
Tel: 01463 220501
Email: info@invernessmarina.com
www.invernessmarina.com

VHF Ch 12
ACCESS H24

The marina is situated in the Inverness firth just one mile from the city centre and half a mile from the entrance to the Caledonian Canal. It has a minimum depth of 3m, 24hr access and 150 fully serviced berths. On site are a chandlery and services including rigging, engineering, electronics and boat repair.

Inverness has excellent transport networks to the rest of the UK and Europe and, as the gateway to the Highlands is a great location as a base for a touring golf courses, historic sites and the Whisky Trail. The marina is a perfect base for cruising Orkney, Shetland and Scandinavia.

FACILITIES AT A GLANCE

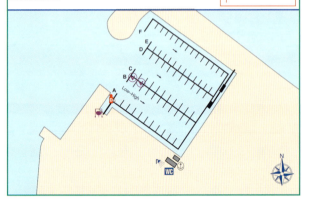

SEAPORT MARINA

Seaport Marina
Muirtown Wharf, Inverness, IV3 5LE
Tel: 01463 725500 Fax: 01463 710942
Email: enquiries@scottishcanals.co.uk
www.scottishcanals.co.uk

VHF Ch 74
ACCESS HW±4

Photo courtesy of D Edes

Seaport Marina is based at Muirtown Basin at the eastern entrance of the Caledonian Canal; a 60 mile coast-to-coast channel slicing through the majestic Great Glen. Only a 15 minute walk from the centre of Inverness, the Marina is an ideal base for visiting the Highlands.

There are shops and amenities nearby, as well as chandlers, boat repair services and a slipway. The marina also offers a variety of winter mooring packages and details of transit and short term licences, including the use of the Caledonian Canal can be found on the above website.

FACILITIES AT A GLANCE

Key
a Office, toilets, showers, laundry, disabled toilets
b Waste oil disposal

CALEY MARINA

Caley Marina
Canal Road, Inverness, IV3 8NF
Tel: 01463 236539 Fax: 01463 238323
Email: info@caleymarina.com
www.caleymarina.com

VHF Ch 74
ACCESS H24

Caley Marina is a family run business based near Inverness. With the four flight Muirtown locks and the Kessock Bridge providing a dramatic backdrop, the marina runs alongside the Caledonian Canal which, opened in 1822, is regarded as one of the most spectacular waterways in Europe. Built as a short cut between the North Sea and the Atlantic Ocean, thus avoiding the potentially dangerous Pentland Firth on the north coast of Scotland, the canal is around 60 miles long and takes about three days to cruise from east to west. With the prevailing winds behind you, it takes slightly less time to cruise in the other direction.

FACILITIES AT A GLANCE

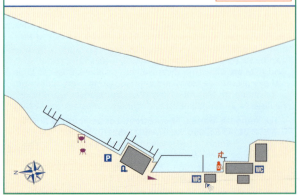

WICK MARINA

Wick Marina
Harbour Office, Wick, Caithness, KW1 5HA
Tel: 01955 602030 Fax: 01955 605936
Email: malcolm.bremner@wickharbour.co.uk

VHF Ch 14, 16
ACCESS H24

This is the most northerly marina on the British mainland and the last stop before the Orkney and Shetland Islands. Situated an easy five minutes walk from the town centre Wick Marina accommodates 70 fully serviced berths with all the support facilities expected in a modern marina including a boat lift.

This part of Scotland with its rugged coastline and rich history is easily accessible by air and a great starting point for cruising in the northern isles, Moray Firth, Caledonian Canal and Scandinavia, a comfortable 280-mile sail.

FACILITIES AT A GLANCE

MARINA GUIDE 2018

NORTH EAST SCOTLAND AREA 7

KIRKWALL MARINA

Kirkwall Marina
Harbour Street, Kirkwall, Orkney, KW15
Tel: 07810 465835   Fax: 01856 871313
Email: info@orkneymarinas.co.uk   www.orkneymarinas.co.uk

VHF Ch 14
ACCESS H24

The Orkney Isles, comprising 70 islands in total, provides some of the finest cruising grounds in Northern Europe. The Main Island, incorporating the ancient port of Kirkwall, is the largest, although 16 others have lively communities and are rich in archaeological sites as well as spectacular scenery and wildlife.

Kirkwall Marina, an all year facility, is located within the harbour and just yards from the visitor attractions of this ancient port. Local shops, hotels and restaurants are all within walking distance.

STROMNESS MARINA

Stromness Marina
Stromness, Orkney, KW16
Tel: 07810 465825   Fax: 01856 871313
Email: info@orkneymarinas.co.uk
www.orkneymarinas.co.uk

VHF Ch 14
ACCESS H24

Stromness lies on the south-western tip of the Orkney Isles' Mainland. Sitting beneath the rocky ridge known as Brinkie's Brae, it is considered one of Orkney's major seaports, with sailors first attracted to the fine anchorage provided by the bay of Hamnavoe.

Stromness offers comprehensive facilities including a chandlery and repair services. Also on hand are an internet café, a fitness suite and swimming pool as well as car and bike hire.

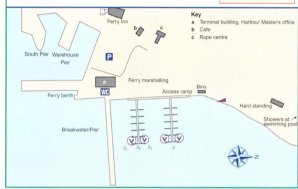

DUNCAN'S
SCOTLAND'S No.1

- 1ST for Service
- 1ST for Value
- 1ST for Choice
- 1ST for Advice
- 1ST for Price

Why not pay us a visit and see our vast range of chandlery, electronics, inflatables, outboards, clothing, footwear, life jackets, buoyancy aids and lots, lots more...

OPENING HOURS
Mon to Fri 9am - 5.30pm
Sat 9am - 4pm
Sun 10am - 3pm

PARKING
FREE & EASY
Parking in our own Car Park

PROUDLY SUPPORTING BOATING SINCE 1961

7 Scotland Street, Glasgow G5 8NL   Tel: 0141 429 6044   Fax: 0141 429 3078
Email: sales@duncanyachtchandlers.co.uk   www.duncanyacht.co.uk

CRUISE AMONGST OVER 70 MEMBER MARINAS

transeurope MARINAS

VISITORS BERTHING 50% DISCOUNT

www.transeuropemarinas.com

TransEurope Marinas

1. **Kinsale** Castlepark Marina
2. **Greystones** Greystones Harbour Marina
3. **Malahide** Malahide Marina
4. **Bangor** Bangor Marina
5. **Rhu** Rhu Marina
6. **Troon** Troon Yacht Haven
7. **North Shields** Royal Quays Marina
8. **Whitehaven** Whitehaven Marina
9. **Fleetwood** Fleetwood Haven Marina
10. **Liverpool** Liverpool Marina
11. **Deganwy** Deganwy Marina
12. **Conwy** Conwy Quays Marina
13. **Milford Haven** Neyland Yacht Haven
14. **Penarth** Penarth Quays Marina
15. **Upton-upon-Severn** Upton Marina
16. **Portishead** Portishead Quays Marina
17. **Falmouth** Mylor Yacht Harbour
18. **Plymouth** Mayflower Marina
19. **Dartmouth** Dart Marina
20. **Poole** Poole Quay Boathaven
21. **Beaulieu** Buckler's Hard Yacht Harbour
22. **Southampton** Town Quay Marina
23. **Hamble River** Universal Marina
24. **Cowes** Cowes Yacht Haven
25. **Gosport** Royal Clarence Marina
26. **Emsworth** Emsworth Yacht Harbour
27. **Chichester** Birdham Pool
28. **Dover** Dover Marina
29. **Gillingham** Gillingham Marina
30. **River Crouch** Fambridge Yacht Haven
31. **Tollesbury** Tollesbury Marina
32. **Ipswich** Fox's Marina
33. **Norfolk** Brundall Bay Marina
34. **Hull** Hull Marina
35. **Den Oever** Marina Den Oever
36. **Monnickendam** Jachthaven Waterland
37. **Wetterwille** Jachthaven Wetterwille
38. **Ouddorp** Marina Port Zélande
39. **Drimmelen** Jachthaven Biesbosch
40. **Kortgene** Delta Marina
41. **Nieuwpoort** VVW Nieuwpoort
42. **Dunkerque** Port de Dunkerque
43. **Saint-Valéry sur Somme** Port Saint-Valéry
44. **Fécamp** Port de plaisance de Fécamp
45. **Dives-Cabourg-Houlgate** Port de plaisance
46. **Ouistreham/Caen** Port de plaisance
47. **Guernsey** Beaucette Marina (Channel Islands)
48. **Granville** Port de Hérel
49. **Saint-Quay Portrieux** Saint Quay Port d'Armor
50. **Perros-Guirec** Port de plaisance
51. **Roscoff** Port de plaisance
52. **Brest** Moulin Blanc / Marina du Château
53. **Douarnenez** Port Tréboul / Port Rhu
54. **Loctudy** Port de plaisance de Loctudy
55. **Concarneau** Port de plaisance de Concarneau
56. **La Rochelle** Port de plaisance de La Rochelle
57. **Gijón** Puerto Deportivo Gijón
58. **Combarro** Marina Combarro
59. **Pontevedra** Nauta Sanxenxo
60. **Vigo** Marina Davila Sport
61. **Porto** Douro Marina
62. **Portimão** Marina Portimão
63. **Madeira** Quinta do Lorde Marina
64. **La Palma** Marina La Palma
65. **Lanzarote** Puerto Calero Marina
66. **La Linea** Marina Alcaidesa
67. **Valencia** Pobla Marina
68. **Barcelona** Port Ginesta
69. **Port-Saint-Louis-du-Rhône** Port Napoléon
70. **Rome** Porto Romano
71. **Venice** Venezia Certosa Marina
72. **Punat** Marina Punat, Croatia
73. **Kos Island** Kos Marina, Greece

TRANSEUROPE MARINAS 30 YEARS 1987 - 2017

AREA 8

NORTH WEST SCOTLAND – Cape Wrath to Crinan Canal

Reeds PDF ebooks

In response to popular demand, all the Reeds Almanacs are now available as searchable, highlightable PDF ebooks. (All ebooks incorporate the Marina Guide.)

Visit www.reedsnauticalalmanac.co.uk for further information

Key to Marina Plans symbols

	Bottled gas	P	Parking
	Chandler		Pub/Restaurant
	Disabled facilities		Pump out
	Electrical supply		Rigging service
	Electrical repairs		Sail repairs
	Engine repairs		Shipwright
	First Aid		Shop/Supermarket
	Fresh Water		Showers
	Fuel - Diesel		Slipway
	Fuel - Petrol	WC	Toilets
	Hardstanding/boatyard		Telephone
@	Internet Café		Trolleys
	Laundry facilities	V	Visitors berths
	Lift-out facilities		Wi-Fi

Area 8 - North West Scotland

MARINAS
Telephone Numbers
VHF Channel
Access Times

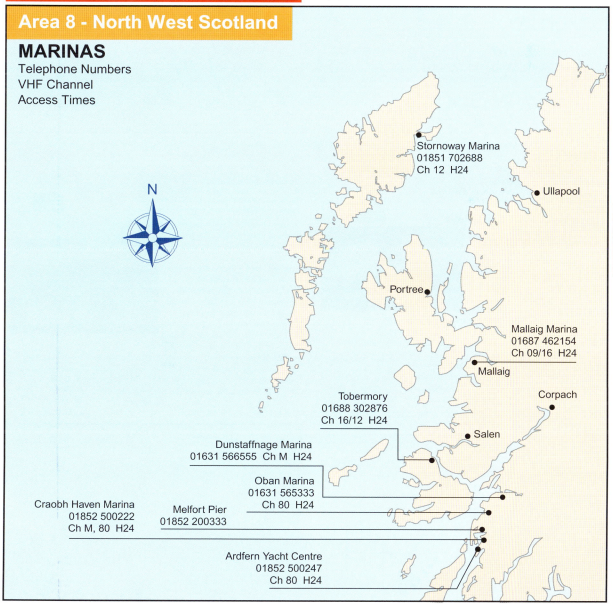

Stornoway Marina
01851 702688
Ch 12 H24

Ullapool

Portree

Mallaig Marina
01687 462154
Ch 09/16 H24

Mallaig

Corpach

Tobermory
01688 302876
Ch 16/12 H24

Salen

Dunstaffnage Marina
01631 566555 Ch M H24

Oban Marina
01631 565333
Ch 80 H24

Craobh Haven Marina
01852 500222
Ch M, 80 H24

Melfort Pier
01852 200333

Ardfern Yacht Centre
01852 500247
Ch 80 H24

MARINA GUIDE 2018

MARINAS & SERVICES

STORNOWAY MARINA

Stornoway Port Authority
Amity House, Esplanade Quay,
Stornoway, Isle of Lewis, HS1 2XS
Tel: 01851 702688 Fax: 01851 705714
Email: sypa@stornowayport.com

VHF Ch 12
ACCESS HW24

Stornoway Marina is sheltered and has easy access at all states of the tide and weather conditions. Vessels up to 24 metres in length and 3 metres draft can be accommodated.

The 80-berth marina provides a safe haven for island hoppers and days sailors. The marina is particularly popular as it is located right in the heart of the bustling town centre. Fresh water, electricity, wi-fi, toilet, shower and laundry facilities are available quayside for all visitors.

MALLAIG MARINA

Mallaig Marina
East Bay, Mallaig, Inverness-shire, PH41 4QS
Tel: 07824 331031 Fax: 01687 462172
Email: info@mallaigharbourauthority.com

VHF Ch 09, 16
ACCESS H24

Mallaig Marina is truly the gateway to the Western Isles. Now in its fourth year of operation the 50 berth Marina – part funded by EC Sail West project – provides the ideal location for experiencing and exploring the magnificent sailing opportunities available on the West Coast of Scotland. Shower/toilet/laundrette facilities are housed in the Mallaig Marina Centre.

The village centre, only 300m from the Marina, offers plenty of options for the discerning diner, shopper or tourist. Fishing boats still operate from the busy harbour, ferries, large and small, sail to Skye/Small Isles/Inverie and there is the daily arrival of The Jacobite Steam Train.

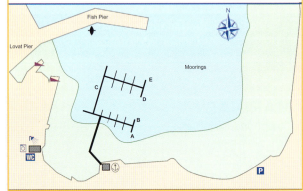

TOBERMORY

Tobermory Harbour Association
Taigh Solais, Tobermory, Isle of Mull, PA75 6NR
Mob: 07917 832497   Tel: 01688 302876
www.tobermoryharbour.co.uk
Email: jim.traynor@tobermoryharbour.co.uk

VHF Ch 16/12
ACCESS 0800–2000

Tobermory Harbour pontoons are located in the west shore of Tobermory Bay with access directly to the town. Swinging moorings for hire, look for the blue moorings with white top. A full range of excellent facilities ashore and afloat.

Tobermory is the iconic Scottish west coast destination, a natural historic harbour and protected anchorage. The town offers an exceptional array of shops, bars and restaurants. Mull Aquarium in the Harbour Building is Europe's first Catch and Release Aquarium.

Situated adjacent to the main car par, the pontoon has easy access to public transport links to and from mainland ferry links or destination tours throughout the Island of Mull.

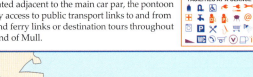

Key
a Tobermory Harbour Association office
b Recycling
c Cruise ship tenders and charter boats
d Large vessels
e Shallow draft vessels

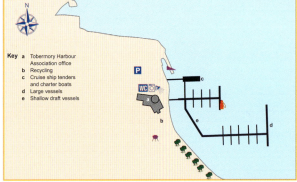

DUNSTAFFNAGE MARINA

Dunstaffnage Marina Ltd
Dunbeg, by Oban, Argyll, PA37 1PX
Tel: 01631 566555 Fax: 01631 571044
Email: info@dunstaffnagemarina.com

VHF Ch M
ACCESS H24

Located just two to three miles north of Oban, Dunstaffnage Marina has been renovated to include an additional 36 fully serviced berths, a new breakwater providing shelter from NE'ly to E'ly winds and an increased amount of hard standing. Also on site is the Wide Mouthed Frog, offering a convivial bar, restaurant and accommodation with stunning views of the 13th century Dunstaffnage Castle.

The marina is perfectly placed to explore Scotland's west coast and Hebridean Islands. Only 10M NE up Loch Linnhe is Port Appin, while sailing 15M S, down the Firth of Lorne, brings you to Puldohran where you can walk to an ancient hostelry situated next to the C18 Bridge Over the Atlantic.

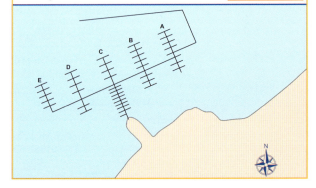

NORTH WEST SCOTLAND — AREA 8

OBAN MARINA

Oban Marina & Yacht Services Ltd
Isle of Kerrera, Oban, Argyll, PA34 4SX
Tel: 01631 565333
Email: info@obanmarina.com   www.obanmarina.com

VHF Ch 80   ACCESS H24

Oban Marina is perfectly situated at the gateway to the Western Isles on the picturesque Isle of Kerrera. In sight of the town of Oban, it is a well serviced and popular marina offering access at all tides.

With 100 pontoons berths and 30 moorings, easily accessible diesel fuel berth, free wifi, shower block and laundry, this friendly, small marina offers visitors a warm welcome. A complimentary 2-hourly ferry service runs to and from Oban – must be pre-booked – where all the major facilities including restaurants, chandlery, banks and transport links are available.

FACILITIES AT A GLANCE

Key
a Reception
b Showers/toilets
c Bar & grill
d Shed

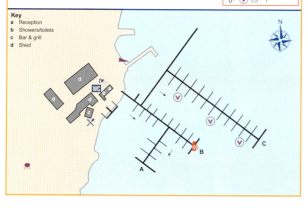

MELFORT PIER AND HARBOUR

Melfort Pier and Harbour
Kilmelford, by Oban, Argyll
Tel: 01852 200333
Email: melharbour@aol.com   www.mellowmelfort.com

VHF   ACCESS

Melfort Pier & Harbour is situated on the shores of Loch Melfort, one of the most peaceful lochs on the south west coast of Scotland. Overlooked by the Pass of Melfort and the Braes of Lorn, it lies approximately 18 miles north of Lochgilphead and 16 miles south of Oban. Its onsite facilities include showers, laundry, free Wi-Fi access and parking – pets welcome. Fuel, power and water are available at nearby Kilmelford Yacht Haven.

For those who want a few nights on dry land, Melfort Pier & Harbour offers lochside houses, each one equipped with a sauna, spa bath and balcony offering stunning views over the loch - available per night.

FACILITIES AT A GLANCE

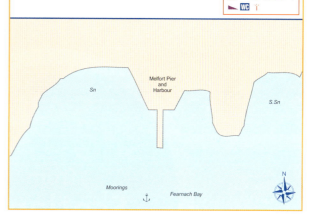

CRAOBH MARINA

Craobh Marina
By Lochgilphead, Argyll, Scotland, PA31 8UA
Tel: 01852 500222   Fax: 01852 500252
Email: info@craobhmarina.co.uk
www.craobhmarina.co.uk

VHF Ch M, 80   ACCESS H24

Craobh Marina is idyllically situated in the heart of Scotland's most sought after cruising grounds. Not only does Craobh offer ready access to a wonderful choice of scenic cruising throughout the western isles, the marina is conveniently close to Glasgow and its international transport hub.

Craobh Marina has been developed from a near perfect natural harbour, offering secure and sheltered berthing for up to 250 vessels to 40m LOA and with a draft of 4m. With an unusually deep and wide entrance Craobh Marina provides shelter and a warm welcome for all types of craft.

FACILITIES AT A GLANCE

Key
a Holiday cottages
b Village store
c Bar
d Gift shop
e Waste oil
f Boat shed
g Marina office

ARDFERN YACHT CENTRE

Ardfern Yacht Centre
Ardfern, by Lochgilphead, Argyll, PA31 8QN
Tel: 01852 500247   Fax: 01852 500624
www.ardfernyacht.co.uk   Email: office@ardfernyacht.co.uk

VHF Ch 80   ACCESS H24

Developed around an old pier once frequented by steamers, Ardfern Yacht Centre lies at the head of Loch Craignish, one of Scotland's most sheltered and picturesque sea lochs. With several islands and protected anchorages nearby, Ardfern is an ideal place from which to cruise the west coast of Scotland and the Outer Hebrides.

The Yacht Centre comprises pontoon berths and swinging moorings as well as a workshop, boat storage and well-stocked chandlery, while a grocery store and eating places can be found in the village. Among the onshore activities available locally are horse riding, cycling, and walking.

FACILITIES AT A GLANCE

Key
a Workshop
b Showers, toilets and launderette
c Chandlery and office

MARINA GUIDE 2018

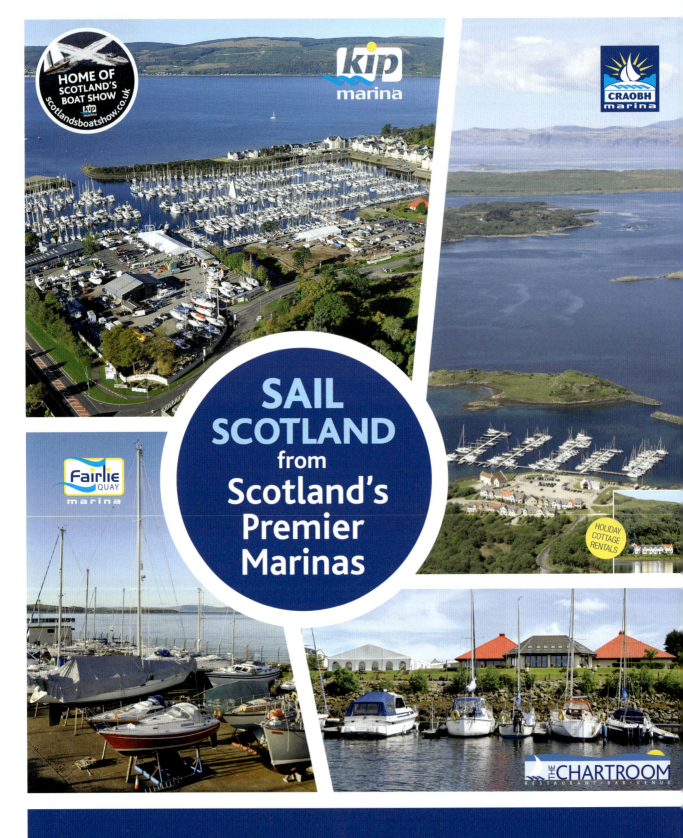

AREA 9

SOUTH WEST SCOTLAND – Crinan Canal to Mull of Galloway

Reeds PDF ebooks

In response to popular demand, all the Reeds Almanacs are now available as searchable, highlightable PDF ebooks. (All ebooks incorporate the Marina Guide.)

Visit www.reedsnauticalalmanac.co.uk for further information

Key to Marina Plans symbols

	Bottled gas		Parking
	Chandler		Pub/Restaurant
	Disabled facilities		Pump out
	Electrical supply		Rigging service
	Electrical repairs		Sail repairs
	Engine repairs		Shipwright
	First Aid		Shop/Supermarket
	Fresh Water		Showers
	Fuel - Diesel		Slipway
	Fuel - Petrol		Toilets
	Hardstanding/boatyard		Telephone
	Internet Café		Trolleys
	Laundry facilities		Visitors berths
	Lift-out facilities		Wi-Fi

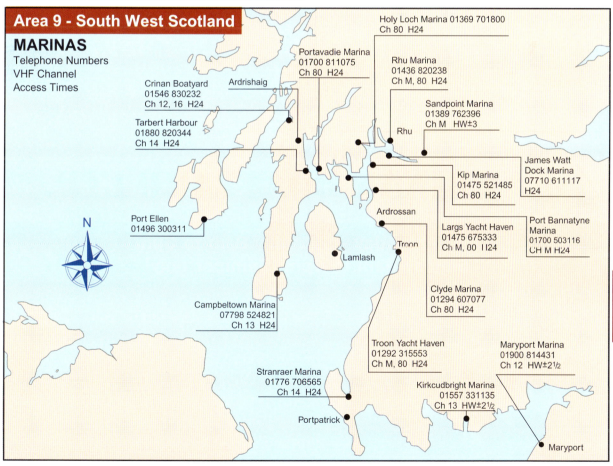

Area 9 - South West Scotland

MARINAS
Telephone Numbers
VHF Channel
Access Times

- Holy Loch Marina 01369 701800 Ch 80 H24
- Portavadie Marina 01700 811075 Ch 80 H24
- Rhu Marina 01436 820238 Ch M, 80 H24
- Crinan Boatyard 01546 830232 Ch 12, 16 H24
- Ardrishaig
- Sandpoint Marina 01389 762396 Ch M HW±3
- Tarbert Harbour 01880 820344 Ch 14 H24
- Rhu
- Kip Marina 01475 521485 Ch 80 H24
- James Watt Dock Marina 07710 611117 H24
- Port Ellen 01496 300311
- Ardrossan
- Largs Yacht Haven 01475 675333 Ch M, 00 H24
- Port Bannatyne Marina 01700 503116 CH M H24
- Lamlash
- Troon
- Clyde Marina 01294 607077 Ch 80 H24
- Campbeltown Marina 07798 524821 Ch 13 H24
- Troon Yacht Haven 01292 315553 Ch M, 80 H24
- Maryport Marina 01900 814431 Ch 12 HW±2½
- Stranraer Marina 01776 706565 Ch 14 H24
- Kirkcudbright Marina 01557 331135 Ch 13 HW±2½
- Portpatrick
- Maryport

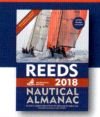

Subscribe annually and receive the Almanac for just £32.50 (rrp £49.99)

Visit www.reedsnauticalalmanac.co.uk/subscribetoreeds

MARINA GUIDE 2018

MARINAS & SERVICES

PORT ELLEN MARINA

Port Ellen Marina
Port Ellen, Islay, Argyll, PA42 7DB
Tel: 07464 151200 www.portellenmarina.co.uk
Email: portellenmarina@outlook.com

VHF / **ACCESS** H24

A safe and relaxed marina for visitors to the *Malt Whisky Island*. There are seven classic distilleries and yet another still (private) to start production soon. If you are planning a cruise to the north then superb sailing will take you onward via Craighouse on Jura. Meeting guests or short term storage is trouble free with the excellent air and ferry services connecting to Glasgow. Once on Islay you will be tempted to extend your stay so be warned, check www.portellenmarina.com for the many reasons to visit, from golf to music.

FACILITIES AT A GLANCE

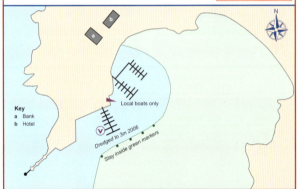

Key
a Bank
b Hotel

CRINAN BOATYARD

Crinan Boatyard Ltd
Crinan, Lochgilphead, Argyll, PA31 8SW
Tel: 01546 830232 Fax: 01546 830281
Email: info@crinanboatyard.co.uk
www.crinanboatyard.co.uk

VHF Ch 12, 16 / **ACCESS** H24

Situated at the westerly entrance of the scenic Crinan Canal, Crinan Boatyard offers swinging moorings nightly or longer term, a fuelling/loading berth, a well stocked Chandlery, heads, showers, laundry and an experienced work force for repair work all on site. A hotel and coffee shop, just a short walk away at the Canal basin, great walking and the historic Kilmartin Glen close by are some of the attractions on shore.

The nearby town of Lochgilphead 7 miles away offers shopping and good travel links to Glasgow (85 miles) and its International Airport.

FACILITIES AT A GLANCE
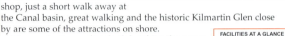

CRINAN BOATYARD LTD.

Open Monday - Saturday 8am to 5pm
Sunday 9am to 4pm (Summer only)

The boatyard is situated on the Argyll coast near the Western end of the Crinan Canal - about 7 miles north of Lochgilphead and 35 miles south of Oban by road.
It is a convenient and well equipped stopping point for cruising boats.

**Admiralty Charts - Marine Hardware
Safety Gear - Navigation Equipment
Moorings - Boat Repair Services
Gas & Diesel - Showers
Basic Provisions - Clothing - Gifts**

Crinan, Argyll PA31 8SW
Tel: 01546 830 232

MARINA GUIDE 2018

SOUTH WEST SCOTLAND — AREA 9

TARBERT HARBOUR

Tarbert Harbour Authority
Harbour Office, Garval Road, Tarbert, Argyll, PA29 6TR
Tel: 01880 820344 Fax: 01880 820719
Email: info@tarbertharbour.co.uk

VHF Ch 14 ACCESS H24

East Loch Tarbert is situated on the western shores of Loch Fyne. The naturally sheltered harbour is accessible H24 through an easily navigated narrow entrance, and is a prefect stopping point for those heading north to the Crinan Canal.

The pontoons can accommodate up to 100 visiting vessels of various sizes, with fresh water, electricity and wi-fi available FOC. Toilet, shower and laundry facilities are accessible 24/7, and the unique recreation area and community marquee are available to use - perfect for families, gatherings and musters. The marina pontoons are situated at the heart of the heritage village of Tarbert, which boasts a busy festival calendar and offers a wide range of amenities.

FACILITIES AT A GLANCE

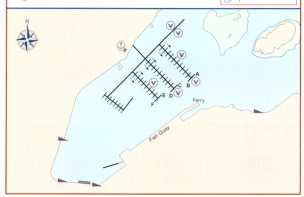

PORT BANNATYNE MARINA

Port Bannatyne Marina
Marine Road, Port Bannatyne, PA20 0LT
Tel: 01700 503116 Fax: 01700 503549
Email: portbannatynemarina@btconnect.com

VHF Ch M ACCESS H24

Nestled in the bay at Port Bannatyne on the Isle of Bute, the marina is set in breathtakingly beautiful surroundings. The shore facilities include toilets and showers, lifting and winter storage and all boat repairs. Free wi-fi is available throughout the marina. Protected by a breakwater and accessible H24 the marina is dredged to –2.4m CD.

The village of Port Bannatyne offers a Post Office for essential groceries and three pubs. There are frequent bus services to both Rothesay and Ettrick Bay where a walk along a beautiful beach with amazing views can be completed with either a meal or tea and cake at the beach side restaurant.

FACILITIES AT A GLANCE

PORTAVADIE MARINA

Portavadie Marina
Portavadie, Loch Fyne, Argyll, PA21 2DA
Tel: 01700 811075 Fax: 01700 811074
Email: info@portavadiemarina.com

VHF Ch 80 ACCESS H24

Portavadie Marina offers deep and sheltered berthing to residential and visiting boats in an area renowned for its superb cruising waters. Situated on the east side of Loch Fyne in close proximity to several islands and the famous Kyles of Bute, Portavadie is within easy sailing distance of the Crinan Canal, giving access to the Inner and Outer Hebrides. The marina has 230 berths 60 of which are reserved for visitors, plus comprehensive on shore facilities, including a choice of restaurants, bars and self catering accommodation. There is also a shop and small chandlery overlooking the marina, a dedicated fuel berth for petrol and diesel and bike hire.

This unspoiled area of Argyll which is less than two hours by road from Glasgow offers an ideal base for boat owners looking for a safe and secure haven.

FACILITIES AT A GLANCE

Key
a Reception, offices, conference room, open deck viewing platform
b Bar & restaurant
c WC, Showers & laundry
d Luxury self-catering apartments
e Leisure complex

Berthing
A-H pontoons
Odd numbers on the north side
Even numbers on the south side
Numbers start at the inner end

Visitor S pontoon
Mostly alongside with just S46 to S60 at the access bridge remaining

Visitor N pontoon
Runs from N1 at the north end to N19 at the access bridge

CAMPBELTOWN MARINA

Campbeltown Marina Ltd
Dubh Artach, Roading, Campbeltown, PA28 6LU
Tel: 07798 524821
Email: campbeltownmarina@btinternet.com

VHF Ch 13 ACCESS H24

Campbeltown Marina is a brand new facility opened in June 2015 and is situated in the town centre at the head of the deep, sheltered waters of Campbeltown Loch on the SE aspect of the Kintyre Peninsula. It is within easy reach of the Antrim Coast, Ayrshire and the Upper Clyde. Diesel is available at the Old Quay and gas is across the road. Petrol can be bought a 5-minute walk away and a well stocked chandlery is situated in the town centre.

Campbeltown is the perfect getaway destination with plenty to offer the whole family. Golf, cycling and walking routes, modern swimming pool and horse riding are some of the activities on offer. Situated directly in the town centre there is a wide choice of shops, cafes, bars, restaurants and supermarkets within easy walking distance.

FACILITIES AT A GLANCE

MARINA GUIDE 2018

MARINAS & SERVICES

HOLY LOCH MARINA

Holy Loch Marina
Rankin's Brae, Sandbank, Dunoon, PA23 8FE
Tel: 01369 701800
Email: info@holylochmarina.co.uk   www.holylochmarina.co.uk

VHF Ch 80
ACCESS H24

Holy Loch Marina, the marine gateway to Loch Lomond and the Trossachs National Park, lies on the south shore of the loch, roughly half a mile west of Lazaretto Point. Holy Loch is among the Clyde's most beautiful natural harbours and, besides being a peaceful location, offers an abundance of wildlife, places of local historical interest as well as excellent walking and cycling through the Argyll Forest Park. The marina can be entered in all weather conditions and is within easy sailing distance of Loch Long and Upper Firth.

FACILITIES AT A GLANCE

GOACHER SAILS

- **Sails**
- **Covers**
- **Canopies**
- **Upholstery**
- **Repairs & Service**

The complete service from the leading loft in the North

A trusted name since 1986

Designed. Manufactured. Tested

Lowside, Bowness-on-Windermere
Cumbria   015394 88686
loft@goachersails.co.uk
www.goachersails.co.uk

RHU MARINA

Rhu Marina
Rhu, Dunbartonshire, G84 8LH
Tel: 01436 820238   Fax: 01436 821039
Email: rhumarina@quaymarinas.com

VHF Ch M, 80
ACCESS H24

Located on the north shore of the Clyde Estuary, Rhu Marina is accessible at all states of the tide and can accommodate yachts up to 24m in length. It also operates 40 swinging moorings in the bay adjacent to the marina, with a ferry service provided.

Within easy walking distance of the marina is Rhu village, a conservation village incorporating a few shops, a pub and the beautiful Glenarn Gardens as well as the Royal Northern & Clyde Yacht Club. A mile or two to the east lies the holiday town of Helensburgh, renowned for its attractive architecture and elegant parks and gardens, while Glasgow city is just 25 miles away and can be easily reached by train.

FACILITIES AT A GLANCE

SANDPOINT MARINA

Sandpoint Marina Ltd
Sandpoint, Woodyard Road, Dumbarton, G82 4BG
Tel: 01389 762396   Fax: 01389 732605
Email: sales@sandpoint-marina.co.uk
www.sandpoint-marina.co.uk

VHF
ACCESS HW±3

Lying on the north bank of the Clyde estuary on the opposite side of the River Leven from Dumbarton Castle, Sandpoint Marina provides easy access to some of the most stunning cruising grounds in the United Kingdom. It is an independently run marina, offering a professional yet personal service to every boat owner. Among the facilities to hand are an on site chandlery, storage areas, a 40 ton travel hoist and 20 individual workshop units.

Within a 20-minute drive of Glasgow city centre, the marina is situated close to the shores of Loch Lomond, the largest fresh water loch in Britain.

FACILITIES AT A GLANCE

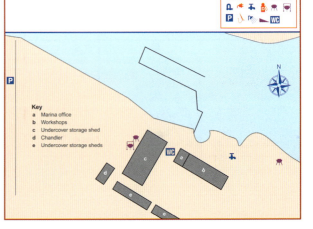

SOUTH WEST SCOTLAND — AREA 9

KIP MARINA

Kip Marina, The Yacht Harbour
Inverkip, Renfrewshire, Scotland, PA16 0AS
Tel: 01475 521485   Fax: 01475 521298
www.kipmarina.co.uk   Email: info@kipmarina.co.uk

VHF Ch 80   ACCESS H24

Inverkip is a small village which lies on the south shores of the River Kip as it enters the Firth of Clyde. Once established for fishing, smuggling and, in the 17th century, witch-hunts, it became a seaside resort in the 1860s as a result of the installation of the railway. Today it is a yachting centre, boasting a state-of-the-art marina with over 600 berths and full boatyard facilities. With the capacity to accommodate yachts of up to 23m LOA, Kip Marina offers direct road and rail access to Glasgow and its international airport, therefore making it an ideal location for either a winter lay up or crew changeover.

FACILITIES AT A GLANCE

Key
a Boat sales, chandlery and reception
b Workshop and contractors
c Chartroom bar and restaurant

JAMES WATT DOCK MARINA

James Watt Dock Marina
East Hamilton Street
Greenock, Renfrewshire, PA15 2TD
Tel: 01475 729838
www.jwdmarina.co.uk   Email: info@jwdmarina.co.uk

VHF 80   ACCESS H24

Based in the historic James Watt Dock alongside the stunning Victorian Sugar Shed, this new marina opened in May 2011 and is the first step in establishing an exciting new River Clyde waterfront development only 23 miles from Glasgow and 15 miles from the airport. James Watt Dock will have all the usual amenities expected of a modern marina.

Within easy reach of Greenock's cinema, pool, ice rink, restaurants and shops, and with nearby transport connections, the marina will be a great location for both visitors and regular berthers.

FACILITIES AT A GLANCE

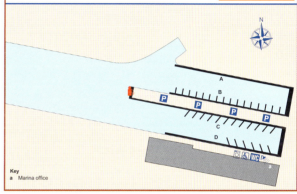

Key
a Marina office

DUNCAN'S
SCOTLAND'S NO.1

1ST for Service
1ST for Value
1ST for Choice
1ST for Advice
1ST for Price

Why not pay us a visit and see our vast range of chandlery, electronics, inflatables, outboards, clothing, footwear, life jackets, buoyancy aids and lots, lots more...

OPENING HOURS
Mon to Fri 9am - 5.30pm
Sat 9am - 4pm
Sun 10am - 3pm

PARKING
FREE & EASY
Parking in our own Car Park

YACHT CHANDLERS

PROUDLY SUPPORTING BOATING SINCE 1961

7 Scotland Street, Glasgow G5 8NL   Tel: 0141 429 6044   Fax: 0141 429 3078
Email: sales@duncanyachtchandlers.co.uk   www.duncanyacht.co.uk

MARINAS & SERVICES

LARGS YACHT HAVEN

Largs Yacht Haven Ltd
Irvine Road, Largs, Ayrshire, KA30 8EZ
Tel: 01475 675333 Fax: 01475 672245
Email: largs@yachthavens.com www.yachthavens.com

VHF Ch M, 80
ACCESS H24

Largs Yacht Haven offers a superb location among lochs and islands, with numerous fishing villages and harbours nearby. Sheltered cruising can be enjoyed in the inner Clyde, while the west coast and Ireland are only a day's sail away. With a stunning backdrop of the Scottish mountains, Largs incorporates 700 fully serviced berths and provides a range of on site facilities including chandlers, sailmakers, divers, engineers, shops, restaurants and club.

A 20-minute coastal walk brings you to the town of Largs, which has all the usual amenities as well as good road and rail connections to Glasgow.

FACILITIES AT A GLANCE

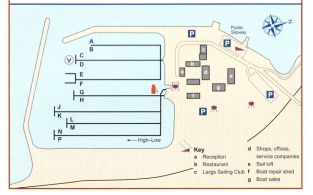

Key
- a Reception
- b Restaurant
- c Largs Sailing Club
- d Shops, offices, service companies
- e Sail loft
- f Boat repair shed
- g Boat sales

CLYDE MARINA

Clyde Marina Ltd
The Harbour, Ardrossan, Ayrshire, KA22 8DB
Tel: 01294 607077 Fax: 01294 607076
www.clydemarina.com Email: info@clydemarina.com

VHF Ch 80
ACCESS H24

Situated on the Clyde Coast between Irvine and Largs, Clyde Marina is Scotland's third largest marina and boatyard. It is set in a landscaped environment boasting a 50T hoist and active boat sales. A deep draft marina berthing vessels up to 30m LOA, draft up to 5m. Peviously accommodated vessels include tall ships and Whitbread 60s plus a variety of sail and power craft. Fully serviced pontoons plus all the yard facilities you would expect from a leading marina including boatyard and boatshed for repairs or storage. Good road and rail connections and only 30 minutes from Glasgow and Prestwick airports.

FACILITIES AT A GLANCE

key
- a Winter storage shed
- b Secure winter hard standing area

Numbering starts from shoreside
For pontoons B-E from shoreside:
Even nos - starboard side of pontoon
Odd nos - port side of pontoon

Adlard Coles Maritime Classics
Start your collection today

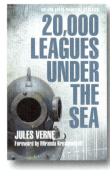
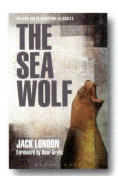
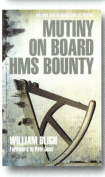

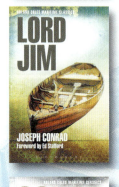
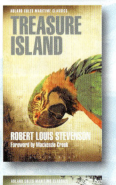
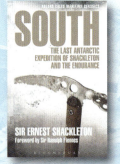
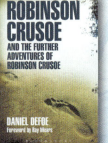

Visit **www.adlardcoles.com**
to buy at discount

MARINA GUIDE 2018

SOUTH WEST SCOTLAND

AREA 9

TROON YACHT HAVEN

Troon Yacht Haven Ltd
The Harbour, Troon, Ayrshire, KA10 6DJ
Tel: 01292 315553
Email: troon@yachthavens.com
www.yachthavens.com

VHF Ch 80
ACCESS H24

Troon Yacht Haven, situated on the Southern Clyde Estuary, benefits from deep water at all states of the tide. Tucked away in the harbour of Troon, it is well sheltered and within easy access of the town centre.

There are plenty of cruising opportunities to be had from here, whether it be hopping across to the Isle of Arran, with its peaceful anchorages and mountain walks, sailing round the Mull or through the Crinan Canal to the Western Isles, or heading for the sheltered waters of the Clyde.

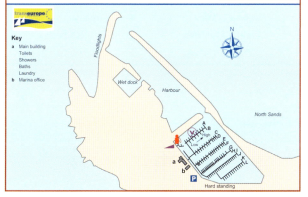

STRANRAER MARINA

Stranraer Marina
Militia House, English Street, Dumfries, DG1 2HR
Tel: 01776 706565 Mob: 07734 073421
Email: dgfirst-harbouradministration@dumgal.gov.uk

VHF Ch 14
ACCESS H24

Stranraer marina is at the southern end of beautiful Loch Ryan with H24 access and modern facilities. The town centre with full facilities is only a short walk from the marina. A new 30T boat crane, boat transporter and hard standing will become operational during 2016. The marina provides an excellent base for touring the picturesque Mull of Galloway.

It should be noted that the marina is exposed in strong N winds. Two ferry terminals are located on the E side of the loch approximately 6M N of the marina and extra care should be taken in this area.

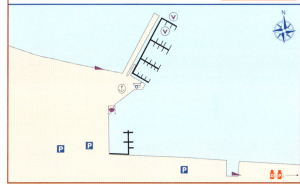

KIRKCUDBRIGHT MARINA

Kirkcudbright Marina
Militia House, English Street, Dumfries, DG1 2HR
Tel: 01557 331135 Mob: 07709 479663
Email: dgfirst-harbouradministration@dumgal.gov.uk

VHF Ch 16, 73
ACCESS HW±2.5

A very well sheltered picturesque marina accessed HW+/ 2.5 hrs via a 3.5 mile long, narrow channel that is well marked and lit, contact should be made with Range Safety vessel 'Gallovidian' prior to approach. Limited visitors berths so vessels should contact the harbour master in advance.

The marina is only 250m from the centre of Kirkcudbright, an historic 'artist's' town where visitors may enjoy a wide range of facilities and tourist attractions including castle, museum, tollbooth, art galleries and traditional shops. There is a superb programme of summer festivities.

MARYPORT MARINA

Maryport Development Ltd
Marine Road, Maryport, Cumbria, CA15 8AY
Tel: 01900 814431
www.maryportmarina.com
Email: enquires@maryportmarina.com

VHF Ch 12,16
ACCESS HW±2.5

Maryport Marina is located in the historic Senhouse Dock, which was originally built for sailing clippers in the late 19th century. The old stone harbour walls provide good shelter to the 190 berths from the prevailing south westerlies.

Maryport town centre and its shops, pubs and other amenities is within easy walking distance from the marina. Maryport a perfect location from which to explore the west coast of Scotland as well as the Isle of Man and the Galloway Coast. For those who wish to venture inland, then the Lake District is only seven miles away.

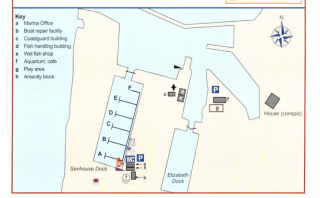

MARINA GUIDE 2018

MARINAS & SERVICES

NW ENGLAND, ISLE OF MAN & N WALES – Mull of Galloway to Bardsey Is

Reeds PDF ebooks

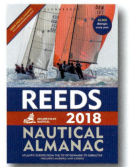

In response to popular demand, all the Reeds Almanacs are now available as searchable, highlightable PDF ebooks. (All ebooks incorporate the Marina Guide.)

Visit www.reedsnauticalalmanac.co.uk for further information

Key to Marina Plans symbols

	Bottled gas	P	Parking
	Chandler		Pub/Restaurant
	Disabled facilities		Pump out
	Electrical supply		Rigging service
	Electrical repairs		Sail repairs
	Engine repairs		Shipwright
	First Aid		Shop/Supermarket
	Fresh Water		Showers
	Fuel - Diesel		Slipway
	Fuel - Petrol	WC	Toilets
	Hardstanding/boatyard		Telephone
@	Internet Café		Trolleys
	Laundry facilities	V	Visitors berths
	Lift-out facilities		Wi-Fi

Area 10 - North West England & Wales

MARINAS
Telephone Numbers
VHF Channel
Access Times

Workington

Whitehaven Marina
01946 692435
Ch 12 HW±4
• Whitehaven

ENGLAND

Isle of Man
• Ramsey

Peel Marina
01624 842338
Ch 12 HW±2
• Peel

Douglas
01624 867543
Ch 12 HW±2
• Ronaldsway
• Port St Mary

Walney Is

Glasson Basin Marina
01524 751491
Ch 69 HW-1 to HW
• Glasson Dock

Fleetwood Haven Marina
01253 879062
Ch 12 HW±1½
• Fleetwood
• Blackpool
• Preston

Preston Marina
01772 733595
Ch 80 HW±2

• Liverpool

Liverpool Marina
0151 707 6777
Ch M HW±2

• Holyhead

Holyhead Marina
01407 764242
Ch M, M1 H24

Anglesey
• Conwy
Menai Strait

Deganwy Quays Marina
01492 576888
Ch 80 HW±2

Conwy Marina
01492 593000
Ch 80 LW±3½

Pwllheli Marina
01758 701219
Ch 80 H24
• Pwllheli
• Porthmadog
• Abersoch
• Barmouth

WALES

MARINA GUIDE 2018

NORTH WEST ENGLAND AND NORTH WALES — AREA 10

WHITEHAVEN MARINA

Whitehaven Marina Ltd
Harbour Office, Bulwark Quay, Whitehaven, Cumbria, CA28 7HS
Tel: 01946 692435
Email: enquiries@whitehavenmarina.co.uk
www.whitehavenmarina.co.uk

VHF Ch 12
ACCESS HW±4

Whitehaven Marina can be found at the south-western entrance to the Solway Firth, providing a strategic departure point for those yachts heading for the Isle of Man, Ireland or Southern Scotland. The harbour is one of the more accessible ports of refuge in NW England, affording a safe entry in most weathers. The approach channel across the outer harbour is dredged to about 1.0m above chart datum, allowing entry into the inner harbour via a sea lock at around HW±4. Over 100 new walk ashore berths were installed in 2013.

Conveniently situated for visiting the Lake District, Whitehaven is an attractive Georgian town, renowned in the C18 for its rum and slave imports.

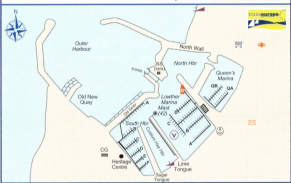

BWML GLASSON BASIN MARINA

BWML, Glasson Basin Marina
School Lane, Glasson Dock, Lancaster, LA2 0AW
Tel: 01524 751491   Fax: 01524 752626
Email: barnaby.hayward@bwml.co.uk
www.bwml.co.uk

VHF Ch 69
ACCESS HW-1 to HW

Glasson Basin Marina lies on the River Lune, west of Sunderland Point. Access is via the outer dock which opens 45 minutes before HW. Liverpool and thence via BWB lock into the inner basin. It is recommended to leave Lune No. 1 Buoy approx 1.5 hrs before HW. Contact the dock on Channel 69. The Marina can only be contacted by telephone. All the necessary requirements can be found either on site or within easy reach of Glasson Dock, including boat, rigging and sail repair services as well as a launderette, ablution facilities, shops and restaurants.

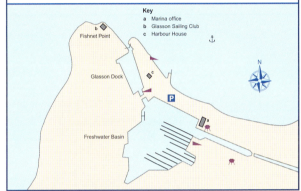

Glasson Basin Marina
Lancashire

- Fully serviced pontoons
- Visitors welcome
- Comprehensive chandlery
- Fully serviced boatyard and workshops with 50 tonne hoist
- Professional workshop services including rigging and spray painting
- **We are a proud agent of Z Spars UK for yacht masts and rigging requirements**

01524 751491   bwml.co.uk   barnaby.hayward@bwml.co.uk

MARINAS & SERVICES

DOUGLAS MARINA

Douglas Marina
Sea Terminal Building, Douglas, IM1 2RF
Tel: 01624 686627 Fax: 01624 686612
www.gov.im/harbours/
Email: enquiries.harboursdoi@gov.im

VHF Ch 12, 16
ACCESS HW±2

Douglas Marina is accessible HW±2 with 2.5m retained at LW. The depth of water inside the marina can vary so please advise draft. The maximum length accommodated on pontoons is 15m. Wall berths are also available. Douglas Marina Operations Centre requires clearance for entrance to the outer harbour due to commercial traffic. Please inform arrival on VHF Ch 12 10 minutes before port entry.

The marina has many facilities including electricity, fresh water, diesel, lift out, drying pad, gas, chandlery and showers/toilet facilities.

Douglas Marina is in the heart of the Isle of Man's capital so all local amenities and excellent transport links such as the Steam Railway are just a short walk away.

FACILITIES AT A GLANCE

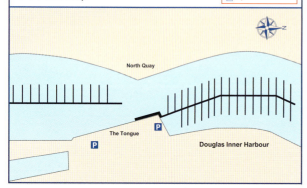

PEEL MARINA

Peel Marina
The Harbour Office, East Quay, Peel, IM5 1AR
Tel: 01624 842338 Fax: 01624 843610
www.gov.im/harbours/
Email: harbours@gov.im

VHF Ch 12
ACCESS HW±2

The Inner harbour has provision on pontoons for visiting vessels up 15m with rafting also available on the harbour walls. Access is available HW±2hrs with a maximum draft of 2.5m retained at low water but this does vary so please advise vessel dimensions on approach via VHF Ch 12.

Fresh water and electricity are available on all pontoon and some wall berths. Diesel fuel is available at the quayside with petrol sourced from a local forecourt in Peel.

Peel is a lovely active fishing port with many local amenities and a beautiful castle overlooking the harbour.

FACILITIES AT A GLANCE

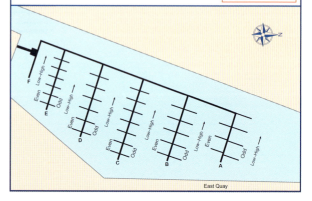

East Quay

GOACHER SAILS

- **Sails**
- **Covers**
- **Canopies**
- **Upholstery**
- **Repairs & Service**

The complete service from the leading loft in the North

A trusted name since 1986

Lowside, Bowness-on-Windermere
Cumbria 015394 88686
loft@goachersails.co.uk
www.goachersails.co.uk

FLEETWOOD HAVEN MARINA

Fleetwood Haven Marina
c/o ABP, Port & Marina Office, Fleetwood, FY7 8BP
Tel: 01253 879062 Fax: 01253 879063
Email: fleetwoodhaven@abports.co.uk

VHF Ch 12
ACCESS HW±1.5

Fleetwood Haven Marina provides a good location from which to cruise Morecambe Bay and the Irish Sea. To the north west is the Isle of Man, the north is the Solway Firth and the Clyde Estuary, while to the south west is Conwy, the Menai Straits and Holyhead.

Tucked away in a protected dock which dates to 1835, the marina has 340 full service berths and offers extensive facilities including a 75-tonne boat hoist, laundry and a first class shower/bathroom block.

Call Fleetwood Dock Radio on VHF Channel 12 (Tel 01253 872351) for permission to enter the dock channel.

FACILITIES AT A GLANCE

NORTH WEST ENGLAND AND NORTH WALES

AREA 10

PRESTON MARINA

Preston Marine Services Ltd
The Boathouse, Navigation Way, Preston, PR2 2YP
Tel: 01772 733595 Fax: 01772 731881
Email: info@prestonmarina.co.uk www.prestonmarina.co.uk

VHF Ch 80
ACCESS HW±2

Preston Marina forms part of the comprehensive Riversway Docklands development, meeting all the demands of modern day boat owners. With the docks' history dating back over 100 years, today the marina comprises 40 acres of fully serviced pontoon berths sheltered behind the refurbished original lock gates.

Lying 15 miles up the River Ribble, which itself is an interesting cruising ground with an abundance of wildlife, Preston is well placed for sailing to parts of Scotland, Ireland or Wales. The Docklands development includes a wide choice of restaurants, shops and cinemas as well as being in easy reach of all the cultural and leisure facilities provided by a large town.

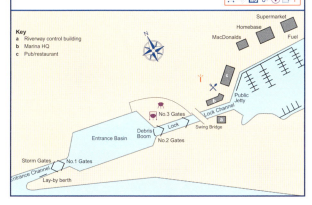

PRESTON MARINA
Sheltered pontoon berthing
for the Irish Sea and Morecambe Bay

Ask about our summer berthing deal
£10 per metre per month (April to September)

- Pontoon berthing
- Hard-standing
- Chandlery
- Brokerage
- Coffee Shop
- Restaurants
- RYA Training

RYA Active Marina

Preston Marina, Riversway Docklands,
Navigation Way, Preston, Lancashire, PR2 2YP
T: 01772 733595   E: info@prestonmarina.co.uk

www.prestonmarina.co.uk   /prestonmarina

LIVERPOOL MARINA

Liverpool Marina
Coburg Wharf, Sefton Street, Liverpool, L3 4BP
Tel: 0151 707 6777 Fax: 0151 707 6770
Email: mail@liverpoolmarina.co.uk

VHF Ch M
ACCESS HW±2

Liverpool Marina is ideally situated for yachtsmen wishing to cruise the Irish Sea. Access is through a computerised lock that opens two and a half hours either side of high water between 0600 and 2200 daily. Once in the marina, you can enjoy the benefits of the facilities on offer, including a first class club bar and restaurant.

Liverpool is now a thriving cosmopolitan city, with attractions ranging from numerous bars and restaurants to museums, art galleries and the Beatles Story.

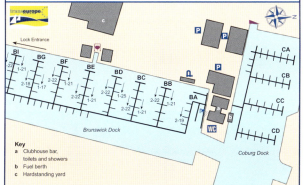

CONWY MARINA

Conwy Marina
Conwy, LL32 8EP
Tel: 01492 593000 Fax: 01492 564828
Email: jroberts@quaymarinas.com
www.quaymarinas.com

VHF Ch 80
ACCESS LW±3.5

Situated in an area of outstanding natural beauty, with the Mountains of Snowdonia National Park providing a stunning backdrop, Conwy is the first purpose-built marina to be developed on the north coast of Wales. Enjoying a unique site next to the 13th century Conwy Castle, the third of Edward I's great castles, it provides a convenient base from which to explore the cruising grounds of the North Wales coast. The unspoilt coves of Anglesey and the beautiful Menai Straits prove a popular destination, while further afield are the Lleyn Peninsula and the Islands of Bardsey and Tudwells. The marina incorporates about 500 fully serviced berths which are accessible through a barrier gate between half tide and high water.

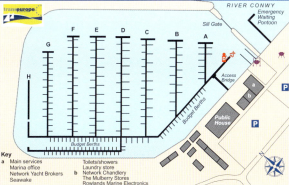

MARINA GUIDE 2018

MARINAS & SERVICES

DEGANWY QUAYS MARINA

Deganwy Quays Marina
Deganwy, Conwy, LL31 9DJ
Tel: 01492 576888 Fax: 01492 580066
Email: jjones@quaymarinas.com www.quaymarinas.com

VHF Ch 80
ACCESS HW±3

Deganwy Quays Marina is located in the centre of the north Wales coastline on the estuary of the Conwy River and sits between the river and the small town of Deganwy with the beautiful backdrop of the Vardre hills. The views from the Marina across the Conwy River are truly outstanding with the medieval walled town and Castle of Conwy outlined against the foothills of the Snowdonia National Park.

Deganwy Quays Marina opened in 2004 and has 165 fully serviced berths which are accessed via a tidal gate between half tide and high water.

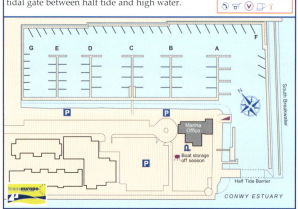

HOLYHEAD MARINA

Holyhead Marina Ltd
Newry Beach, Holyhead, Gwynedd, LL65 1YA
Tel: 01407 764242 Fax: 01407 769152
Email: info@holyheadmarina.co.uk

VHF Ch M
ACCESS H24

One of the few natural deep water harbours on the Welsh coast, Anglesey is conveniently placed as a first port of call if heading to North Wales from the North, South or West. Its marina at Holyhead, accessible at all states of the tide, is sheltered by Holyhead Mountain as well as an enormous harbour breakwater and extensive floating breakwaters, therefore offering good protection from all directions.

Anglesey boasts numerous picturesque anchorages and beaches in addition to striking views over Snowdonia, while only a tide or two away are the Isle of Man and Eire.

PWLLHELI MARINA

Pwllheli Marina
Glan Don, Pwllheli, North Wales, LL53 5YT
Tel: 01758 701219 Fax: 01758 701443
Email: wilwilliams@gwynedd.gov.uk

VHF Ch 80
ACCESS

Pwllheli is an old Welsh market town providing the gateway to the Llyn Peninsula, which stretches out as far as Bardsey Island to form an 'Area of Outstanding Natural Beauty'. Enjoying the spectacular backdrop of the Snowdonia Mountains, Pwllheli's numerous attractions include an open-air market every Wednesday, 'Neuadd Dwyfor', offering a mix of live theatre and latest films, and beautiful beaches.

Pwllheli Marina is situated on the south side of the Llyn Peninsula. One of Wales' finest marinas and sailing centres, it has over 400 pontoon berths and excellent onshore facilities.

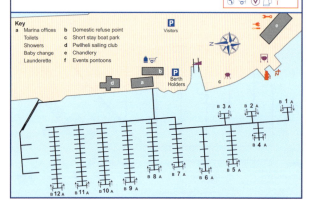

VISIT HAFAN PWLLHELI

A European Centre of Sailing Excellence
www.hafanpwllheli.co.uk

Hafan Pwllheli is your key to unlocking some of the best sailing waters in the UK.

Enjoy excellent facilities and easy access at virtually all states of the tide. With plenty of room for visiting yachts, it's the perfect base to discover the Lleyn Peninsula or start your cruise to Ireland, Scotland and beyond.

Glan Don, Pwllheli, Gwynedd LL53 5YT
Tel: (01758) 701219   VHF: Ch80
Email: hafanpwllheli@Gwynedd.gov.uk

AREA 11

SOUTH WALES & BRISTOL CHANNEL – Bardsey Island to Land's End

Reeds PDF ebooks

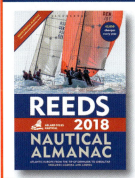

In response to popular demand, all the Reeds Almanacs are now available as searchable, highlightable PDF ebooks. (All ebooks incorporate the Marina Guide.)

Visit www.reedsnauticalalmanac.co.uk for further information

Key to Marina Plans symbols

	Bottled gas	P	Parking
	Chandler		Pub/Restaurant
	Disabled facilities		Pump out
	Electrical supply		Rigging service
	Electrical repairs		Sail repairs
	Engine repairs		Shipwright
	First Aid		Shop/Supermarket
	Fresh Water		Showers
	Fuel - Diesel		Slipway
	Fuel - Petrol	WC	Toilets
	Hardstanding/boatyard		Telephone
@	Internet Café		Trolleys
	Laundry facilities	V	Visitors berths
	Lift-out facilities		Wi-Fi

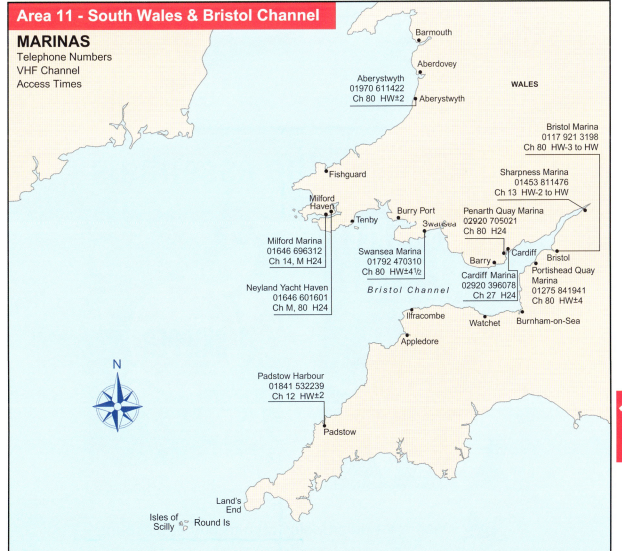

Area 11 - South Wales & Bristol Channel

MARINAS
Telephone Numbers
VHF Channel
Access Times

Barmouth
Aberdovey

Aberystwyth
01970 611422
Ch 80 HW±2

WALES

Bristol Marina
0117 921 3198
Ch 80 HW-3 to HW

Sharpness Marina
01453 811476
Ch 13 HW-2 to HW

Fishguard

Milford Haven
Tenby
Burry Port
Swansea

Penarth Quay Marina
02920 705021
Ch 80 H24

Milford Marina
01646 696312
Ch 14, M H24

Swansea Marina
01792 470310
Ch 80 HW±4½

Barry Cardiff Bristol

Cardiff Marina
02920 396078
Ch 27 H24

Portishead Quay Marina
01275 841941
Ch 80 HW±4

Neyland Yacht Haven
01646 601601
Ch M, 80 H24

Bristol Channel

Ilfracombe Watchet Burnham-on-Sea
Appledore

Padstow Harbour
01841 532239
Ch 12 HW±2

Padstow

Land's End
Isles of Scilly Round Is

MARINA GUIDE 2018

MARINAS & SERVICES

ABERYSTWYTH MARINA

Aberystwyth Marina, IMP Developments
Trefechan, Aberystwyth, Ceredigion, SY23 1AS
Tel: 01970 611422 Fax: 01970 624122
Email: aber@themarinegroup.co.uk

VHF Ch 80 **ACCESS** HW±2

Aberystwyth Marina offers 160 first class berths providing safe, secure and sheltered moorings for motor boats and yachts. The marina is at the heart of the historic fishing port on the 23 acre harbour site.

The location of Aberystwyth Marina, in a historic, university town, provides a range of cultural, active and educational activities within close proximity to the marina for berth holders to benefit from. Aberystwyth has a range of cafes, restaurants, pubs and bars, many a short walk from the marina.

FACILITIES AT A GLANCE

Key
a Offices
b Offices
c Marina office
d Apartments
e Aberystwyth BC

MILFORD MARINA

Milford Marina
Milford Docks, Milford Haven, Pembrokeshire, SA73 3AF
Tel: 01646 696312 Fax: 01646 696314
Email: enquiries@milfordmarina.com www.milfordmarina.com

VHF Ch 14 **ACCESS** H24

Set within one of the deepest natural harbours in the world, Milford Marina is situated in a non-tidal basin within the UK's only coastal National Park, the ideal base for discovering the fabulous coastline in Pembrokeshire, Wales and Ireland. Continued investment has meant that the marina provides safe, secure and sheltered boat berths with a full range of shoreside facilities in the heart of SW Wales.

Accessed via an entrance lock (with waiting pontoons both inside and outside the lock), the marina is perfect for exploring the picturesque upper reaches of the River Cleddau or cruising out beyond St Ann's Head to the unspoilt islands of Skomer, Skokholm and Grassholm.

FACILITIES AT A GLANCE

Key
a Neil Hart Joinery
b Mustang Marine
c Neyland Marine Services
d Fish Processing
e Fish Markets
f Galley Café
g MPSC
h Servitec
i MITEC Building
j Seal Hospital
k Sail loft
l Charlies Bar
m Norrad Electrics
n All Pets Vet Care
o Locks on Line
p Museum
q Marina Control
  Martha's Vineyard
  Dyfed Electronics
r Phoenix Bowl
s Windjammer Marine

Set sail with the essentials

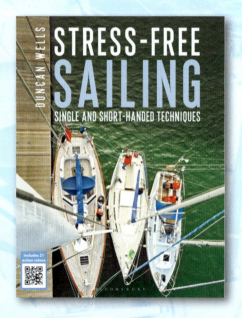

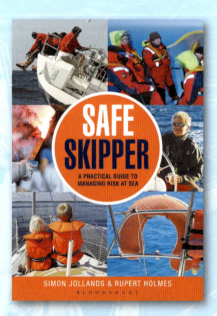

Visit www.adlardcoles.com to buy at discount

MARINA GUIDE 2018

SOUTH WALES AND BRISTOL CHANNEL — AREA 11

NEYLAND YACHT HAVEN

Neyland Yacht Haven Ltd
Brunel Quay, Neyland, Pembrokeshire, SA73 1PY
Tel: 01646 601601
Email: neyland@yachthavens.com   www.yachthavens.com

VHF Ch M, 80
ACCESS H24

Approximately 10 miles from the entrance to Milford Haven lies Neyland Yacht Haven. Tucked away in a well protected inlet just before the Cleddau Bridge, this marina has 420 berths and can accommodate yachts up to 25m LOA with draughts of up to 2.5m. The marina is divided into two basins, with the lower one enjoying full tidal access, while entry to the upper one is restricted by a tidal sill. Visitor and annual berthing enquiries welcome.

Offering a comprehensive range of services, Neyland Yacht Haven is within a five minute walk of the town centre where the various shops and takeaways cater for most everyday needs; bicycle hire is also available. The Yacht Haven is a member of the TransEurope Group.

FACILITIES AT A GLANCE

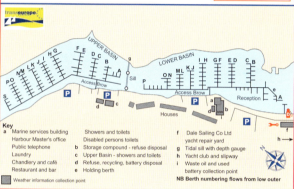

Key
a Marine services building
   Harbour Master's office
   Public telephone
   Laundry
   Chandlery and café
   Restaurant and bar
   Weather information collection point
b Storage compound - refuse disposal
c Upper Basin - showers and toilets
d Refuse, recycling, battery disposal
e Holding berth
   Showers and toilets
   Disabled persons toilets
f Dale Sailing Co Ltd yacht repair yard
g Tidal sill with depth gauge
h Yacht club and slipway
i Waste oil and used battery collection point
NB Berth numbering flows from low outer

www.yachthavens.com

Neyland Yacht Haven

Full Tidal Access

Visitors Welcome

HAVEN POD — FLOATING ACCOMMODATION

– Pembrokeshire's Picturesque Marina
– Full tidal access within a well-protected creek
– TransEurope Member – visitor discounts
– Café, Bar/Restaurant & Chandlery
– Full marina services
– Free Wi-Fi
– Bike Hire

Neyland Yacht Haven Tel: 01646 601601   VHF Ch 37 & 80
Email: neyland@yachthavens.com

NEYLAND Marine Services Ltd
Electronic & Electrical Engineers

We provide unequalled sales and service to the pleasure boating, fishing and shipping industry.

Your complete repair and supply service for electrical and electronic equipment, engineering installations and components.

Supply, service and dealers for most manufacturers.

Tel: 01646 600358 Fax: 01646 600323
email: info@neylandmarine.co.uk
www.neylandmarine.co.uk

Unit 52 Honeyborough Business Park, Neyland, Pembrokeshire SA73 1SE

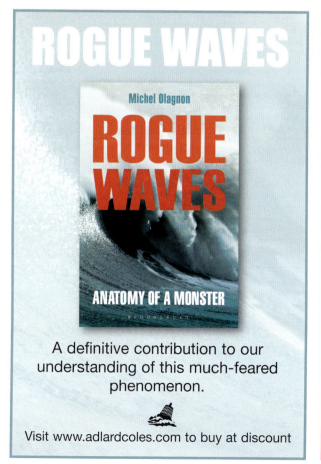

ROGUE WAVES
Michel Olagnon
ROGUE WAVES
ANATOMY OF A MONSTER
BLOOMSBURY

A definitive contribution to our understanding of this much-feared phenomenon.

Visit www.adlardcoles.com to buy at discount

Ratseys

SAILMAKING
state of the art racing and cruising sails - professional repairs

RIGGING
standing and running rigging - furling systems
booms and spars - guard rails - deck hardware
Dyneema and other ropes - supply and installation

COVERS
of all types for motor and sailing craft

Stephen Ratsey Sailmakers
8 Brunel Quay, Neyland, Milford Haven,
Pembrokeshire SA73 1PY
Tel 01646 601561 Fax 01646 601968
Email ratseys@btconnect.com

www.ratseys.co.uk
www.ratseysyachtrigging.co.uk

MARINAS & SERVICES

SWANSEA MARINA

Swansea Marina
Lockside, Maritime Quarter, Swansea, SA1 1WG
Tel: 01792 470310 Fax: 01792 463948
www.swansea.gov.uk/swanseamarina
Email: swanmar@swansea.gov.uk

VHF Ch 80
ACCESS HW±4.5

At the hub of the city's redeveloped and award winning Maritime Quarter, Swansea Marina can be accessed HW±4½ hrs via a lock. Surrounded by a plethora of shops, restaurants and marine businesses to cater for most yachtsmen's needs, the marina is in close proximity to the picturesque Gower coast, where there is no shortage of quiet sandy beaches off which to anchor. It also provides the perfect starting point for cruising to Ilfracombe, Lundy Island, the North Cornish coast or West Wales.

Within easy walking distance of the marina is the city centre, boasting a covered shopping centre and market. For those who prefer walking or cycling, take the long promenade to the Mumbles fishing village from where there are plenty of coastal walks.

FACILITIES AT A GLANCE

Key
a Leisure Centre
b Maritime Museum
c Pumphouse Restaurant
d Yacht Club
e Repair shed
f Mariott Hotel

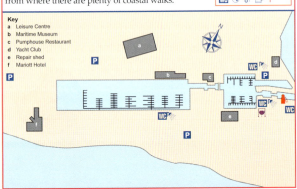

PENARTH QUAYS MARINA

Penarth Quays Marina
Penarth, Vale of Glamorgan, CF64 1TQ
Tel: 02920 705021
Email: sjones@quaymarinas.com
www.quaymarinas.com

VHF Ch 80
ACCESS H24

Penarth Quays Marina has been established in the historic basins of Penarth Docks for over 20 years and is the premier boating facility in the region. The marina is Cardiff Bay's only 5 Gold Anchor marina and provides an ideal base for those using the Bay and the Bristol Channel. With 24hr access there is always water available for boating. Penarth and Cardiff boast an extensive range of leisure facilities, shops and restaurants making this marina an ideal base or destination. The marina has a blue flag and is a member of the TransEurope Group.

FACILITIES AT A GLANCE

Key
a Marina office
b Inner basin services building
c Boat shed
d Refuse compound/recycling
e Boat sales/Café
f Restaurant

CARDIFF MARINA

Cardiff Marina
Watkiss Way, Cardiff, CF11 0SY
Tel: 02920 396078 Fax: 02920 345116
Email: info@themarinegroup.co.uk
www.themarinegroup.co.uk

VHF Ch M
ACCESS H24

Situated on the River Ely on the Cardiff International Sports Village, Cardiff Marina is perfectly positioned to provide safe, secure and sheltered moorings for motor boats and yachts. Cardiff Bay is an attractive and approachable environment for boat users of all standards and provides 200 hectares of freshwater to explore with the Barrage allowing H24 access to the Bristol Channel.

The location of Cardiff Marina, in the Welsh capital city, ensures there are lots of activities within close proximity to the marina to provide an exciting and dynamic location to berth your boat.

FACILITIES AT A GLANCE

Key
a Marina Office
b Showers, toilets
c Workshop

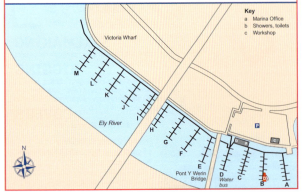

SHARPNESS MARINA

Sharpness Marina
Berkeley, Gloucestershire GL13 9UN
Tel & fax: 01453 811476
Email: sharpnessmarine@gmx.com

VHF Ch 13
ACCESS HW-2

Sharpness is a small port on the River Severn lying at the entrance to the Gloucester and Sharpness Canal. At the time of its completion in 1827, the canal was the largest and deepest ship canal in the world. However, although once an important commercial waterway, it is now primarily used by pleasure boats. Yachts approaching the marina from seaward can do so via a lock two hours before high water, but note that the final arrival should be timed as late as possible to avoid strong tides in the entrance. From the lock, a passage under two swing bridges and a turn to port brings you to the marina, where pontoon berths are equipped with electricity and water supplies.

FACILITIES AT A GLANCE

82 MARINA GUIDE 2018

SOUTH WALES AND BRISTOL CHANNEL

AREA 11

BRISTOL MARINA

Bristol Marina Ltd
Hanover Place, Bristol, BS1 6UH
Tel: 0117 921 3198 Fax: 0117 929 7672
Email: info@bristolmarina.co.uk

VHF	Ch 80
ACCESS	HW-3 to HW

Situated in the heart of the city, Bristol is a fully serviced marina providing over 100 pontoon berths for vessels up to 20m LOA. Among the facilities are a new fuelling berth and pump out station as well as an on site chandler and sailmaker. It is situated on the south side of the Floating Harbour, about eight miles from the mouth of the River Avon. Accessible from seaward via the Cumberland Basin, passing through both Entrance Lock and Junction Lock, it can be reached approximately three hours before HW.

Shops, restaurants, theatres and cinemas are all within easy reach of the marina, while local attractions include the SS *Great Britain*, designed by Isambard Kingdom Brunel, and the famous Clifton Suspension Bridge, which has an excellent visitors' centre depicting its fascinating story.

FACILITIES AT A GLANCE

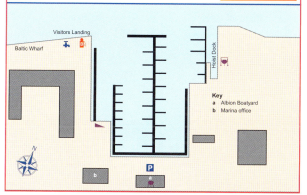

PORTISHEAD QUAYS MARINA

Portishead Quays Marina
Newfoundland Way, Portishead, North Somerset, BS20 7DF
Tel: 01275 841941 Fax: 01275 841942
Email: portisheadmarina@quaymarinas.com
www.quaymarinas.com

VHF	Ch 80
ACCESS	HW±3.5

Portishead Marina is a popular destination for cruising in the Bristol Channel. Providing an excellent link between the inland waterways at Bristol and Sharpness and offering access to the open water and marinas down channel. The entrance to the Marina is via a lock, with a minimum access of HW+/- 3.5hrs. Contact the Marina on VHF Ch 80 ahead of time for next available lock. The Marina provides 270 fully serviced berths and can accommodate vessels up to 40m LOA, draft up to 5.5m. The marina has a 35 tonnes boat hoist and the boatyard offers all the facilities you would expect from a Quay Marinas site.

FACILITIES AT A GLANCE

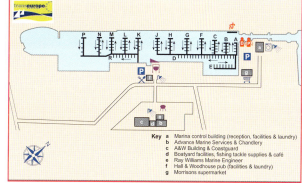

PADSTOW HARBOUR

Padstow Harbour Commissioners
The Harbour Office, Padstow, Cornwall, PL28 8AQ
Tel: 01841 532239 Fax: 01841 533346
Email: padstowharbour@btconnect.com
www.padstow-harbour.co.uk

VHF	Ch 12, 16
ACCESS	HW±2

Padstow is a small commercial port with a rich history situated 1.5 miles from the sea within the estuary of the River Camel. The inner harbour is serviced by a tidal gate – part of the 1988–1990 flood defence scheme, which is open approximately two hours either side of high water. A minimum of 3m of water is maintained in the inner harbour at all times. Onshore facilities are excellent, please enquire at the Harbour Office.

This is a thriving fishing port, so perhaps it wasn't surprising that celebrity chefs like Rick Stein and Jamie Oliver would set up shop in the town. This is a great resting point for everything Cornish from surf and coastal walks to fish and chips and cream teas.

FACILITIES AT A GLANCE

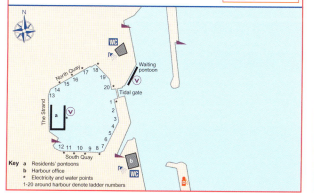

PADSTOW HARBOUR COMMISSIONERS

Tel: 01841 532239
Fax: 01841 533346
E-Mail: padstowharbour@btconnect.com

Services include showers, toilets, diesel, water and ice, CCTV security.

Free Wi-fi internet access.

Inner harbour controlled by tidal gate -
open HW ±2 hours -
minimum depth 3 metres

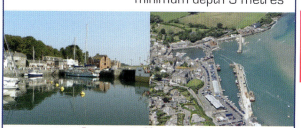

Harbour Office Padstow,
Cornwall PL28 8AQ
Website: www.padstow-harbour.co.uk

MARINA GUIDE 2018

MARINAS & SERVICES

SOUTH IRELAND – Malahide, clockwise to Liscannor Bay

Reeds PDF ebooks

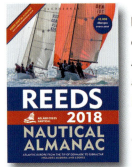

In response to popular demand, all the Reeds Almanacs are now available as searchable, highlightable PDF ebooks. (All ebooks incorporate the Marina Guide.)

Visit www.reedsnauticalalmanac.co.uk for further information

Key to Marina Plans symbols

Symbol	Description	Symbol	Description
	Bottled gas		Parking
	Chandler		Pub / Restaurant
	Disabled facilities		Pump out
	Electrical supply		Rigging service
	Electrical repairs		Sail repairs
	Engine repairs		Shipwright
	First Aid		Shop / Supermarket
	Fresh Water		Showers
	Fuel - Diesel		Slipway
	Fuel - Petrol		Toilets
	Hardstanding/boatyard		Telephone
	Internet Café		Trolleys
	Laundry facilities		Visitors berths
	Lift-out facilities		Wi-Fi

Area 12 - South Ireland

MARINAS
Telephone Numbers
VHF Channel
Access Times

Malahide 01 845 4129 Ch M, 80 HW±4

Howth YC Marina 01 839 2777 Ch M, 80 H24

Dun Laoghaire Marina 01202 0040 Ch M, 16 H24

Arklow Marina 0402 39901 H24

Kilrush 065 9052072 Ch 80 H24

Dingle Marina 066 9151629 Ch M H24

Fenit Marina 066 713 6231 Ch M H24

Cahersiveen Marina 066 947 2777 Ch M H24

Waterford City Marina 051 849503 Ch 12 H24

Kilmore Quay 053 29955 Ch 09, 16 H24

Cork Harbour Marina 087 366 9009 H24
Crosshaven BY Marina 021 483 1161 Ch M H24
East Ferry Marina 086 735 7785 H24
Royal Cork YC Marina 021 483 1023 Ch M H24
Salve Marine 021 483 1145 Ch M H24

Kinsale YC Marina 021 477 2196 Ch M H24
Castlepark Marina 021 477 4959 Ch 06 H24

Lawrence Cove 027 75044 Ch 16 H24

SOUTH IRELAND   AREA 12

MALAHIDE MARINA

Malahide Marina
Malahide, Co. Dublin
Tel: +353 1 845 4129 Fax: +353 1 845 4255
Email: info@malahidemarina.net
www.malahidemarina.net

VHF: Ch M, 80
ACCESS: HW±4

Malahide Marina, situated just 10 minutes from Dublin Airport and 20 minutes north of Dublin's city centre, is a fully serviced marina accommodating up to 350 yachts. Capable of taking vessels of up to 75m in length, its first class facilities include a boatyard with hard standing for approximately 170 boats and a 30-ton mobile hoist. Its on site restaurant provides a large seating area in convivial surroundings. The village of Malahide has plenty to offer the visiting yachtsmen, with a wide variety of eating places, nearby golf courses and tennis courts as well as a historic castle and botanical gardens.

FACILITIES AT A GLANCE

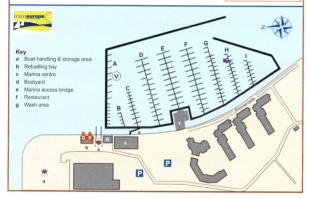

Key
a Boat handling & storage area
b Refuelling bay
c Marina centre
d Boatyard
e Marina access bridge
f Restaurant
g Wash area

HOWTH MARINA

Howth Marina
Howth Marina, Harbour Road, Howth, Co. Dublin
Tel: +353 1 8392777 Fax: +353 1 8392430
Email: marina@hyc.ie
www.hyc.ie

VHF: Ch M, 80
ACCESS: H24

Based on the north coast of the rugged peninsula that forms the northern side of Dublin Bay, Howth Marina is ideally situated for north or south-bound traffic in the Irish Sea. Well sheltered in all winds, it can be entered at any state of the tide. Overlooking the marina is Howth Yacht Club, which has in recent years been expanded and is now said to be the largest yacht club in Ireland. With good road and rail links, Howth is in easy reach of Dublin's airport and ferry terminal, making it an obvious choice for crew changeovers.

FACILITIES AT A GLANCE

Key
a Harbour office
b RNLI boathouse
c Clubhouse
d Drying pad
e Waiting pontoons (A&B)

Berth numbering starts at hammerheads

Gripping true life adventures

SEA FEVER
The true adventures that inspired our greatest maritime authors, from Conrad to Masefield, Melville and Hemingway
SAM JEFFERSON

SAM JEFFERSON
GORDON BENNETT
AND THE FIRST YACHT RACE ACROSS THE ATLANTIC

THE CAPE HORNERS' CLUB
Adrian Flanagan

RESCUE PILOT
CHEATING THE SEA
JERRY GRAYSON AFC

Visit www.adlardcoles.com to buy at discount

MARINA GUIDE 2018

DUN LAOGHAIRE MARINA

Dun Laoghaire Marina
Harbour Road, Dun Laoghaire, Co Dublin, Eire
Tel: +353 1 202 0040 Fax: +353 1 202 0043
Email: info@dlmarina.com   www.dlmarina.com

VHF Ch M, 16
ACCESS H24

Dun Laoghaire Marina – Gateway to Dublin and the first marina in the Republic of Ireland to be awarded five Gold anchors by THYA and also achieved the ICOMIA 'Clean Marina' accreditation – is the largest marina in Ireland. 24 hour access in all weather conditions. The town centre is located within 400m. Serviced berthing for 820 boats from 6m to 23m with visitors mainly on the hammerheads.

Larger vessels up to 30m and 80 tonne displacement can be accommodated alongside breakwater pontoons. Minimum draft is 3.6m LWS. With adjacent ferry terminal and rail station, Dublin 12kms and airport 35kms, the marina is an ideal location for crew change etc. Easy access to Dublin Bay, home to the biennial Dun Laoghaire Regatta.

An essential boater's companion

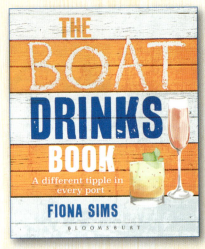

An expert look at enjoyable things to drink in key sailing spots around the world

Visit www.adlardcoles.com to buy at discount

ARKLOW MARINA

Arklow Marina
North Quay, Arklow, Co. Wicklow, Eire
Mobiles: 087 2375189 or 087 2588078
Email: personnel@asl.ie
www.arklowmarina.com

VHF
ACCESS H24

Arklow is a popular fishing port and seaside town situated at the mouth of the River Avoca, 16 miles south of Wicklow and 11 miles north east of Gorey. The town is ideally placed for visiting the many beauty spots of County Wicklow including Glenmalure, Glendalough and Clara Lara, Avoca (Ballykissangel).

Arklow Marina is on the north bank of the river (dredged 2014) just upstream of the commercial quays, with 42 berths in an inner harbour and 30 berths on pontoons outside the marina entrance. Vessels over 14m LOA should moor on the river pontoons.

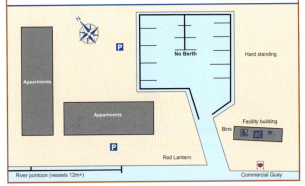

KILMORE QUAY

Kilmore Quay
Wexford, Ireland
Tel: +353 53 9129955 Fax: +353 53 9129955 www.wexford.ie
Email: assistant.marineofficer@wexfordcoco.ie

VHF Ch 09, 16
ACCESS H24

Located in the SE corner of Ireland, Kilmore Quay is a small rural fishing village situated approximately 14 miles from the town of Wexford and 12 miles from Rosslare ferry port.

Its 55-berthed marina, offering shelter from the elements as well as various on shore facilities, including diesel available 24/7, has become a regular port of call for many cruising yachtsmen. With several nearby areas of either historical or natural significance accessible using local bike hire, Kilmore is renowned for its 'green' approach to the environment.

SOUTH IRELAND — AREA 12

WATERFORD CITY MARINA

Waterford City Marina
Waterford, Ireland
Tel: +353 87 238 4944
Email: jcodd@waterfordcouncil.ie

VHF Ch 12
ACCESS H24

Famous for its connections with Waterford Crystal, manufactured in the city centre, Waterford is the capital of the SE region of Ireland. As a major city, it benefits from good rail links with Dublin, and Limerick, a regional airport with daily flights to Britain and an extensive bus service to surrounding towns and villages. The marina is found on the banks of the River Suir, in the heart of this historic Viking city dating back to the ninth century. Yachtsmen can make the most of Waterford's wide range of shops, restaurants and bars without having to walk too far from their boats. With 100 fully serviced berths and first rate security, Waterford City Marina now provides shower, toilet and laundry facilities in its new reception building.

FACILITIES AT A GLANCE

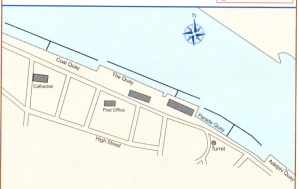

CROSSHAVEN BOATYARD MARINA

Crosshaven Boatyard Marina
Crosshaven, Co Cork, Ireland
Tel: +353 214 831161 Fax: +353 214 831603
Email: info@crosshavenboatyard.com

VHF Ch M
ACCESS H24

One of three marinas at Crosshaven, Crosshaven Boatyard was founded in 1950 and originally made its name from the construction of some of the most world-renowned yachts, including *Gypsy Moth* and Denis Doyle's *Moonduster*. Nowadays, however, the yard has diversified to provide a wide range of services to both the marine leisure and professional industries. Situated on a safe and sheltered river only 12 miles from Cork City Centre, the marina boasts 100 fully-serviced berths along with the capacity to accommodate yachts up to 35m LOA with a 4m draught. In addition, it is ideally situated for cruising the stunning south west coast of Ireland.

FACILITIES AT A GLANCE

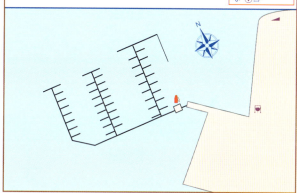

SALVE MARINE

Salve Marine
Crosshaven, Co Cork, Ireland
Tel: +353 21 483 1145 Fax: +353 21 483 1747
Email: salvemarine@eircom.net

VHF Ch M
ACCESS H24

Crosshaven is a picturesque seaside resort providing a gateway to Ireland's south and south west coasts. Offering a variety of activities to suit all types, its rocky coves and quiet sandy beaches stretch from Graball to Church Bay and from Fennell's Bay to nearby Myrtleville. Besides a selection of craft shops selling locally produced arts and crafts, there are plenty of pubs, restaurants and takeaways to suit even the most discerning of tastes. Lying within a few hundred metres of the village centre is Salve Marine, accommodating yachts up to 43m LOA with draughts of up to 4m. Its comprehensive services range from engineering and welding facilities to hull and rigging repairs.

FACILITIES AT A GLANCE

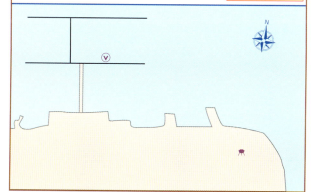

CORK HARBOUR MARINA

Cork Harbour Marina
Monkstown, Co Cork, Ireland
Tel: +353 87 366 9009
Email: info@corkharbourmarina.ie   www.corkharbourmarina.ie

VHF
ACCESS H24

Located in the picturesque town of Monkstown, Cork Harbour Marina is in the heart of Cork Harbour. The marina can cater for all boat types with a draft of up to 7m and the marina is accessible at all phases of the tide.

Within strolling distance from the marina is the 'Bosun' restaurant and 'Napoli', an Italian delicatessen. There is also a sailing club, tennis club and golf club located nearby. Monkstown is just a short riverside walk from Passage West, with all the amenities one might require.

There is a frequent bus service from the marina gates to Cork City. Cork Harbour Marina is 15km from Cork International Airport.

FACILITIES AT A GLANCE

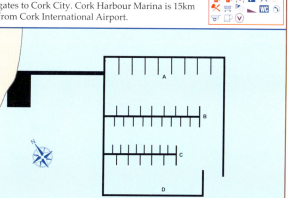

MARINA GUIDE 2018

MARINAS & SERVICES

ROYAL CORK YACHT CLUB

Royal Cork Yacht Club Marina
Crosshaven, Co Cork, Ireland
Tel: +353 21 483 1023 Fax: +353 21 483 2657
Email: mark@royalcork.com www.royalcork.com

VHF Ch M
ACCESS H24

Founded in 1720, the Royal Cork Yacht Club is one of the oldest and most prominent yacht clubs in the world. Organising, among many other events, the prestigious biennial Ford Cork Week, it boasts a number of World, European and national sailors among its membership.

The Yacht Club's marina is situated at Crosshaven, on the hillside at the mouth of the Owenabue River, just inside the entrance to Cork Harbour. The harbour is popular with yachtsmen as it is accessible and well sheltered in all weather conditions. It also benefits from the Gulf Stream producing a temperate climate practically all year round.

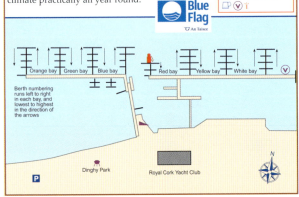

KINSALE YACHT CLUB MARINA

Kinsale Yacht Club Marina
Kinsale, Co Cork, Ireland
Tel: +353 21 4772196 Fax: +353 21 4774455
Email: kyc@iol.ie

VHF Ch M
ACCESS H24

Kinsale is a natural, virtually land-locked harbour on the estuary of the Bandon River, approximately 12 miles south west of Cork harbour entrance. Home to a thriving fishing fleet as well as frequented by commercial shipping, it boasts two fully serviced marinas, with the Kinsale Yacht Club & Marina being the closest to the town. Visitors to this marina automatically become temporary members of the club and are therefore entitled to make full use of the facilities, which include a fully licensed bar and restaurant serving evening meals on Wednesdays, Thursdays and Saturdays. Fuel, water and repair services are also available.

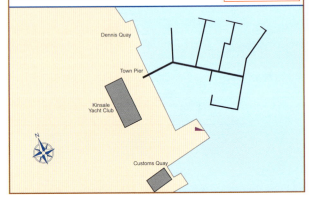

CASTLEPARK MARINA

Castlepark Marina Centre
Kinsale, Co Cork, Ireland
Tel: +353 21 4774959
Email: info@castleparkmarina.com

VHF Ch 16, 14
ACCESS H24

Situated on the south side of Kinsale Harbour, Castlepark is a small marina with deep water pontoon berths that are accessible at all states of the tide. Surrounded by rolling hills, it boasts its own beach as well as being in close proximity to the parklands of James Fort and a traditional Irish pub. The attractive town of Kinsale, with its narrow streets and slate-clad houses, lies just 1.5 miles away by road or five minutes away by ferry. Known as Ireland's 'fine food centre', it incorporates a number of gourmet food shops and high quality restaurants as well as a wine museum.

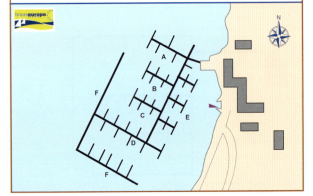

LAWRENCE COVE MARINA

Lawrence Cove Marina
Lawrence Cove, Bere Island, Co Cork, Ireland
Tel: +353 27 75044 Fax: +353 27 75044
Email: lcm@iol.ie
www.lawrencecovemarina.com

VHF Ch 16
ACCESS H24

Lawrence Cove enjoys a peaceful location on an island at the entrance to Bantry Bay. Privately owned and run, it offers sheltered and secluded waters as well as excellent facilities and fully serviced pontoon berths. A few hundred yards from the marina you will find a shop, pub and restaurant, while the mainland, with its various attractions, can be easily reached by ferry. Lawrence Cove lies at the heart of the wonderful cruising grounds of Ireland's south west coast and, just two hours from Cork airport, is an ideal place to leave your boat for long or short periods.

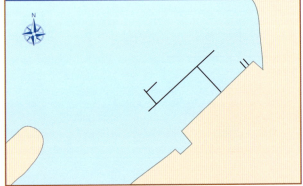

SOUTH IRELAND   AREA 12

CAHERSIVEEN MARINA

Cahersiveen Marina
The Pier, Cahersiveen, Co. Kerry, Ireland
Tel: +353 66 9472777   Fax: +353 66 9472993
Email: acard@eircom.net
www.cahersiveenmarina.ie

VHF Ch M
ACCESS H24

Situated two miles up Valentia River from Valentia Harbour, Cahersiveen Marina is well protected in all wind directions and is convenient for sailing to Valentia Island and Dingle Bay as well as for visiting some of the spectacular uninhabited islands in the surrounding area. Boasting a host of sheltered sandy beaches, the region is renowned for salt and fresh water fishing as well as being good for scuba diving.

Within easy walking distance of the marina lies the historic town of Cahersiveen, incorporating an array of convivial pubs and restaurants.

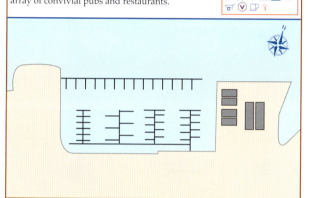

DINGLE MARINA

Dingle Marina
c/o Dingle Fishery Harbour Centre, Strand Street, Dingle, Co Kerry, Ireland
Tel: +353 (0)87 925 4115   Fax: +353 (0)69 5152546
Email: dingleharbour@agriculture.gov.ie
www.dinglemarina.ie

VHF Ch 14
ACCESS H24

Dingle is Ireland's most westerly marina, lying at the heart of the sheltered Dingle Harbour, and is easily reached both day and night via a well buoyed approach channel. The surrounding area is an interesting and unfrequented cruising ground, with several islands, bays and beaches for the yachtsman to explore.

The marina lies in the heart of the old market town, renowned for its hospitality and traditional Irish pub music. Besides enjoying the excellent seafood restaurants and 52 pubs, other recreational pastimes include horse riding, golf, climbing and diving.

Key
a Marina centre building - cafe, dive centre, sailing and rowing centre, chandlery and showers
b Sea Life Centre
c Commercial berths - FVs & ferries
d Marina office

FENIT HARBOUR MARINA

Fenit Harbour & Marina
Fenit, Tralee, Co. Kerry, Republic of Ireland
Tel: +353 66 7136231   Fax: +353 66 7136473
Email: info@fenitharbour.com   www.fenitharbour.com

VHF Ch M
ACCESS H24

Fenit Harbour Marina is tucked away in Tralee Bay, not far south of the Shannon Estuary. Besides offering a superb cruising ground, being within a day's sail of Dingle and Kilrush, the marina also provides a convenient base from which to visit inland attractions such as the picturesque tourist towns of Tralee and Killarney. This 120-berth marina accommodates boats up to 15m LOA and benefits from deep water at all states of the tide.

The small village of Fenit incorporates a grocery shop as well a several pubs and restaurants, while among the local activities are horse riding, swimming from one of the nearby sandy beaches and golfing.

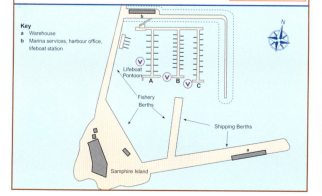

Key
a Warehouse
b Marina services, harbour office, lifeboat station

KILRUSH MARINA

Kilrush Marina Ltd
Kilrush, Co. Clare, Ireland
Tel: +353 65 9052072   Mobile: +353 86 2313870
Fax: +353 65 9051692   Email: info@kilrushmarina.ie

VHF Ch 80
ACCESS H24

Kilrush Marina and boatyard is well placed for exploring the unspoilt west coast of Ireland, including Galway Bay, Dingle, W Cork and Kerry. It also provides a gateway to over 150 miles of cruising on Lough Derg, the R Shannon and the Irish canal system. Accessed via lock gates, the marina lies at one end of the main street in Kilrush, the marina centre provides all the facilities for the visiting sailor. Kilrush is a vibrant market town with a long maritime history. A 15-minute ferry ride from the marina takes you to Scattery Is, once a 6th century monastic settlement but now only inhabited by wildlife. The Shannon Estuary is reputed for being the country's first marine Special Area of Conservation (SAC) and is home to Ireland's only known resident group of bottlenose dolphins.

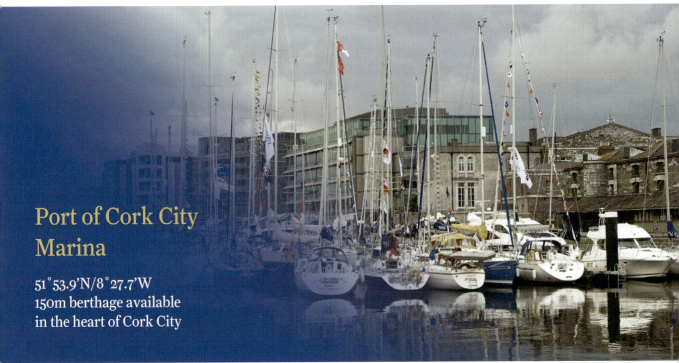

Port of Cork City Marina

51°53.9'N/8°27.7'W
150m berthage available
in the heart of Cork City

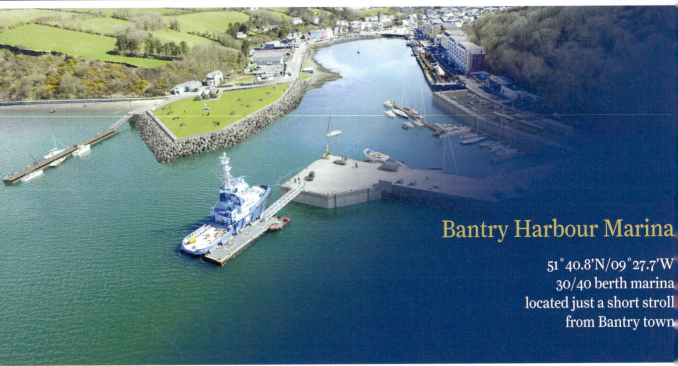

Bantry Harbour Marina

51°40.8'N/09°27.7'W
30/40 berth marina
located just a short stroll
from Bantry town

- Fresh water supply
- 220V
- Security/CCTV

To submit a berth request visit
www.portofcork.ie
Cork Harbour Master Dept.
+353 21 4273125 or Bantry Harbour Master +353 27 53277

AREA 13

NORTH IRELAND – Liscannor Bay, clockwise to Lambay Island

Reeds PDF ebooks

In response to popular demand, all the Reeds Almanacs are now available as searchable, highlightable PDF ebooks. (All ebooks incorporate the Marina Guide.)

Visit www.reedsnauticalalmanac.co.uk for further information

Key to Marina Plans symbols

Symbol	Meaning	Symbol	Meaning
	Bottled gas	P	Parking
	Chandler	✕	Pub/Restaurant
	Disabled facilities		Pump out
	Electrical supply		Rigging service
	Electrical repairs		Sail repairs
	Engine repairs		Shipwright
	First Aid		Shop/Supermarket
	Fresh Water		Showers
D	Fuel - Diesel		Slipway
P	Fuel - Petrol	WC	Toilets
	Hardstanding/boatyard		Telephone
@	Internet Café		Trolleys
	Laundry facilities	V	Visitors berths
	Lift-out facilities		Wi-Fi

Area 13 - North Ireland

MARINAS
Telephone Numbers
VHF Channel
Access Times

Coleraine Harbour Town Centre Marina
028 7034 2012 Ch 12 H24
Coleraine Marina
028 7034 4768 Ch M H24
Seatons Marina
028 7083 2086 Ch M H24

Foyle Marina
028 7180 0313
Ch 14 H24

Ballycastle Marina
028 2076 8525 Ch 80 H24

Lough Swilly
Lough Foyle
• Portrush
• Coleraine
Londonderry

Carrickfergus
028 9336 6666
Ch M H24

NORTHERN IRELAND

• Killybegs

Larne •

BELFAST

Bangor Marina 028 9145 3297
Ch M, 80 H24

Portaferry Marina
028 4272 9598
Ch 80 H24

Strangford
Ardglass

• Sligo

Ardglass
Phennick Cove
028 4484 2332
Ch M, 80 H24

Galway City Marina
+353 91 561874
Ch 12 H24

Carlingford •

Carlingford Marina
042 937 3072
Ch M H24

MARINA GUIDE 2018

MARINAS & SERVICES

GALWAY CITY MARINA

Galway City Marina
Galway Harbour Co, Harbour Office, Galway, Ireland
Tel: +353 91 561874   Fax: +353 91 563738
Email: info@theportofgalway.com

VHF Ch 12
ACCESS HW-2 to HW

The Galway harbour Company operates a small marina in the confines of Galway Harbour with an additional 60m of pontoon-walkway. Freshwater and electrical power is available at the pontoons. Power cars can be purchased from the harbour office during the day. A number of visitors pontoons are available for hire during the summer and for winter layup. Sailors intending to call to Galway Harbour should first make contact with the Harbour office to determine if a berth is available — advisable as demand is high in this quiet and beautiful part of Ireland.

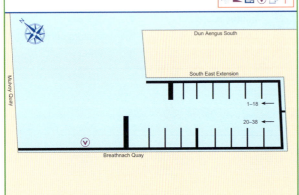

FOYLE MARINA

Foyle Marina
Londonderry Port, Lisahally, L'Derry, BT47 6FL
Tel: 02871 860555   Fax: 02871 861656
www.londonderryport.com/leisure
Email: info@londonderryport.com

VHF Ch 14
ACCESS H24

Foyle Marina lies in the heart of the city, 17M from the mouth of Lough Foyle, is accessible at any state of the tide and is sheltered from all directions of wind. Approach is via well-marked navigation channel with a maintained depth of 8m.

The marina has recently undergone extensive improvements with over 680m of secure pontoon mooring now available. Foyle Marina now offers full facilities to visiting vessels. Toilets and showers on site, water and electricity at each berth. Vessels up to 130m LOA can be accommodated. Craft can berth either side of the pontoons in depths of 5–7m at LW.

The pontoons are within easy walking distance of the city centre where you will find restaurants, bars, cinemas, shopping and a host of tourist attractions.

Key
a Council offices
b Apartments
c Doctor's surgery

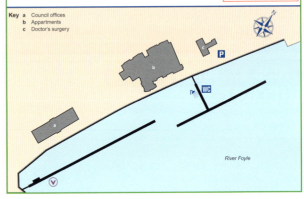

COLERAINE MARINA

Coleraine Marina
64 Portstewart Road, Coleraine,
Co Londonderry, BT52 1RR
Tel: 028 7034 4768   Email: rickiemac@talktalk.net

VHF Ch M
ACCESS H24

Coleraine Marina complex enjoys a superb location in sheltered waters just one mile north of the town of Coleraine and four and a half miles south of the River Bann Estuary and the open sea. Besides accommodating vessels up to 18m LOA, this modern marina with 105 berths offers hard standing, fuel, a chandlery and shower facilities.

Among one of the oldest known settlements in Ireland, Coleraine is renowned for its linen, whiskey and salmon. Its thriving commercial centre includes numerous shops, a four-screen cinema and a state-of-the-art leisure complex.

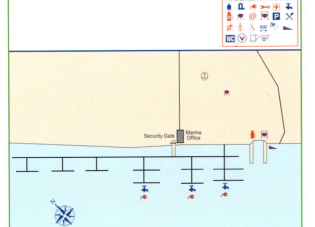

SEATONS MARINA

Seatons Marina
Drumslade Rd, Coleraine, Londonderry, BT52 1SE
Tel: 028 7083 2086   Mobile 07718 883099
Email: jill@seatonsmarina.co.uk   www.seatonsmarina.co.uk

VHF Ch M
ACCESS H24

Seatons Marina is a privately owned business on the north coast of Ireland, which was established by Eric Seaton in 1962. It lies on the east bank of the River Bann, approximately two miles downstream from Coleraine and three miles from the sea. Long term pontoon berths are available for yachts up to 11.5 with a maximum draft of 2.4m; fore and aft moorings are available for larger vessels. Lift out and mast stepping facilities are provided by a 12 tonne trailer hoist.

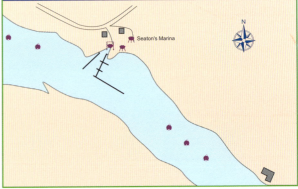

NORTH IRELAND AREA 13

COLERAINE HARBOUR MARINA

Coleraine Harbour Town Centre Marina
Coleraine Harbour Office, 4 Riverside Road, Coleraine, BT52 1XA
Tel: 028 7034 2012   Fax: 028 7034 2000
Email: info@coleraineharbour.com
www.coleraineharbour.com

VHF Ch 12
ACCESS H24

The Marina lies upstream about five miles from the sea ideally situated in the centre of the town, just a few minutes stroll from a selection of shops, restaurants and bars.

In addition to the pontoon berths there is a 40 tonne Roodberg slipway launch/recovery trailer. Hard standing and covered storage are available.

Coleraine is an ideal base for exploring the many nearby attractions including the Old Bushmills Distillery and the Giants Causeway.

FACILITIES AT A GLANCE

Coleraine Harbour Town Centre Marina

The ideal place to berth a yacht when visiting the River Bann. Pontoon berths for visitors. Situated in the centre of town. Excellent facilities including free showers and all your marina needs.

Access via the lifting bridge – Telephone the Harbour Master on 028 70 34 2012 or Channel 12 VHF

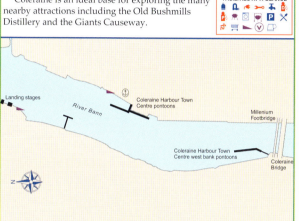

BALLYCASTLE MARINA

Ballycastle Marina
Bayview Road, Ballycastle, Northern Ireland
Tel: 028 2076 8525/07803 505084   Fax: 028 2076 6215
Email: info@moyle-council.org

VHF Ch 80
ACCESS H24

Ballycastle is a traditional seaside town situated on Northern Ireland's North Antrim coast. The 74-berthed, sheltered marina provides a perfect base from which to explore the well known local attractions such as the Giant's Causeway world heritage site, the spectacular Nine Glens of Antrim, and Rathlin, the only inhabited island in Northern Ireland. The most northern coastal marina in Ireland, Ballycastle is accessible at all states of the tide, although yachts are required to contact the marina on VHF Ch 80 before entering the harbour. Along the seafront are a selection of restaurants, bars and shops, while the town centre is only about a five minute walk away.

FACILITIES AT A GLANCE

CARRICKFERGUS MARINA

Carrickferus Marina
3 Quayside, Carrickfergus, Co. Antrim, BT38 8BJ
Tel: 028 9336 6666   Fax: 028 9335 0505
Email: marinarec@carrickfergus.org
www.carrickfergus.org

VHF Ch M
ACCESS H24

Located on the north shore of Belfast Lough, Carrickfergus Marina and harbour incorporates two sheltered areas suitable for leisure craft. The harbour is dominated by a magnificent 12th century Norman Castle which, recently renovated, includes a film theatre, banqueting room and outdoor models depicting the castle's chequered history.

With a wide range of services available to the visitor, the marina is located 250m west of the harbour and has become increasingly popular since its opening in 1985. An interesting variety of shops and restaurants along the waterfront caters for most yachtsmen's needs.

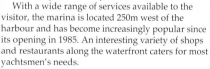

FACILITIES AT A GLANCE

Key
a Development site
b Hotel/bar/restaurant
c Marina office
d Cinema/café/restaurant
e Retail superstore

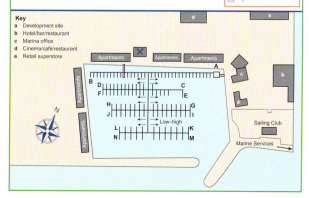

MARINA GUIDE 2018

MARINAS & SERVICES

BANGOR MARINA

Quay Marinas Limited
Bangor Marina, Bangor, Co. Down, BT20 5ED
Tel: 028 9145 3297   Fax: 028 9145 3450
Email: kbaird@quaymarinas.com
www.quaymarinas.com

VHF Ch 11, 80
ACCESS H24

Situated on the south shore of Belfast Lough, Bangor is located close to the Irish Sea cruising routes. The marina is right at the town's centre, within walking distance of shops, restaurants, hotels and bars. The Tourist information centre is across the road from marina reception and there are numerous visitors' attractions in the Borough. The Royal Ulster Yacht Club and the Ballyholme Yacht Club are both nearby and welcome visitors.

Key
a Boat hoist - BJ Marine
b Boat yard - BJ Marine
c Bregenz House
d Chandlery/brokerage BJ Marine
e Dinghy berths
f Access bridge
g Lifeboat slipway
h Domestic waste facilities
i Waste oil tank
j Disabled berthing
NB Berth numbers low outer to high inner, odd numbers on right, even left

CARLINGFORD MARINA

Carlingford Marina
Co. Louth, Ireland
Tel: +353 (0)42 937 3072   Fax: +353 (0)42 937 3075
Email: info@carlingfordmarina.ie
www.carlingfordmarina.ie

VHF Ch M
ACCESS H24

Carlingford Lough is an eight-mile sheltered haven between the Cooley Mountains to the south and the Mourne Mountains to the north. The marina is situated on the southern shore, about four miles from Haulbowline Lighthouse, and can be easily reached via a deep water shipping channel. Among the most attractive destinations in the Irish Sea, Carlingford is only 60 miles from the Isle of Man and within a day's sail from Strangford Lough and Ardglass. Full facilities in the marina include a first class bar and restaurant offering superb views across the water.

Key
a Bar and restaurant
b Toilets, showers and laundry
c Refuse
d Office
e Chandlery
f Marina office
g Waiting pontoon

ARDGLASS MARINA

Ardglass Marina
19 Quay Street, Ardglass, BT30 7SA
Tel & fax: 028 4484 2332
Email: ardglassmarina@tiscali.co.uk
www.ardglassmarina.co.uk

VHF Ch M, 80
ACCESS H24

Situated just south of Strangford, Ardglass has the capacity to accommodate up to 22 yachts as well as space for small craft. Despite being relatively small in size, the marina boasts an extensive array of facilities, either on site or close at hand. Recent access improvements have been made for wheelchair users in the shower/WC and reception. Grocery stores, a post office, chemist and off-licence, are all within a five-minute walk from the marina. Among the local onshore activities are golf, mountain climbing in Newcastle, which is 18 miles south, as well as scenic walks at Ardglass and Delamont Park.

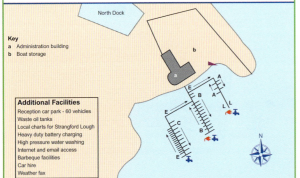

Key
a Administration building
b Boat storage

Additional Facilities
Reception car park - 60 vehicles
Waste oil tanks
Local charts for Strangford Lough
Heavy duty battery charging
High pressure water washing
Internet and email access
Barbeque facilities
Car hire
Weather fax

PORTAFERRY MARINA

Portaferry Marina
1 Mill View, Portaferry, BT22 1LQ
Mobile: 07703 209780   Fax: 028 4272 9784
Email: info@portaferrymarina.co.uk

VHF Ch 80
ACCESS H24

Portaferry Marina lies on the east shore of the Narrows, the gateway to Strangford Lough on the north east coast of Ireland. A marine nature reserve of outstanding natural beauty, the Lough offers plenty of recreational activities. The marina, which caters for draughts of up to 2.5m, is fairly small, accommodating around 30 yachts. The office is situated about 200m from the marina itself, where you will find ablution facilities along with a launderette.

Portaferry incorporates several pubs and restaurants as well as a few convenience stores, while one of its prime attractions is the Exploris Aquarium. Places of historic interest in the vicinity include Castleward, an 18th century mansion in Strangford, and Mount Stewart House & Garden in Newtownards.

AREA 14

CHANNEL ISLANDS – Guernsey & Jersey

Reeds PDF ebooks

In response to popular demand, all the Reeds Almanacs are now available as searchable, highlightable PDF ebooks. (All ebooks incorporate the Marina Guide.)

Visit www.reedsnauticalalmanac.co.uk for further information

Key to Marina Plans symbols

Symbol	Description	Symbol	Description
	Bottled gas		Parking
	Chandler		Pub/Restaurant
	Disabled facilities		Pump out
	Electrical supply		Rigging service
	Electrical repairs		Sail repairs
	Engine repairs		Shipwright
	First Aid		Shop/Supermarket
	Fresh Water		Showers
	Fuel - Diesel		Slipway
	Fuel - Petrol		Toilets
	Hardstanding/boatyard		Telephone
@	Internet Café		Trolleys
	Laundry facilities		Visitors berths
	Lift-out facilities		Wi-Fi

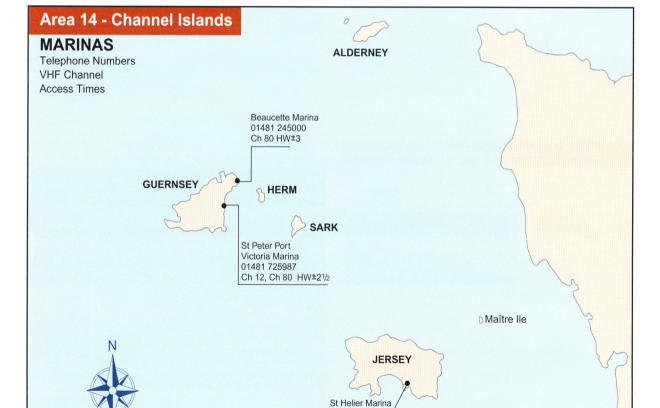

Area 14 - Channel Islands

MARINAS
Telephone Numbers
VHF Channel
Access Times

ALDERNEY

Beaucette Marina
01481 245000
Ch 80 HW±3

GUERNSEY   HERM

SARK

St Peter Port
Victoria Marina
01481 725987
Ch 12, Ch 80 HW±2½

Maître Ile

JERSEY

St Helier Marina
01534 447730
Ch 14 HW±3

Now available as an app!

A selection of Adlard Coles Nautical titles are now available as apps. Download these titles direct to your smart phone or tablet and take our expert authors with you wherever you go:
www.adlardcoles.com

MARINAS & SERVICES

BEAUCETTE MARINA

Beaucette Marina
Vale, Guernsey, GY3 5BQ
Tel: 01481 245000 Fax: 01481 247071
Mobile: 07781 102302
Email: info@beaucettemarina.com

VHF Ch 80
ACCESS HW±3

Situated on the north east tip of Guernsey, Beaucette enjoys a peaceful, rural setting in contrast to the more vibrant atmosphere of Victoria Marina. Now owned by a private individual and offering a high standard of service, the site was originally formed from an old quarry.

There is a general store close by, while the bustling town of St Peter Port is only 20 minutes away by bus.

FACILITIES AT A GLANCE

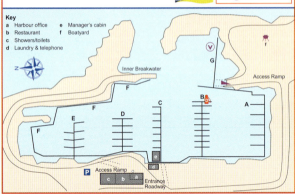

ST PETER PORT

Guernsey Harbours
PO Box 631, St Julian's Emplacement, St Peter Port
Tel: 01481 720229 Fax: 01481 714177
Email: guernsey.harbour@gov.gg

VHF Ch 12, 80
ACCESS HW±2.5

The harbour of St Peter Port comprises the Queen Elizabeth II Marina to the N and Victoria and Albert Marinas to the S, with visiting yachtsmen usually accommodated in Victoria Marina.

St Peter Port is the capital of Guernsey. Its regency architecture and picturesque cobbled streets filled with restaurants and boutiques help to make it one of the most attractive harbours in Europe. Among the places of interest are Hauteville House, home of the writer Victor Hugo, and Castle Cornet. There are regular bus services to all parts of the island for visitors to explore a rich heritage.

FACILITIES AT A GLANCE

ST PETER PORT VICTORIA MARINA

Guernsey Harbours
PO Box 631, St Julian's Emplacement, St Peter Port
Tel: 01481 720229 Fax: 01481 714177
Email: guernsey.harbour@gov.gg

VHF Ch 80
ACCESS HW±2.5

Victoria Marina in St Peter Port accommodates some 300 visiting yachts. In the height of the season it gets extremely busy, but when full visitors can berth on 5 other pontoons in the Pool or pre-arrange a berth in the QE II or Albert marinas. There are no visitor moorings in the Pool. Depending on draught, the marina is accessible approximately two and a half hours either side of HW, with yachts crossing over a sill drying to 4.2m. The marina dory will direct you to a berth on arrival or else will instruct you to moor on one of the waiting pontoons just outside.

Guernsey is well placed for exploring the rest of the Channel Islands and nearby French ports.

FACILITIES AT A GLANCE

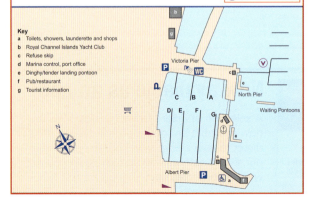

49° 27' 290"N 02° 31' 738"W
Your next port of call

how to find us

our services
- Admiralty Publications
- Boat Lifting
- Boat Repairs
- Boatyard Services
- Chandlery
- Fishing Tackle
- Gas Bottles
- Leisure Clothing
- Marine Diesel
- Marine Petrol
- Nautical Publications
- Osmosis Treatment
- Provisions
- Technical Clothing
- Yacht Rigging

Boatworks+
Castle Emplacement,
St. Peter Port, Guernsey, GY1 1AU
Tel: +44 (0) 1481 726071 (Shop Enquiries)
Tel: +44 (0) 7781 145641 (24hr Emergency)
Email: info@boatworksguernsey.com
Web: www.boatworksguernsey.com

MARINAS & SERVICES

AUTO MARINE JERSEY

- Deck shoes
- Clothing
- Wetsuits
- Fishing equipment
- Rope, chain & anchors
- Fenders
- Charts & books
- Outboard motors & ribs
- Watersports
- Souvenirs & gifts
- Kayaks
- Chandlery
- Dinghies
- Paint & antifouling
- Life jackets
- Trailer parts
- Electronics
- BBQ's & cookers
- Lobster pots
- Compasses
- Bilge pumps & hose
- Bags & gloves
- Boat care products
- Outboard oils
- Flags
- .. and lots more!

Where to find us along Commercial Buildings

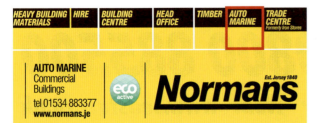

AUTO MARINE
Commercial Buildings
tel 01534 883377
www.normans.je

ST HELIER HARBOUR

St Helier Harbour
Maritime House, La Route du Port Elizabeth
St Helier, Jersey, JE1 1HB
Tel: 01534 447708
www.portofjersey.je Email: marinas@ports.je

VHF Ch 14
ACCESS HW±3

Set in the Norman Breton Gulf, Jersey is the most southerly of the Channel Islands, offering over 200 visitor berths on a flexible daily, weekly or monthly basis. With its close proximity to the adjacent French coast and with sheltered bays and anchorages there are plenty of opportunities to explore new cruising areas, making Jersey an ideal base. Jersey airport is only 15 minutes away from St Helier Marina by bus or car.

Visiting craft are directed into St Helier Marina which is located in the town with access is HW±3. Alternatively, there is a holding pontoon just outside of the marina entrance providing full services and walk ashore access. Visiting vessels of up to 20m may be directed into Elizabeth Marina by prior arrangement.

FACILITIES AT A GLANCE

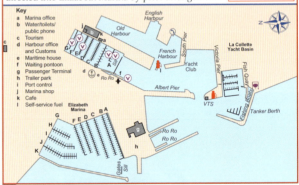

Key
a Marina office
b Water/toilets/public phone
c Tourism
d Harbour office and Customs
e Maritime house
f Waiting pontoon
g Passenger Terminal
h Trailer park
i Port control
j Marina shop
k Cafe
l Self-service fuel

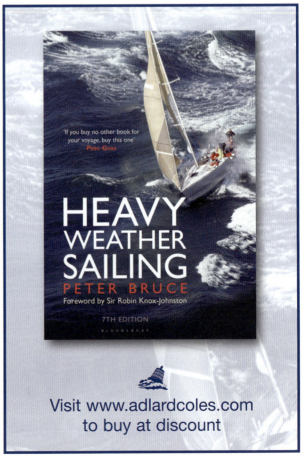

'If you buy no other book for your voyage, buy this one'
Pete Goss

HEAVY WEATHER SAILING
PETER BRUCE
Foreword by Sir Robin Knox-Johnston
7TH EDITION

Visit www.adlardcoles.com to buy at discount

MARINA GUIDE 2018

MARINA SUPPLIES AND SERVICES GUIDE

Adhesives 100	Electronic Devices & Equipment 109	Safety Equipment 119
Associations 100	Engines & Accessories 110	Sailmakers & Repairs 119
Berths & Moorings 100	Foul Weather Gear 111	Solar Power 120
Boatbuilders & Repairs 100	General Marine Equipment & Spares. 111	Sprayhoods & Dodgers 120
Boatyard Services & Supplies ... 101	Harbour Masters 111	Surveyors & Naval Architects 120
Boat Deliveries & Storage 103	Harbours 113	Tape Technology 121
Books & Charts/Publishers 104	Insurance & Finance 113	Transport/Yacht Deliveries 121
Bow Thrusters 104	Liferaft & Inflatables 113	Tuition/Sailing Schools 121
Breakdown 104	Marinas 113	Waterside Accommodation &
Chandlers 104	Marine Engineers 115	Restaurants 123
Chart Agents 108	Masts/Spars & Rigging 117	Weather Info 124
Clothing 108	Navigational Equipment - General 118	Wood Fittings 124
Code of Practice Examiners ... 108	Paint & Osmosis 118	Yacht Brokers 124
Computers & Software 108	Propellers & Sterngear/Repairs 118	Yacht Charters & Holidays 124
Deck Equipment 108	Radio Courses/Schools 118	Yacht Clubs 125
Diesel Marine & Fuel Additives ... 108	Reefing Systems 118	Yacht Designers 128
Divers 108	Repair Materials & Accessories 118	Yacht Management 128
Electrical & Electronic Engineers ... 109	Rope & Wire 119	Yacht Valeting 128

SECTION 2
MARINE SUPPLIES AND SERVICES GUIDE

ADHESIVES – BOATYARD SERVICES & SUPPLIES

ADHESIVES

Casco Adhesives
Darwen   07710 546899
CC Marine Services Ltd
West Mersea   07751 734510
Industrial Self Adhesives Ltd
Nottingham   0115 9681895
Sika Ltd Garden City   01707 394444
Technix Rubber & Plastics Ltd
Southampton   01489 789944
Tiflex Liskeard   01579 320808
Trade Grade Products Ltd
Poole   01202 820177
UK Epoxy Resins
Burscough   01704 892364
Wessex Resins & Adhesives Ltd
Romsey   01794 521111
3M United Kingdom plc
Bracknell   01344 858315

ASSOCIATIONS/ AGENCIES

Cruising Association
London   020 7537 2828
Fishermans Mutual Association (Eyemouth) Ltd
Eyemouth   01890 750373
Maritime and Coastguard Agency
Southampton   0870 6006505
Royal Institute of Navigation
London   020 7591 3130
Royal National Lifeboat Institution
Poole   01202 663000
Royal Yachting Association (RYA) Southampton   0845 345 0400

BERTHS & MOORINGS

ABC Powermarine
Beaumaris   01248 811413
Aqua Bell Ltd Norwich   01603 713013
Ardfern Yacht Centre
Lochgilphead   01852 500247/500636
Ardmair Boat Centre
Ullapool   01854 612054
Arisaig Marine Ltd
Inverness-shire   01687 450224
Bristol Boat Ltd Bristol   01225 872032
British Waterways
Argyll   01546 603210
Burgh Castle Marine
Norfolk   01493 780331
Cambrian Marine Services Ltd
Cardiff   029 2034 3459
Chelsea Harbour Ltd
London   020 7225 9108
Clapson & Son (Shipbuilders) Ltd
Barton-on-Humber   01652 635620
Crinan Boatyard, Crinan   01546 830232
Dartside Quay Brixham   01803 845445
Douglas Marine
Preston   01772 812462
Dublin City Moorings
Dublin   +353 1 8183300

Emsworth Yacht Harbour
Emsworth   01243 377727
Exeter Ship Canal   01392 274306

HAFAN PWLLHELI
Glan Don, Pwllheli, Gwynedd LL53 5YT
Tel: (01758) 701219
Fax: (01758) 701443 VHF Ch80
Hafan Pwllheli has over 400 pontoon berths and offers access at virtually all states of the tide. Ashore, its modern purpose-built facilities include luxury toilets, showers, launderette, a secure boat park for winter storage, 40-ton travel hoist, mobile crane and plenty of space for car parking. Open 24-hours a day, 7 days a week.

Highway Marine
Sandwich   01304 613925
Iron Wharf Boatyard
Faversham   01795 537122
Jalsea Marine Services Ltd
Northwich   01606 77870
Jersey Harbours
St Helier   01534 447788
Jones (Boatbuilders), David
Chester   01244 390363
Lawrenny Yacht Station
Kilgetty   01646 651212
MacFarlane & Son
Glasgow   01360 870214

NEPTUNE MARINA LTD
Neptune Quay, Ipswich, Suffolk IP4 1AX
Tel: (01473) 215204
Fax: (01473) 215206
e-mail:
enquiries@neptune-marina.com
www.neptune-marina.com
The quay to the heart of Ipswich! Call Ipswich lock gates on Channel 68 and Neptune Marina on Channel 80. Bring your crew to the wonderful Ipswich waterfront, with plenty of watering holes and town centre activities. You won't want to leave!

Orkney Marinas Ltd
Kirkwall   07810 465835
V Marine
Shoreham-by-Sea   01273 461491
Sutton Harbour Marina
Plymouth   01752 204186
WicorMarine Fareham   01329 237112
Winters Marine Ltd
Salcombe   01548 843580
Yarmouth Marine Service
Yarmouth   01983 760521
Youngboats
Faversham   01795 536176

BOAT BUILDERS & REPAIRS

ABC Hayling Island   023 9246 1968
ABC Powermarine
Beaumaris   01248 811413
Advance Yacht Systems
Southampton   023 8033 7722
Aqua-Star Ltd
St Sampsons   01481 244550
Ardoran Marine
Oban   01631 566123
Baumbach Bros Boatbuilders
Hayle   01736 753228
Beacon Boatyard
Rochester   01634 841320
Bedwell & Co
Walton on the Naze   01255 675873
Blackwell, Craig
Co Meath   +353 87 677 9605
Boyd Boat Building
Falmouth   07885 436722
Boatcraft
Ardrossan   01294 603047
B+ St Peter Port   01481 726071
Brennan, John
Dun Laoghaire   +353 1 280 5308
Burghead Boat Centre
Findhorn   01309 690099
Carrick Marine Projects
Co Antrim   02893 355884
Chapman & Hewitt Boatbuilders
Wadebridge   01208 813487
Chicks Marine Ltd
Guernsey   01481 723716
Clarence Boatyard
East Cowes   01983 294243
Cooks Maritime Craftsmen - Poliglow
Lymington   01590 675521
Creekside Boatyard (Old Mill Creek)
Dartmouth   01803 832649
CTC Marine & Leisure
Middlesbrough   01642 372600
Davies Marine Services
Ramsgate   01843 586172
Dickie International
Bangor   01248 363400
Dickie International
Pwllheli   01758 701828
East Llanion Marine Ltd
Pembroke Dock   01646 686866
Emblem Enterprises
East Cowes   01983 294243
Fairlie Quay
Fairlie   01475 568267
Fairweather Marine
Fareham   01329 283500
Farrow & Chambers Yacht Builders
Humberston
                            www.farrowandchambers.co.uk
Fast Tack Plymouth   01752 255171

MARINA SUPPLIES AND SERVICES GUIDE

Fergulsea Engineering Ayr	01292 262978	
Ferrypoint Boat Co Youghal	+353 24 94232	
Floetree Ltd (Loch Lomond Marina) Balloch	01389 752069	
Freshwater Boatyard Truro	01326 270443	
Frogmore Boatyard Kingsbridge	01548 531257	
Furniss Boat Building Falmouth	01326 311766	
Gallichan Marine Ltd Jersey	01534 746387	
Garvel Clyde Greenock	01475 725372	
Goodchild Marine Services Great Yarmouth	01493 782301	
Gosport Boatyard Gosport	023 9252 6534	
Gweek Quay Boatyard Helston	01326 221657	
Halls Walton on the Naze	01255 675596	
Harris Pye Marine Barry	01446 720066	
Haven Boatyard Lymington	01590 677073	
Hayling Yacht Company Hayling Island	023 9246 3592	
Hoare Ltd, Bob Poole	01202 736704	
Holyhead Boatyard Holyhead	01407 760111	
Jackson Marine Lowestoft	01502 539772	
Jackson Yacht Services Jersey	01534 743819	
JEP Marine Canterbury	01227 710102	
JWS Marine Services Southsea	023 9275 5155	
Kimelford Yacht Haven Oban	01852 200248	
Kingfisher Marine Weymouth	01305 766595	
Kingfisher Ultraclean UK Ltd Tarporley	0800 085 7039	
King's Boatyard Pin Mill	01473 780258	
Kinsale Boatyard Kinsale	+353 21477 4774	
Kippford Slipway Ltd Dalbeattie	01556 620249	
Lavis & Son, CH Exmouth	01395 263095	
Lawrenny Yacht Station Lawrenny	01646 651212	

Lencraft Boats Ltd Dungarvan +353 58 682220
Mackay Boatbuilders Arbroath 01241 872879
Marine Services Norwich 01692 582239
Mashford Brothers Torpoint 01752 822232
Mayor & Co Ltd, J Preston 01772 812250
Mears, HJ Axmouth 01297 23344
Mill, Dan, Galway +353 86 337 9304
Miller Marine Tyne & Wear 01207 542149
Morrison, A Killyleagh 028 44828215
Moss (Boatbuilders), David Thornton-Cleveleys 01253 893830
Multi Marine Composites Ltd Torpoint 01752 823513
Newing, Roy E Canterbury 01227 860345
Noble and Sons, Alexander Girvan 01465 712223
Northney Marine Services Hayling Island 023 9246 9246
Northshore Sport & Leisure King's Lynn 01485 210236
O'Sullivans Marine Ltd Tralee +353 66 7124957
Oyster Marine Ltd Ipswich 01473 688888
Pachol, Terry Brighton 01273 620192
Partington Marine Ltd, William Pwllheli 01758 612808
Pasco's Boatyard Truro 01326 270269
Penrhos Marine Aberdovey 01654 767478
Penzance Marine Services Penzance 01736 361081
PJ Bespoke Boat Fitters Ltd Crewe 01270 812244
Preston Marine Services Ltd Preston 01772 733595
Red Bay Boats Ltd Cushendall 028 2177 1331
Reliance Marine Wirral 0151 625 5219
Retreat Boatyard Ltd Exeter 01392 874720/875934
Richardson Boatbuilders, Ian Stromness 01856 850321
Richardson Yacht Services Ltd Newport 01983 821095

Cordell Grove Middlesbrough 01642 226226
Roberts Marine Ltd, S Liverpool 0151 707 8300
Rothman Pantall & Co Fareham 01329 280221
Rustler Yachts Falmouth 01326 310210
Salterns Boatyard Poole 01202 707391
Sea & Shore Ship Chandler Dundee 01382 450666

SEAFIT MARINE SERVICES LTD
Falmouth Marina, North Parade,
Falmouth, Cornwall TR11 2TD
Tel: (01326) 313713
Fax: (01326) 313713
Mob: 07971 196175
Email: mary.townsend@homecall.co.uk
For installation maintenance and repair work - electrical, plumbing, hulls, rigs etc.

Seamark-Nunn & Co Felixstowe 01394 275327
Seapower Woolverstone 01473 780090
Slipway Cooperative Ltd Bristol 0117 907 9938
Smith, GB, & Sons Rock 01208 862815
Spicer Boatbuilder, Nick Weymouth Marina 01305 767118
Storrar Marine Store Newcastle upon Tyne 0191 266 1037
TT Marine Ashwell 01462 742449
Waterfront Marine Bangor 01248 352513
Way, A&R, Boat Building Tarbert, Loch Fyne 01546 606657
WestCoast Marine Troon 01292 318121
Western Marine Dublin +353 1 280 0321
Wigmore Wright Marine Services Penarth 029 2070 9983
Williams, Peter Fowey 01726 870987
WQI Ltd Bournemouth 01202 771292
Yarmouth Marine Service 01983 760521
Youngboats Faversham 01795 536176

BOATYARD SERVICES & SUPPLIES

A & P Ship Care Ramsgate 01843 593140

BOATYARD SERVICES & SUPPLIES – BOAT DELIVERIES & STORAGE

ABC Marine
Hayling Island 023 9246 1968

Abersoch Boatyard Services Ltd
Abersoch 01758 713900

Amble Boat Co Ltd
Amble 01665 710267

Amsbrisbeg Ltd
Port Bannatyne 01700 831215

Ardmair Boat Centre
Ullapool 01854 612054

Ardmaleish Boat Building Co Rothesay 01700 502007

www.ardoran.co.uk
West coast Scotland. All marine facilities.

Ardrishaig Boatyard
Lochgilphead 01546 603280

Arklow Slipway
Arklow +353 402 33233

Baltic Wharf Boatyard
Totnes 01803 867922

Baltimore Boatyard
Baltimore +353 28 20444

Bedwell and Co
Walton-on-the-Naze 01255 675873

Berthon Boat Co
Lymington 01590 673312

Birdham Shipyard
Chichester 01243 512310

BJ Marine Ltd Bangor 028 91271434

Blagdon, A
Plymouth 01752 561830

Boatcraft
Ardrossan 01294 603047

Boatworks + Ltd
St Peter Port 01481 726071

Brennan, John
Dun Laoghaire +353 1 280 5308

Brighton Marina Boatyard
Brighton 01273 819919

Bristol Marina (Yard)
Bristol 0117 921 3198

Buckie Shipyard Ltd
Buckie 01542 831245

Bucklers Hard Boat Builders Ltd
Brockenhurst 01590 616214

C & J Marine Services
Newcastle Upon Tyne 0191 295 0072

Caley Marina Inverness 01463 236539

Cambrian Boat Centre
Swansea 01792 467263

Cambrian Marine Services Ltd
Cardiff 029 2034 3459

Cantell and Son Ltd
Newhaven 01273 514118

Canvey Yacht Builders Ltd
Canvey Island 01268 696094

Carroll's Ballyhack Boatyard
New Ross +353 51 389164

Castlepoint Boatyard
Crosshaven +353 21 4832154

Chabot, Gary
Newhaven 07702 006767

Chapman & Hewitt Boatbuilders
Wadebridge 01208 813487

Chippendale Craft Rye 01797 227707

Clapson & Son (Shipbuilders) Ltd
Barton on Humber 01652 635620

Clarence Boatyard
East Cowes 01983 294243

Coastal Marine Boatbuilders
(Berwick upon Tweed)
Eyemouth 01890 750328

Coastcraft Ltd
Cockenzie 01875 812150

Coates Marine Ltd
Whitby 01947 604486

Coombes, AA
Bembridge 01983 872296

Corpach Boatbuilding Company
Fort William 01397 772861

Craobh Marina
By Lochgilphead 01852 500222

Creekside Boatyard (Old Mill Creek)
Dartmouth 01803 832649

Crinan Boatyard
By Lochgilphead 01546 830232

Crosshaven Boatyard Co Ltd
Crosshaven +353 21 831161

Dale Sailing Co Ltd
Neyland 01646 603110

Darthaven Marina
Kingswear 01803 752242

Dartside Quay Brixham 01803 845445

Dauntless Boatyard Ltd
Canvey Island 01268 793782

Davis's Boatyard Poole 01202 674349

Dinas Boat Yard Ltd
Y Felinheli 01248 671642

Dorset Yachts
Poole 01202 674531

Douglas Boatyard
Preston 01772 812462

Dover Yacht Co Dover 01304 201073

Dun Laoghaire Marina
Dun Laoghaire +353 1 2020040

Elephant Boatyard
Southampton 023 8040 3268

Elton Boatbuilding Ltd
Kirkcudbright 01557 330177

Felixstowe Ferry Boatyard
Felixstowe 01394 282173

Ferguson Engineering
Wexford +353 6568 66822133

Ferry Marine South
Queensferry 0131 331 1233

Findhorn Boatyard
Findhorn 01309 690099

Firmhelm Ltd Pwllheli 01758 612251

Fleming Engineering, J
Stornoway 01851 703488

Forrest Marine Ltd
Exeter 08452 308335

Fowey Boatyard
Fowey 01726 832194

Fox's Marina Ipswich 01473 689111

Frank Halls & Son
Walton on the Naze 01255 675596

Freeport Marine
Jersey 01534 888100

Furniss Boat Building
Falmouth 01326 311766

Garval Clyde
Greenock 01475 725372

Goodchild Marine Services
Great Yarmouth 01493 782301

Gosport Boatyard
Gosport 023 9252 6534

Gweek Quay Boatyard
Helston 01326 221657

Haines Boatyard
Chichester 01243 512228

Harbour Marine
Plymouth 01752 204691

Harbour Marine Services Ltd
Southwold 01502 724721

Harris Pye Marine
Barry 01446 720066

Hartlepool Marine Engineering
Hartlepool 01429 867883

Hayles, Harold
Yarmouth, IoW 01983 760373

Henderson, J Shiskine 01770 860259

Heron Marine
Whitstable 01227 361255

Hewitt, George
Binham 01328 830078

Holyhead Marina & Trinity Marine Ltd
Holyhead 01407 764242

Instow Marine Services
Bideford 01271 861081

Ipswich Haven Marina
Ipswich 01473 236644

Iron Wharf Boatyard
Faversham 01795 537122

Island Boat Services
Port of St Mary 01624 832073

Isle of Skye Yachts
Ardvasar 01471 844216

Jalsea Marine Services Ltd Weaver
Shipyard, Northwich 01606 77870

JBS Group
Peterhead 01779 475395

J B Timber Ltd
North Ferriby 01482 631765

Jersey Harbours Dept
St Helier 01534 885588

Kilnsale Boatyard
Kinsale +353 21 4774774

MARINA SUPPLIES AND SERVICES GUIDE

Kilrush Marina & Boatyard – Ireland	+353 65 9052072
Kingfisher Ultraclean UK Ltd Tarporley	01928 787878
Kinsale Boatyard	+353 21477 4774
KPB Beaucette	07781 152581
Lake Yard Poole	01202 674531
Lallow, C Isle of Wight	01983 292112
Latham's Boatyard Poole	01202 748029
Laxey Towing Douglas, Isle of Man	07624 493592
Leonard Marine, Peter Newhaven	01273 515987
Lincombe Marine Salcombe	01548 843580
Lomax Boatbuilders Cliffony	+353 71 66124
Lymington Yt Haven	01590 677071
MacDougalls Marine Services Isle of Mull	01681 700294
Macduff Shipyard Ltd Macduff	01261 832234
Madog Boatyard Porthmadog	01766 514205/513435
Mainbrayce Marine Alderney	01481 822772
Malakoff and Moore Lerwick	01595 695544
Mallaig Boat Building and Engineering Mallaig	01687 462304
Maramarine Helensburgh	01436 810971
Marindus Engineering Kilmore Quay	+353 53 29794
Mariners Farm Boatyard Gillingham	01634 233179
McGruar and Co Ltd Helensburgh	01436 831313
Mevagh Boatyard Mulroy Bay	+353 74 915 4470
Mill, Dan, Galway	+353 86 337 9304
Mitchell's Boatyard Poole	01202 747857
Mooney Boats Killybegs	+353 73 31152/31388
Moore & Son, J St Austell	01726 842964
Morrison, A Killyleagh	028 44828215
Moss (Boatbuilders), David Thornton-Cleveleys	01253 893380
Mustang Marine Milford Haven	01646 696320
New Horizons Rhu	01436 821555
Noble and Sons, Alexander Girvan	01465 712223
North Pier (Oban) Oban	01631 562892
North Wales Boat Centre Conwy	01492 580740
Northam Marine Brightlingsea	01206 302003
Northshore Yacht Yard Chichester	01243 512611
Oban Yachts and Marine Services By Oban	01631 565333
Pearn and Co, Norman Looe	01503 262244
Penrhos Marine Aberdovey	01654 767478
Penzance Dry Dock and Engineering Co Ltd Penzance	01736 363838
Philip & Son Dartmouth	01803 833351
Phillips, HJ Rye	01797 223234
Ponsharden Boatyard Penryn	01326 372215
Powersail and Island Chandlers Ltd East Cowes Marina	01983 299800
Priors Boatyard Burnham-on-Crouch	01621 782160
R K Marine Ltd Swanwick	01489 583572
Rat Island Sailboat Company (Yard) St Mary's	01720 423399
Rennison, Russell Gosport	07734 688819
Retreat Boatyard Ltd Exeter	01392 874720/875934
Rice and Cole Ltd Burnham-on-Crouch	01621 782063
Richardson Boatbuilders, Ian Stromness	01856 850321
Richardsons Boatbuilders Binfield	01983 821095
Riverside Yard Shoreham Beach	01273 592456
River Yar Boatyard Yarmouth, IoW	01983 761000
Robertsons Boatyard Woodbridge	01394 382305
Rossbrin Boatyard Schull	+353 28 37352
Rossiter Yachts Ltd Christchurch	01202 483250
Rossreagh Boatyard Rathmullan	+353 74 9150182
Rudders Boatyard & Moorings Milford Haven	01646 600288
Ryan & Roberts Marine Services Askeaton	+353 61 392198
Rye Harbour Marina Rye	01797 227667
Rynn Engineering, Pat Galway	+353 91 562568
Salterns Boatyard Poole	01202 707391
Sandbanks Yacht Company Poole	01202 611262
Scarborough Marine Engineering Ltd Scarborough	01723 375199
Severn Valley Cruisers Ltd (Boatyard) Stourport-on-Severn	01299 871165
Shepards Wharf Boatyard Ltd Cowes	01983 297821
Shipshape King's Lynn	01553 764058
Shotley Marina Ltd Ipswich	01473 788982
Shotley Marine Services Ltd Ipswich	01473 788913
Silvers Marina Ltd Helensburgh	01436 831222
Skinners Boat Yard Baltimore	+353 28 20114
Smith, GB, & Sons Rock	01208 862815
Smith & Gibbs Eastbourne	07802 582009
Sparkes Boatyard Hayling Island	023 92463572
Spencer Sailing Services, Jim Brightlingsea	01206 302911
Standard House Boatyard Wells-next-the-Sea	01328 710593
Storrar Marine Store Newcastle upon Tyne	0191 266 1037
Strand Shipyard Rye	01797 222070
Surry Boatyard Shoreham-by-Sea	01273 461491
The Shipyard Littlehampton	01903 713327
Titchmarsh Marina Walton-on-the-Naze	01255 672185
Tollesbury Marina Tollesbury	01621 869202
T J Rigging Conwy	07780 972411
Toms and Son Ltd, C Fowey	01726 870232
Tony's Marine Service Coleraine	028 7035 6422
Torquay Marina Torquay	01803 200210
Trinity Marine & Holyhead Marina Holyhead	01407 763855
Trouts Boatyard (River Exe) Topsham	01392 873044
Upson and Co, RF Aldeburgh	01728 453047
Versatility Workboats Rye	01797 224422
Weir Quay Boatyard Bere Alston	01822 840474
West Solent Boatbuilders Lymington	01590 642080
WicorMarine Fareham	01329 237112
Woodrolfe Boatyard Maldon	01621 869202
Yarmouth Marine Services Yarmouth, IoW	01983 760521

BOAT DELIVERIES & STORAGE

ABC Marine Hayling Island	023 9246 1968

MARINA GUIDE 2018

BOAT DELIVERIES & STORAGE – CHANDLERS

Abersoch Boatyard Services Ltd Pwllheli	01758 713900	
Ambrisbeg Ltd Port Bannatyne	01700 502719	
Arisaig Marine Inverness-shire	01687 450224	
Bedwell and Co Walton-on-the-Naze	01255 675873	
Berthon Boat Company Lymington	01590 673312	
Boat Shifters	07733 344018/01326 210548	
C & J Marine Services Newcastle upon Tyne	0191 295 0072	
Caley Marine Inverness	01463 233437	
Carrick Marine Projects Co Antrim	02893 355884	
Challenger Marine Penryn	01326 377222	
Coates Marine Ltd Whitby	01947 604486	
Convoi Exceptionnel Ltd Hamble	023 8045 3045	
Creekside Boatyard (Old Mill Creek) Dartmouth	01803 832649	
Crinan Boatyard Ltd Crinan	01546 830232	
Dale Sailing Co Ltd Neyland	01646 603110	
Dart Marina Ltd Dartmouth	01803 833351	
Dartside Quay Brixham	01803 845445	
Dauntless Boatyard Ltd Canvey Island	01268 793782	
Debbage Yachting Ipswich	01473 601169	
Douglas Marine Preston	01772 812462	
East & Co, Robin Kingsbridge	01548 531257	
East Coast Offshore Yachting	01480 861381	
Emsworth Yacht Harbour Emsworth	01243 377727	
Exeter Ship Canal	01392 274306	
Exmouth Marina	01395 269314	
Firmhelm Ltd Pwllheli	01758 612244	
Forrest Marine Ltd Exeter	08452 308335	
Fowey Boatyard Fowey	01726 832194	
Freshwater Boatyard Truro	01326 270443	
Hafan Pwllheli Pwllheli	01758 701219	
Houghton Boat Transport Tewkesbury	07831 486710	
Gweek Quay Boatyard Helston	01326 221657	
Iron Wharf Boatyard Faversham	01795 537122	

Jalsea Marine Services Ltd Northwich	01606 77870
KG McColl Oban	01852 200248
Latham's Boatyard Poole	01202 748029
Lavis & Son, CH Exmouth	01395 263095
Lincombe Boat Yard Salcombe	01548 843580
MCL Transboat	08455 201900
Marine Resource Centre Ltd Oban	01631 720291
Marine & General Engineers Guernsey	01481 245808
Milford Marina Milford Haven	01646 696312/3
Moonfleet Sailing Poole	01202 682269
Southerly Chichester	01243 512611
Pasco's Boatyard Truro	01326 270269
Pearn and Co, Norman Looe	01503 262244
Performance Yachting Plymouth	01752 565023
Peters & May Ltd Southampton	023 8048 0480
Ponsharden Boatyard Penryn	01326 372215
Portsmouth Marine Engineering Fareham	01329 232854
Priors Boatyard Burnham-on-Crouch	01621 782160
Reeder School of Seamanship, Mike Lymington	01590 674560
Rossiter Yachts Christchurch	01202 483250
Seafix Boat Transfer North Wales	0845 528 0139
Sealand Boat Deliveries Ltd Liverpool	01254 705225
Shearwater Sailing Southampton	01962 775213
Shepards Wharf Boatyard Cowes Harbour Commission Cowes	01983 297821
Silvers Marina Ltd Helensburgh	01436 831222
Southcoasting Navigators Devon	01626 335626
Waterfront Marine Bangor	01248 352513
West Country Boat Transport	01566 785651
WicorMarine Fareham	01329 237112
Winters Marine Ltd Salcombe	01548 843580
Wolff, David	07659 550131 **Yacht**

Solutions Ltd Portsmouth	023 9275 5155
Yarmouth Marine Service Yarmouth, IoW	01983 760521
Youngboats Faversham	01795 536176

BOOKS, CHARTS & PUBLISHERS

Adlard Coles Nautical London	020 7631 5600
Brown Son & Ferguson Ltd Glasgow	0141 429 1234
Cooke & Son Ltd, B Hull	01482 223454
Dubois Phillips & McCallum Ltd Liverpool	0151 236 2776
Imray, Laurie, Norie & Wilson Huntingdon	01480 462114
Kelvin Hughes Southampton	023 8063 4911
Lilley & Gillie Ltd, John	0191 257 2217
Marine Chart Services Wellingborough	01933 441629
Price & Co Ltd, WF Bristol	0117 929 2229
QPC Fareham	01329 287880
Stanford Charts Bristol	0117 929 9966
Stanford Charts London	020 7836 1321
Stanford Charts Manchester	0845 880 3730 / 0870 890 3730
Wiley Nautical Chichester	01243 779777

BOW THRUSTERS

ARS Anglian Diesels Ltd Wakefield	01924 332492
Buckler's Hard Boat Builders Ltd Beaulieu	01590 616214
JS Mouldings International Bursledon	023 8063 4400

BREAKDOWN

BJ Marine Ltd Bangor, Ireland	028 9127 1434
Seafit Marine Services Falmouth	01326 313713

CHANDLERS

ABC Powermarine Beaumaris	01248 811413
Admiral Marine Supplies Bootle	01469 575909
Allgadgets.co.uk Exmouth	01395 227727
Alpine Room & Yacht Equipment Chelmsford	01245 223563

MARINA SUPPLIES AND SERVICES GUIDE

Aquatogs Cowes		01983 295071
Arbroath Fishermen's Association Arbroath		01241 873132
Ardfern Yacht Centre Ltd Argyll		01852 500247
Ardoran Marine Oban		01631 566123
Arthurs Chandlery Gosport		023 9252 6522
Arun Canvas and Rigging Ltd Littlehampton		01903 732561
Aruncraft Chandlers Littlehampton		01903 713327
ASAP Supplies – Equipment & Spares Worldwide Beccles		0845 1300870
Auto Marine Southsea		02392 825601
Bayside Marine Brixham		01803 856771
Bedwell and Co Walton on the Naze		01255 675873
BJ Marine Ltd Bangor		028 9127 1434
Bluecastle Chandlers Portland		01305 822298
Blue Water Marine Ltd Pwllheli		01758 614600
Boatacs Westcliffe on Sea		01702 475057
Boathouse, The Penryn		01326 374177
Boston Marina		01205 364420
Bosun's Locker, The Falmouth		01326 312212
Bosun's Locker, The Ramsgate		01843 597158
Bosuns Locker, The South Queensferry		0131 331 3875/4496
B+ St Peter Port		01481 726071
Bridger Marine, John Exeter		01392 250970
Bristol Boat Ltd Bristol		01225 872032
Brixham Yacht Supplies Ltd Brixham		01803 882290
Brunel Chandlery Ltd Neyland		01646 601667
Buccaneer Ltd Macduff		01261 835199
Bucklers Hard Boat Builders Beaulieu		01590 616214
Burghead Boat Centre Findhorn		01309 690099
Bussell & Co, WL Weymouth		01305 785633
Buzzard Marine Yarmouth		01983 760707
C & M Marine Bridlington		01262 672212
Cabin Yacht Stores Rochester		01634 718020
Caley Marina Inverness		01463 236539
Cambrian Boat Centre Swansea		01792 467263
Cantell & Son Ltd Newhaven		01273 514118
Carne (Sales) Ltd, David Penryn		01326 374177
Carrickcraft Malahide		+353 1 845 5438
Caters Carrick Ltd Carrickfergus		028 93351919
CH Marine (Cork) Cork		+353 21 4315700
CH Marine Skibbereen		+353 28 23190
Charity & Taylor Ltd Lowestoft		01502 581529
Chertsey Marine Ltd Penton Hook Marina		01932 565195
Chicks Marine Ltd Guernsey		01481 723716
Christchurch Boat Shop Christchurch		01202 482751
Clapson & Son (Shipbuilders) Ltd South Ferriby Marina		01652 635620
Clarke, Albert, Marine Newtownards		028 9187 2325
Clyde Chandlers Ardrossan		01294 471444
CMC Campbeltown		01586 551441
Coastal Marine Boatbuilders Ltd (Dunbar) Eyemouth		01890 750328
Coates Marine Ltd Whitby		01947 604486
Collins Marine St Helier		01534 732415
Compass Marine Lancing		01903 761773
Cosalt International Ltd Aberdeen		01224 588327
Cosalt International Ltd Southampton		023 8063 2824
Cotter, Kieran Baltimore		+353 28 20106
Cox Yacht Charter Ltd, Nick Lymington		01590 673489
C Q Chandlers Ltd Poole		01202 682095
Crinan Boats Ltd Lochgilphead		01546 830232
CTC Marine & Leisure Middlesbrough		01642 372600
Dale Sailing Co Ltd Milford Haven		01646 603110
Danson Marine Sidcup		0208 304 5678
Dartmouth Chandlery Dartmouth		01803 839292
Dartside Quay Brixham		01803 845445
Dauntless Boatyard Ltd Canvey Island		01268 793782
Davis's Yacht Chandler Littlehampton		01903 722778
Denney & Son, EL Redcar		01642 483507
Deva Marine Conwy		01492 572777
Dickie & Sons Ltd, AM Bangor		01248 363400
Dickie & Sons Ltd, AM Pwllheli		01758 701828
Dinghy Supplies Ltd/Sutton Marine Ltd Sutton		+353 1 832 2312
Diverse Yacht Services Hamble		023 80453399
Dixon Chandlery, Peter Exmouth		01395 273248
Doling & Son, GW Barrow In Furness		01229 823708
Dovey Marine Aberdovey		01654 767581
Down Marine Co Ltd Belfast		028 9048 0247
Douglas Marine Preston		01772 812462
Dubois Phillips & McCallum Ltd Liverpool		0151 236 2776
Duncan Ltd, JS Wick		01955 602689
Duncan Yacht Chandlers Ely		01353 663095
East Anglian Sea School Ipswich		01473 659992
Eccles Marine Co Middlesbrough		01642 372600
Ely Boat Chandlers Hayling Island		023 9246 1968
Emsworth Chandlery Emsworth		01243 375500
Force 4 Chandlery Stroud		0845 1300710
Exe Leisure Exeter		01392 879055
Express Marine Services Chichester		01243 773788
Fairways Chandlery Burnham-on-Crouch		01621 782659
Fairweather Marine Fareham		01329 283500
Fal Chandlers Falmouth Marina		01326 212411
Ferrypoint Boat Co Youghal		+353 24 94232
Findhorn Marina & Boatyard Findhorn		01309 690099
Firmhelm Ltd P wllheli		01758 612244
Fisherman's Mutual Asssociation (Eyemouth) Ltd Eyemouth		01890 750373
Floetree Ltd (Loch Lomond Marina) Balloch		01389 752069
Force 4 (Deacons) Bursledon		023 8040 2182
Force 4 Chichester		01243 773788
Force 4 Chandlery Mail order		0845 1300710
Force 4 Chandlery Plymouth		01752 252489

CHANDLERS

Force 4 (Hamble Point) Southampton	023 80455 058	
Force 4 (Mercury) Southampton	023 8045 4849	
Force 4 (Port Hamble) Southampton	023 8045 4858	
Force 4 (Shamrock) Southampton	023 8063 2725	
Force 4 (Swanwick) Swanwick	01489 881825	
Freeport Marine Jersey	01534 888100	
French Marine Motors Ltd Brightlingsea	01206 302133	
Furneaux Riddall & Co Ltd Portsmouth	023 9266 8621	
Gael Force Stornoway	01851 705540	
Gallichan Marine Ltd Jersey	01534 746387	
Galway Marine Chandlers Ltd Galway	+353 91 566568	
GB Attfield & Company Dursley	01453 547185	
Gibbons Ship Chandlers Ltd Sunderland	0191 567 2101	
Goodwick Marine Fishguard	01348 873955	
Gorleston Marine Ltd Great Yarmouth	01493 661883	
GP Barnes Ltd Shoreham	01273 591705/596680	
Great Outdoors Clarenbridge, Galway	+353 87 2793821	
Green Marine, Jimmy Fore St Beer	01297 20744	
Grimsby Rigging Services Ltd Grimsby	01472 362758	
Gunn Navigation Services, Thomas Aberdeen	01224 595045	
Hale Marine, Ron Portsmouth	023 92732985	
Harbour Marine Services Ltd (HMS) Southwold	01502 724721	
Hardware & Marine Supplies Wexford	+353 53 29791	
Harris Marine (1984) Ltd, Ray Barry	01446 740924	
Hartlepool Marine Supplies Hartlepool	01429 862932	
Harwich Chandlers Ltd Harwich	01255 504061	
Harwoods Yarmouth	01983 760258	
Hawkins Marine Shipstores, John Rochester	01634 840812	
Hayles, Harold Yarmouth	01983 760373	
Herm Seaway Marine Ltd St Peter Port	01481 726829	
Highway Marine Sandwich	01304 613925	
Hoare Ltd, Bob, Poole	01202 736704	
Hodges, T Coleraine	028 7035 6422	
Hornsey (Chandlery) Ltd, Chris Southsea	023 9273 4728	
Hunter & Combes Cowes	01983 299599	
Iron Stores Marine St Helier	01534 877755	
Isles of Scilly Steamship Co St Mary's	01720 422710	
Jackson Yacht Services Jersey	01534 743819	
Jamison and Green Ltd Belfast	028 9032 2444	
Jeckells and Son Ltd Lowestoft	01502 565007	
JF Marine Chandlery Rhu	01436 820584	
JNW Services Aberdeen	01224 594050	
JNW Services Peterhead	01779 477346	
JSB Ltd Tarbert, Loch Fyne	01880 820180	
Johnston Brothers Mallaig	01687 462215	
Johnstons Marine Stores Lamlash	01770 600333	
Kearon Ltd, George Arklow	+353 402 32319	
Kelpie Boats Pembroke Dock	01646 683661	
Kelvin Hughes Ltd Southampton	023 80634911	
Kildale Marine Hull	01482 227464	
Kingfisher Marine Weymouth	01305 766595	
Kings Lock Chandlery Middlewich	01606 737564	
Kip Chandlery Inverkip Greenock	01475 521485	
Kirkcudbright Scallop Gear Ltd Kirkcudbright	01557 330399	
Kyle Chandlers Troon	01292 311880	
Landon Marine, Reg Truro	01872 272668	
Largs Chandlers Largs	01475 686026	
Lencraft Boats Ltd Dungarvan	+353 58 68220	
Lincoln Marina Lincoln	01522 526896	
Looe Chandlery West Looe	01503 264355	
Lynch Ltd, PA Morpeth	01670 512291	
Mackay Boatbuilders (Arbroath) Ltd Aberdeen	01241 872879	
Mackay Marine Services Aberdeen	01224 575772	
Mailspeed Marine Burnham-on-Crouch	01342 710618	
Mailspeed Marine Essex Marina	01342 710618	
Mailspeed Marine Warrington	01342 710618	
Mainbrayce Chandlers Braye, Alderney	01481 822772	
Manx Marine Ltd Douglas	01624 674842	
Marine & Leisure Europe Ltd Plymouth	01752 268826	
Marine MegaStore Hamble	023 8045 4400	
Marine MegaStore Morpeth	01670 516151	
Marine Scene Bridgend	01656 671822	
Marine Scene Cardiff	029 2070 5780	
Marine Services Jersey	01534 626930	
Marine Store Wyatts West Mersea	01206 384745	
Marine Store Maldon	01621 854380	
Marine Store Titchmarsh Marina	01621 874495	
Marine Store Walton on the Naze	01255 679028	
Marine Superstore Port Solent Chandlery Portsmouth	023 9221 9843	
MarineCo Torpoint	01752 816005	
Maryport Harbour and Marina Maryport	01900 814431	
Matchett Ltd, HC Widnes	0151 423 4420	
Matthews Ltd, D Cork	+353 214 277633	
McClean Greenock	01475 728234	
McCready Sailboats Ltd Holywood	028 9042 1821	
Moore, Kevin Cowes	01983 289699	
Moore & Son, J Mevagissey	01726 842964	
Morgan & Sons Marine, LH Brightlingsea	01206 302003	
Mount Batten Boathouse Plymouth	01752 482666	
Murphy, Nicholas Dunmore East	+353 51 383259	
Mylor Chandlery & Rigging Falmouth	01326 375482	
Nancy Black Oban	01631 562550	
Nautical World Bangor	028 91460330	
New World Yacht Care Helensburgh	01436 820586	
Newhaven Chandlery Newhaven	01273 612612	
Nifpo Ardglass	028 4484 2144	
Norfolk Marine Great Yarmouth	01692 670272	

MARINA GUIDE 2018

MARINA SUPPLIES AND SERVICES GUIDE

Norfolk Marine Chandlery Shop
Norwich 01603 783150
Northshore Sport & Leisure
Brancaster Staithe 01485 210236
Ocean Leisure Ltd
London 020 7930 5050
One Stop Chandlery
Maldon 01621 853558
O'Sullivans Marine Ltd
Tralee +353 66 7129635
Partington Marine Ltd, William
Pwllheli 01758 612808
Pascall Atkey & Sons Ltd
Isle of Wight 01983 292381
Pennine Marine Ltd
Skipton 01756 792335
Penrhos Marine
Aberdovey 01654 767478
Penzance Marine Services
Penzance 01736 361081
Perry Marine, Rob
Axminster 01297 631314
Pepe Boatyard
Hayling Island 023 9246 1968
Performance Yachting & Chandlery
Plymouth 01752 565023
Peters PLC Chichester 01243 511033
Pinnell & Bax
Northampton 01604 592808
Piplers of Poole Poole 01202 673056
Pirate's Cave, The
Rochester 01634 295233
Powersail Island Chandlers Ltd
East Cowes Marina 01983 299800
Preston Marine Services Ltd
Preston 01772 733595
Price & Co Ltd, WF
Bristol 0117 929 2229
PSM Ltd Alderney 07781 106635
Purcell Marine
Clarenbridge +353 87 279 3821
Purple Sails & Marine
Walsall 08456 435510
Quay West Marine
Poole 01202 732445
Quayside Marine
Salcombe 01548 844300
R&A Fabrication
Kirkcudbright 01557 330399
Racecourse Yacht Basin (Windsor) Ltd
Windsor 01753 851501
Rat Rigs Water Sports
Cardiff 029 2062 1309
Reliance Marine
Wirral 0151 625 5219
Rigmarine Padstow 01841 532657
Riversway Marine
Preston 0844 879 4901

RHP Marine Cowes 01983 290421
RNS Marine Northam 01237 474167
Sail Loft
Bideford 01271 860001
Sailaway
St Anthony 01326 231357
Salcombe Boatstore
Salcombe 01548 843708
Salterns Chandlery
Poole 01202 701556
Shipmate
Salcombe 01548 844555
Sandrock Marine Rye 01797 222679
Schull Watersports Centre
Schull +353 28 28554
Sea & Shore Ship Chandler
Dundee 01382 450666
Sea Cruisers of Rye Rye 01797 222070
Sea Span Edinburgh 0131 552 2224
Sea Teach Ltd Emsworth 01243 375774
Seafare Tobermory 01688 302277
Seahog Boats Preston 01772 633016
Seamark-Nunn & Co
Felixstowe 01394 451000
Seaquest Marine Ltd
St Peter Port 01481 721773
Seaware Ltd Penryn 01326 377948
Seaway Marine Macduff 01261 832877
Sharp & Enright Dover 01304 206295
Shearwater Engineering Services Ltd
Dunoon 01369 706666
Shipshape Marine
King's Lynn 01553 764058
Ship Shape Ramsgate 01843 597000
Shorewater Sports
Chichester 01243 672315
Simpson Marlne Ltd
Newhaven 01273 612612
Simpson Marine Ltd, WA
Dundee 01382 566670
Sketrick Marine Centre
Killinchy 028 9754 1400
Smith AM (Marine) Ltd
London 020 8529 6988
Solent Marine Chandlery Ltd
Gosport 023 9258 4622
South Coast Marine
Christchurch 01202 482695
South Pier Shipyard
St Helier 01534 711000
Southampton Yacht Services Ltd
Southampton 023 803 35266
Sparkes Chandlery
Hayling Island 02392 463572
S Roberts Marine Ltd
Liverpool 0151 707 8300
SSL Marine
Eastbourne 01323 47900

Standard House Chandlery
Wells-next-the-Sea 01328 710593
Stornoway Fishermen's Co-op
Stornoway 01851 702563
Sunset Marine & Watersports
Sligo +353 71 9162792
Sussex Marine
St Leonards on Sea 01424 425882
Sussex Yachts Lyd
Shoreham 01273 605482
Sussex Marine Centre
Shoreham 01273 454737
Sutton Marine (Dublin)
Sutton +353 1 832 2312
SW Nets Newlyn 01736 360254
Tarbert Ltd, JSB Tarbert 01880 820180
TCS Chandlery
Essex Marina 01702 258094
TCS Chandlery Grays 01375 374702
TCS Chandlery
Southend 01702 444423
Thulecraft Ltd Lerwick 01595 693192
Torbay Boating Centre
Paignton 01803 558760
Torquay Chandlers
Torquay 01803 211854
Trafalgar Yacht Services
Fareham 01329 822445
Trident UK
N Shields 0191 490 1736
Union Chandlery
Cork +353 21 4554334
Uphill Boat Services
Weston-Super-Mare 01934 418617
Upper Deck Marine and Outriggers
Fowey 01726 832287
V Ships (Isle of Man)
Douglas 01624 688886
V F Marine Rhu 01436 820584
Viking Marine Ltd
Dun Laoghaire +353 1 280 6654
Waterfront Marine
Bangor 01248 352513
Watersport and Leisure
Kings Lynn 01485 210236
Wayne Maddox Marine
Margate 01843 297157
Western Marine
Dalkey +353 1280 0321
Whitstable Marine
Whitstable 01227 274168
Williams Ltd, TJ Cardiff 029 20 487676
Windjammer Marine
Milford Marina 01646 699070
Yacht & Boat Chandlery
Faversham 01795 531777
Yacht Chandlers Conwy 01492 572777
Yacht Equipment
Chelmsford 01245 223563

CHART AGENTS – ELECTRONIC DEVICES AND EQUIPMENT

Yachtmail Ltd
Lymington 01590 672784
Yachtshop Holyhead 01407 760031
You Boat Chandlery
Gosport 02392 522226

CHART AGENTS

Brown Son & Ferguson Ltd
Glasgow 0141 429 1234
Chattan Security Ltd
Edinburgh 0131 554 7527
Cooke & Son Ltd, B
Hull 01482 223454
Dubois Phillips & McCallum Ltd
Liverpool 0151 236 2776
Imray Laurie Norie and Wilson Ltd
Huntingdon 01480 462114
Kelvin Hughes
Southampton 023 8063 4911
Lilley & Gillie Ltd, John
North Shields 0191 257 2217
MARINE CHART SERVICES
Maritime House, 32 Denington Rd,
Wellingborough NN8 2QH
Tel: 01933 441629
Fax: 01933 442662
www.chartsales.co.uk
Access to many thousands of Navigation Charts & publications in different format.
Price & Co, WF
Bristol 0117 929 2229
Sea Chest Nautical Bookshop
Plymouth 01752 222012
Seath Instruments (1992) Ltd
Lowestoft 01502 573811
Small Craft Deliveries
Woodbridge 01394 382655
Smith (Marine) Ltd, AM
London 020 8529 6988
South Bank Marine Charts Ltd Grimsby 01472 361137
Stanford Charts Bristol 0117 929 9966
Stanford Charts
London 020 7836 1321
Todd Chart Agency Ltd
County Down 028 9146 6640
UK Hydrographics Office
Taunton 01823 337900
Warsash Nautical Bookshop
Warsash 01489 572384

CLOTHING

Absolute
Gorleston on Sea 01493 442259
Aquatogs Cowes 01983 295071
Crew Clothing
London 020 8875 2300
Crewsaver
Gosport 01329 820000

Douglas Gill
Nottingham 0115 9460844
Fat Face fatface.com
Gul International Ltd
Bodmin 01208 262400
Guy Cotten UK Ltd
Liskeard 01579 347115
Harwoods Yarmouth 01983 760258
Helly Hansen
Nottingham 0115 979 5997
Henri Lloyd
Manchester 0161 799 1212
Joules 0845 6066871
Mad Cowes Clothing Co
Cowes 0845 456 5158
Matthews Ltd, D
Cork +353 214 277633
Mountain & Marine
Poynton 01625 859863
Musto Ltd Laindon 01268 491555
Ocean World Ltd
Cowes 01983 291744
Purple Sails & Marine
Walsall 0845 6435510
Quba Sails
Lymington 01590 689362
Quba Sails
Salcombe 01548 844599
Yacht Parts Plymouth 01752 252489

CODE OF PRACTICE EXAMINERS

Booth Marine Surveys, Graham
Birchington-on-Sea 01843 843793
Cannell & Associates, David M
Wivenhoe 01206 823337

COMPUTERS & SOFTWARE

Dolphin Maritime Software
White Cross 01524 841946
Forum Software Ltd
Nr Haverfordwest 01646 636363
Kelvin Hughes Ltd
Southampton 023 8063 4911
Memory-Map
Aldermaston 0844 8110950
PC Maritime Plymouth 01752 254205

DECK EQUIPMENT

Aries Van Gear Spares
Penryn 01326 377467
Ronstan
Gosport 023 9252 5377
Harken UK Lymington 01590 689122
IMP Royston 01763 241300
Kearon Ltd George +353 402 32319
Pro-Boat Ltd
Burnham-on-Crouch 01621 785455
Ryland, Kenneth
Stanton 01386 584270

Smith, EC & Son Ltd
Luton 01582 729721
Timage & Co Ltd
Braintree 01376 343087

DIESEL MARINE/ FUEL ADDITIVES

Corralls Poole 01202 674551
Cotters Marine & General Supplies
Baltimore +353 28 20106
Expresslube Henfield 01444 254115
Gorey Marine Fuel Supplies
Gorey 07797 742384
Hammond Motorboats
Dover 01304 206809
Iron Wharf Boatyard
Faversham 01795 536296
Lallow, Clare Cowes 01983 760707
Marine Support & Towage
Cowes 01983 200716/07860 297633
Quayside Fuel
Weymouth 07747 182181
Rossiter Yachts
Christchurch 01202 483250
Sleeman & Hawken
Shaldon 01626 778266

DIVERS

Abco Divers Belfast 028 90610492
Andark Diving
Burseldon 01489 581755
Argonaut Marine
Aberdeen 01224 706526
Baltimore Diving and Watersports Centre West Cork +353 28 20300
C & C Marine Services
Largs 01475 687180
Cardiff Commercial Boat Operators Ltd
Cardiff 029 2037 7872
Clyde Diving Centre
Inverkip 01475 521281
Divetech UK King's Lynn 01485 572323
Diving & Marine Engineering
Barry 01446 721553
Donnelly, R
South Shields 07973 119455
DV Diving 028 9146 4671
Falmouth Divers Ltd
Penryn 01326 374736
Fathoms Ltd Wick 01955 605956
Felixarc Marine Ltd
Lowestoft 01502 509215
Grampian Diving Services
New Deer 01771 644206
Higgins, Noel +353 872027650
Hudson, Dave
Trearddur Bay 01407 860628

MARINA SUPPLIES AND SERVICES GUIDE

Hunt, Kevin Tralee +353 6671 25979	**Baker, Keith** Brentford 07792 937790	**MES** Falmouth Marina, Falmouth 01326 378497
Kaymac Diving Services Swansea 08431 165523	**Belson Design Ltd, Nick** Southampton 077 6835 1330	**Mount Batten Boathouse** Plymouth 01752 482666
Keller, Hilary Buncrana +353 77 62146	**Biggs, John** Weymouth Marina, Weymouth 01305 778445	**New World Yacht Care** Rhu 01436 820586
Kilkee Diving Centre Kilkee +353 6590 56707	**BJ Marine Ltd** Bangor 028 9127 1434	**Neyland Marine Services Ltd** Milford Haven 01646 600358
Leask Marine Kirkwall 01856 874725	**BM Electrical** Kirkcudbright 07584 657192	**Powell, Martin** Shamrock Quay, Southampton 023 8033 2123
Looe Divers Hannaford 01503 262727	**Boat Electrics** Troon 01292 315355	**R & J Marine Electricians** Suffolk Yacht Harbour Ltd, Ipswich 01473 659737
MacDonald, D Nairn 01667 455661	**Buccaneer Ltd** Macduff 01261 835199	**Radio & Electronic Services** Beaucette Marina, Guernsey 01481 728837
Medway Diving Contractors Ltd Gillingham 01634 851902	**Calibra Marine** Dartmouth 01803 833094	**Redcar Fish Company** Stockton-on-Tees 01642 633638
MMC Diving Services Lake, Isle of Wight 07966 579965	**Campbell & McHardy** Lossiemouth Marina, Lossiemouth 01343 812137	**RHP Marine** Cowes 01983 290421
Mojo Maritime Penzance 01736 762771	**CES Sandown** Sparkes Marina, Hayling Island 023 9246 6005	**Rothwell, Chris** Torquay Marina 01803 850960
Murray, Alex Stornoway 01851 704978	**Colin Coady Marine** Malahide +353 87 265 6496	**Ruddy Marine** Galway +353 87 742 7439
New Dawn Dive Centre Lymington 01590 675656	**Contact Electrical** Arbroath 01241 874528	**Rutherford, Jeff** Largs 01475 568026
Northern Divers (Engineering) Ltd Hull 01482 227276	**DDZ Marine** Ardossan 01294 607077	**SM International** Plymouth 01752 662129
Offshore Marine Services Ltd Bembridge 01983 873125	**EC Leisure Craft** Essex Marina 01702 568482	**Sussex Fishing Services** Rye 01797 223895
Parkinson (Sinbad Marine Services), J Killybegs +353 73 31417	**Energy Solutions** Rochester 01634 290772	**Tony's Marine Service** Coleraine 028 7035 6422
Port of London Authority Gravesend 01474 560311	**Enterprise Marine Electronic & Technical Services Ltd** Aberdeen 01224 593281	**Ultra Marine Systems** Mayflower International Marina, Plymouth 07989 941020
Purcell, D – Crouch Sailing School Burnham 01621 784140/0585 33	**Eurotek Marine** Eastbourne 01323 479144	**Upham, Roger** Chichester 01243 528299
Salvesen UK Ltd Liverpool 0151 933 6038	**Evans, Lyndon** Brentford 07795 218704	**Volspec** Ipswich 01473 780144
Sea-Lift Diving Dover 01304 829956	**Floetree Ltd (Loch Lomond Marina)** Balloch 01389 752069	**Weyland Marine Services** Milford Haven 01646 600358
Southern Cylinder Services Fareham 01329 221125	**Hamble Marine** Hamble 02380 001088	
Sub Aqua Services North Ormesby 01642 230209	**HNP Engineers (Lerwick) Ltd** Lerwick 01595 692493	## ELECTRONIC DEVICES AND EQUIPMENT
Teign Diving Centre Teignmouth 01626 773965	**Jackson Yacht Services** Jersey 01534 743819	**Anchorwatch UK** Edinburgh 0131 447 5057
Tuskar Rock Marine Rosslare +353 53 33376	**Jedynak, A** Salcombe 01548 843321	**Aquascan International Ltd** Newport 01633 841117
Underwater Services Dyffryn Arbwy 01341 247702	**Kippford Slipway Ltd** Dalbeattie 01556 620249	**Atlantis Marine Power Ltd** Plymouth 01752 208810
Wilson Alan c/o Portrush Yacht Club Portrush 028 2076 2225	**Lynch Ltd, PA** Morpeth 01670 512291	**Autosound Marine** Bradford 01274 688990
Woolford, William Bridlington 01262 671710	**Lynch, John** Tralee +353 87 992 3102	**B&G** Romsey 01794 518448
## ELECTRICAL AND ELECTRONIC ENGINEERS	**Mackay Boatbuilders (Arbroath) Ltd** Aberdeen 01241 872879	**Brookes & Gatehouse** Romsey 01794 518448
AAS Marine Aberystwyth 01970 631090	**Marine, AW** Gosport 023 9250 1207	**Boat Electrics & Electronics Ltd** Troon 01292 315355
Allworth Riverside Services, Adrian Chelsea Harbour Marina 07831 574774	**Marine Electrical Repair Service** London 020 7228 1336	**Cactus Navigation & Communication** London 020 7833 3435
ASL Auto Services Boston 01205 761560	**Maxfield Electrical** Doncaster 07976 825349	**CDL** Aberdeen 01224 706655
	MB Marine Troon 01292 311944	**Charity & Taylor Ltd** Lowestoft 01502 581529

ELECTRONIC DEVICES AND EQUIPMENT – HARBOUR MASTERS

Diverse Yacht Services
Hamble 023 8045 3399
Dyfed Electronics Ltd
Milford Haven 01646 694572
Echopilot Marine Electronics Ltd
Ringwood 01425 476211
Enterprise Marine
Aberdeen 01224 593281
Euronav Ltd
Portsmouth 023 9237 3855
Exposure Lights
Pulborough 01798 83930
Furuno UK
Fraserburgh 01346 518300
Havant 023 9244 1000
Garmin (Europe) Ltd
Romsey 0870 850 1242
Golden Arrow Marine Ltd
Southampton 023 8071 0371
Greenham Regis Marine Electronics
Lymington 01590 671144
Greenham Regis Marine Electronics
Poole 01202 676363
Greenham Regis Marine Electronics
Southampton 023 8063 6555
ICS Electronics Arundel 01903 731101
JG Technologies Ltd
Weymouth 0845 458 9616
KM Electronics
Lowestoft 01502 569079
Kongsberg Simrad Ltd
Aberdeen 01224 226500
Kongsberg Simrad Ltd
Wick 01955 603606
Landau UK Ltd Hamble 02380 454040
Enterprise Marine
Aberdeen 01224 593281
Marathon Leisure
Hayling Island 023 9263 7711
Marine Instruments
Falmouth 01326 375483
MB Marine Troon 01292 311944
Microcustom Ltd Ipswich 01473 215777
Nasa Marine Instruments
Stevenage 01438 354033
Navionics UK Plymouth 01752 204735
Ocean Leisure Ltd
London 020 7930 5050
Plymouth Marine Electronics
Plymouth 01752 227711
Radio & Electronic Services Ltd
St Peter Port 01481 728837
Raymarine Ltd
Portsmouth 02392 714700
Redfish Car Company
Stockton-on-Tees 01642 633638
Robertson, MK Oban 01631 563836

Satcom Distribution Ltd
Salisbury 01722 410800
Seaquest Marine Ltd
Guernsey 01481 721773
Seatronics Aberdeen 01224 853100
Selex Communications
Aberdeen 01224 890316
Selex Communications
Bristol 0117 931 3550
Selex Communications
Brixham 01803 882716
Selex Communications
Fraserburgh 01346 518187
Selex Communications
Glasgow 0141 882 6909
Selex Communications
Hull 01482 326144
Selex Communications
Kilkeel 028 4176 9009
Selex Communications
Liverpool 01268 823400
Selex Communications
Lowestoft 01502 572365
Selex Communications
Newcastle upon Tyne 0191 265 0374
Selex Communications
Newlyn 01736 361320
Selex Communications
Penryn 01326 378031
Selex Communications
Plymouth 01752 222878
Selex Communications
Rosyth 01383 419606
Selex Communications
Southampton 023 8051 1868
Silva Ltd Livingston 01506 419555
SM International
Plymouth 01752 662129
Sperry Marine Ltd
Peterhead 01779 473475
Stenmar Ltd Aberdeen 01224 827288
Transas Nautic
Portsmouth 023 9267 4016
Veripos Precise Navigation
Fraserburgh 01346 511411
Wema (UK)
Honiton 01404 881810
Wilson & Co Ltd, DB
Glasgow 0141 647 0161
Woodsons of Aberdeen Ltd
Aberdeen 01224 722884

ENGINES AND ACCESSORIES

Airylea Motors
Aberdeen 01224 872891
Amble Boat Co Ltd
Amble 01665 710267
Anchor Marine Products
Benfleet 01268 566666

Aquafac Ltd Luton 01582 568700
Barrus Ltd, EP
Bicester 01869 363636
British Polar Engines Ltd
Glasgow 0141 445 2455
Bukh Diesel UK Ltd
Poole 01202 668840
CJ Marine Mechanical
Troon 01292 313400
Cleghorn Waring Ltd
Letchworth 01462 480380
Cook's Diesel Service Ltd
Faversham 01795 538553
Southern Shipwright (SSL)
Brighton 01273 601779
Southern Shipwright (SSL)
Eastbourne 01323 479000
Fender-Fix Maidstone 01622 751518
Fettes & Rankine Engineering
Aberdeen 01224 573343
Fleetwood & Sons Ltd, Henry
Lossiemouth 01343 813015
Gorleston Marine Ltd
Great Yarmouth 01493 661883
Halyard Salisbury 01722 710922
Interseals (Guernsey) Ltd
Guernsey 01481 246364
Kelpie Boats
Pembroke Dock 01646 683661
Keypart Watford 01923 330570
Lancing Marine
Brighton 01273 410025
Lencraft Boats Ltd
Dungarvan +353 58 68220
Lewmar Ltd Havant 023 9247 1841
Liverpool Power Boats
Bootle 0151 944 1163
Lynch Ltd, PA
Morpeth 01670 512291
MacDonald & Co Ltd, JN
Glasgow 0141 810 3400
Mariners Weigh
Shaldon 01626 873698
MMS Ardrossan 01294 604831
Mooring Mate Ltd
Bournemouth 01202 421199
Newens Marine, Chas
Putney 020 8788 4587
Ocean Safety
Southampton 023 8072 0800
RK Marine Ltd
Hamble 01489 583585
Swanwick 01489 583572
Sillette Sonic Ltd
Sutton 020 8337 7543

MARINA SUPPLIES AND SERVICES GUIDE

Smith & Son Ltd, EC	
Luton	01582 729721
Sowester Simpson-Lawrence Ltd	
Poole	01202 667700
Timage & Co Ltd	
Braintree	01376 343087
Thorne Boat Services	
Thorne	01405 814197
Vetus Den Ouden Ltd	
Totton	023 8045 4507
Western Marine	
Dublin	+353 1 280 0321
Whitstable Marine	
Whitstable	01227 262525
Yates Marine, Martin	
Galgate	01524 751750
Ynys Marine	
Cardigan	01239 613179

FOUL-WEATHER GEAR

Aquatogs Cowes	01983 295071
Crew Clothing	
London	020 8875 2300
Century	
Finchampstead	0118 9731616
Crewsaver Gosport	01329 820000
Douglas Gill	
Nottingham	0115 946 0844
FBI Leeds	0113 270 7000
Gul International Ltd	
Bodmin	01208 262400
Helly Hansen	
Nottingham	0115 979 5997
Henri Lloyd	
Manchester	0161 799 1212
Musto Ltd	
Laindon	01268 491555
Pro Rainer	
Windsor	07752 903882

GENERAL MARINE EQUIPMENT & SPARES

Ampair	
Ringwood	01425 480780
Aries Vane Gear Spares	
Penryn	01326 377467
Arthurs Chandlery, R	
Gosport	023 9252 6522
Atlantis Marine Power Ltd	
Plymouth	01752 208810
Barden UK Ltd Fareham	01489 570770
Calibra Marine International Ltd	
Southampton	08702 400358
CH Marine (Cork)	
Cork	+353 21 4315700
Chris Hornsey (Chandlery) Ltd	
Southsea	023 9273 4728
Compass Marine (Dartmouth) Dartmouth	01803 835915

Cox Yacht Charter Ltd, Nick	
Lymington	01590 673489
CTC Marine & Leisure	
Middlesbrough	01642 372600
Docksafe Ltd Bangor	028 9147 0453
Exposure Lights	
Pulborough	01798 83930
Frederiksen Boat Fittings (UK) Ltd	
Gosport	023 9252 5377
Furneaux Riddall & Co Ltd	
Portsmouth	023 9266 8621
Hardware & Marine Supplies	
Co Wexford	+353 (53) 29791
Index Marine	
Bournemouth	01202 470149
Kearon Ltd, George	
Arklow	+353 402 32319
Marathon Leisure	
Hayling Island	023 9263 7711
Pro-Boat Ltd	
Burnham-on-Crouch	01621 785455
Pump International Ltd	
Cornwall	01209 831937
Quay West Marine	
Poole	01202 732445
Rogers, Angie Bristol	0117 973 8276
Ryland, Kenneth	
Stanton	01386 584270
Tiflex	
Liskeard	01579 320808
Vetus Boating Equipment	
Southampton	02380 454507
Whitstable Marine	
Whitstable	01227 262525
Yacht Parts	
Plymouth	01752 252489

HARBOUR MASTERS

Aberaeron	01545 571645
Aberdeen	01224 597000
Aberdovey	01654 767626
Aberystwyth	01970 611433
Alderney & Burhou	01481 822620
Amble	01665 710306
Anstruther	01333 310836
Appledore	01237 474569
Arbroath	01241 872166
Ardglass	028 4484 1291
Ardrossan Control Tower	
	01294 463972
Arinagour Piermaster	01879 230347
Arklow	+353 402 32466
Baltimore	+353 28 22145
Banff	01261 815544
Bantry Bay	+353 27 53277

Barmouth	01341 280671
Barry	01446 732665
Beaucette	01481 245000
Beaulieu River	01590 616200
Belfast Lough	028 90 553012
Belfast River Manager	028 90 328507
Bembridge	01983 872828
Berwick-upon-Tweed	01289 307404
Bideford	01237 346131
Blyth	01670 352678
Boston	01205 362328
Bridlington	01262 670148/9
Bridport	01308 423222
Brighton	01273 819919
Bristol	0117 926 4797
Brixham	01803 853321
Buckie	01542 831700
	07842 532360
Bude	01288 353111
Burghead	01343 835337
Burnham-on-Crouch	01621 783602
Burnham-on-Sea	01278 782180
Burtonport	+353 075 42155
Caernarfon	01286 672118
Caernarfon	07786 730865
Camber Berthing Offices – Portsmouth	
	023 92297395
Campbeltown	01586 552552
	07825 732862
Caledonian Canal Off. (Inverness)	01463 725500
Cardiff	029 20400500
Carnlough Harbour	07703 606763
Castletown Bay	01624 823549
Charlestown	01726 67526
Chichester Harbour	01243 512301
Clovelly	01273 431549
	07975 501380
Conwy	01492 596253
Cork	+353 21 4273125
Corpach Canal Sea Lock	
	01397 772249
Courtmacsherry	+353 8673 94299
	+353 23 46311/46600
Coverack	01326 380679
Cowes	01983 293952
Crail	01333 450820
Craobh Haven	01852 502222
Crinan Canal Office	01546 603210
Cromarty Firth	01381 600479

MARINA GUIDE 2018 111

HARBOUR MASTERS – MARINAS

Cromarty Harbour	01381 600493
Crookhaven	+353 28 35319
Cullen	01542 831700
Dingle	+353 66 9151629
Douglas	01624 686628
Dover	01304 240400 Ext 4520
Dublin	+353 1 874871
Dun Laoghaire	+353 1 280 1130/8074
Dunbar	07958 754858
Dundee	01382 224121
Dunmore East	+353 51 383166
East Loch Tarbert	01859 502444
Eastbourne	01323 470099
Eigg Harbour	01687 482428
Elie	01333 330051
Estuary Control - Dumbarton	01389 726211
Exe	01392 274306
Exeter	01392 265791
Eyemouth	01890 750223 / 07885 742505
Felixstowe	07803 476621
Findochty	07842 532360
Fisherrow	0131 665 5900
Fishguard (Lower Harbour)	01348 874726
Fishguard	01348 404425
Fleetwood	01253 872323
Flotta	01856 701411
Folkestone	01303 715354
Fowey	01726 832471/2.
Fraserburgh	01346 515858
Galway Bay	+353 91 561874
Garlieston	01988 600274
Glasson Dock	07910 315606
Gorey Port Control	01534 447788
Gourdon	01569 762741
Great Yarmouth	01493 335501
Grimsby Dockmaster	01472 359181
Groomsport Bay	028 91 278040
Hamble River	01489 576387
Hayle	07500 993867
Helford River	01326 732544
Helmsdale	01431 821692
Holy Island	01289 389217
Holyhead	01407 763071
Hopeman	01343 835337
Howth	+353 1 832 2252
Ilfracombe	01271 862108
Inverness	01463 715715
Ipswich	01473 211771
Irvine	01294 487286
Johnshaven	01561 362262
Kettletoft Bay	01857 600227
Killybegs	+353 73 31032
Kilmore Quay	+353 53 912 9955
Kinlochbervie	01971 521235 / 07901 514350
Kinsale	+353 21 4772503
Kirkcudbright	01557 331135
Kirkwall	01856 872292
Langstone Harbour	023 9246 3419
Larne	02828 872100
Lerwick	01595 692991
Littlehampton	01903 721215
Liverpool	0151 949 6134/5
Loch Gairloch	01445 712140
Loch Inver	01571 844267 / 07958 734610
Looe	01503 262839 / 07918 728955
Lossiemouth (Marina)	07969 213513 / 07969 213521
Lough Foyle	028 7186 0555
Lowestoft	01502 572286
Lyme Regis	01297 442137
Lymington	01590 672014
Lyness	01856 791387
Macduff	01261 832236
Maryport	01900 814431
Menai Strait	01248 712312
Methil	01333 462725
Mevagissey	01726 843305
Milford Haven	01646 696100
Minehead (Mon-Fri)	01643 702566
Montrose	01674 672302
Mousehole	01736 731511
Mullion Cove	01326 240222
Nairn Harbour Office	01667 452453
Newhaven Harbour Admin	01273 612872/612926
Newlyn	01736 731897
Newquay	07737 387217
Newport Harbour Office	01983 525994
North Berwick	00776 467373
Oban	01631 562892
Padstow	01841 532239
Peel	01624 842338
Penrhyn Bangor	01248 352525
Penzance	01736 366113
Peterhead	01779 483630
Pierowall	01857 677216
Pittenweem	01333 312591
Plockton	01599 534589
Polperro	01503 272809
Poole	01202 440233
Port Ellen Harbour Association	01496 302458
Port Isaac	01208 880321 / 07855 429422
Port St Mary	01624 833205
Porth Dinllaen	01758 720276
Porthleven	01326 574207
Porthmadog	01766 512927
Portknockie	01542 840833
Portland	01305 824044
Portpatrick	01776 810355
Portree	01478 612926
Portrush	028 70822307
Portsmouth Harbour Commercial Docks	023 92297395
Portsmouth Harbour Control	023 92723694
Portsmouth Harbour	023 92723124
Preston	01772 726711
Pwllheli	01758 701219
Queenborough	01795 662051
Queens Garelock/Rhu	01436 674321
Ramsey	01624 812245
Ramsgate	01843 572100
River Bann & Coleraine	028 7034 2012
River Blackwater	01621 856487
River Colne (Brightlingsea)	01206 302200
River Dart	01803 832337
River Deben	01473 736257
River Exe Dockmaster	01392 274306
River Humber	01482 327171
River Medway	01795 596593
River Orwell	01473 231010
River Roach	01621 783602
River Stour	01255 243000
River Tyne/North Shields	0191 257 2080
River Yealm	01752 872533
Rivers Alde & Ore	07528 092635
Rosslare Europort	+353 53 915 7921
Rothesay	01700 503842 / 07799 724225

MARINA SUPPLIES AND SERVICES GUIDE

Ryde	01983 613879	Watchet	01643 703704	**Pantaenius UK Ltd** Plymouth	01752 223656
Salcombe	01548 843791	Waterford	+353 51 874907	**Porthcawl Insurance Consultants** Porthcawl	01656 784866
Sark	01481 832323	Wells-next-the-Sea	01328 711646	**Saga Boat Insurance** Folkestone	01303 771135
Scalloway	01595 880574	West Bay (Bridport)	01308 423222 / 07870 240636	**St Margarets Insurances** London	020 8778 6161
Scarborough	01723 373530	Wexford	+353 53 912 2039	**Towergate Insurance** Shrewsbury	0344 892 1987
Scrabster	01847 892779	Weymouth	01305 206423		
Seaham	07786 565205	Whitby	01947 602354		

LIFERAFTS & INFLATABLES

Sharpness, Gloucester Harbour Trustees 01453 811913
Shoreham 01273 598100
Silloth 016973 31358
Sligo +353 91 53819 / +353 86 0870767
Southampton 023 8033 9733
Southend-on-Sea 01702 611889
Southwold 01502 724712
St Helier 01534 447788
St Ives 07793 515460
St Margaret's Hope 01856 831454
St Mary's 01720 422768
St Michael's Mount 07870 400282
St Monans (part-time) 07930 869538
St Peter Port 01481 720229
Stonehaven 01569 762741
Stornoway 01851 702688
Strangford Lough 028 44 881637
Stranraer 07734 073421
Stromness 07810 465825
Stronsay 01857 616317
Sullom Voe 01806 242551
Sunderland 0191 567 2626
Swale 01795 561234
Swansea 01792 653787
Tayport Hbr Trust 01382 553799
Tees & Hartlepool Port Authority 01429 277205
Teignmouth 01626 773165
Tenby 01834 842717
Thames Estuary 01474 562200
Tobermory Moorings Officer 07917 832497
Torquay 01803 292429
Troon 01292 281687
Truro 01872 272130
Ullapool 01854 612091
Waldringfield 01394 736291
Walton-on-the-Naze 01255 851899

Whitehaven 01946 692435
Whitehills 01261 861291
Whitstable 01227 274086
Wick 01955 602030
Wicklow +353 404 67455
Workington 01900 602301
Yarmouth 01983 760321
Youghal +353 24 92626

HARBOURS

Bristol Harbour 0117 903 1484
Clyde Marina – Ardrossan 01294 607077
Jersey Harbours St Helier 01534 885588
Maryport Harbour and Marina Maryport 01900 818447/4431
Peterhead Bay Authority Peterhead 01779 474020
Sark Moorings – Channel Islands 01481 832260

INSURANCE/FINANCE

Admiral Marine Ltd Salisbury 01722 416106
Bishop Skinner Boat Insurance London 0800 7838057
Bluefin London 0800 074 5200
Castlemain Ltd St Peter Port 01481 721319
Clark Insurance, Graham Tyneside 0191 455 8089
Craven Hodgson Associates Leeds 0113 243 8443
Giles Insurance Brokers Irvine 01294 315481
GJW Direct Liverpool 0151 473 8000
Haven Knox-Johnston West Malling 01732 223600
Lombard Southampton 023 8024 2171
Marine & General Insurance Services Ltd Maidstone 01622 201106
Mercia Marine Malvern 01684 564457
Nautical Insurance Services Ltd Leigh-on-Sea 01702 470811
Navigators & General Brighton 01273 863400

Adec Marine Ltd Croydon 020 8686 9717
Avon Inflatables Llanelli 01554 882000
Cosalt International Ltd Aberdeen 01224 826662
Glaslyn Marine Supplies Ltd Porthmadog 01766 513545
Hale Marine, Ron Portsmouth 023 9273 2985
Guernsey Yacht Club St Peter Port 01481 722838
IBS Boats South Woodham Ferrers 01245 323211/425551
KTS Seasafety Kilkeel 028 918 28405
Nationwide Marine Hire Warrington 01925 245788
Norwest Marine Ltd Liverpool 0151 207 2860
Ocean Safety Southampton 023 8072 0800
Polymarine Ltd Conwy 01492 583322
Premium Liferaft Services Burnham-on-Crouch 0800 243673
Ribeye Dartmouth 01803 832060
South Eastern Marine Services Ltd Basildon 01268 534427
Suffolk Marine Safety Ipswich 01473 833010
Whitstable Marine Whitstable 01227 262525

MARINAS

Aberystwyth Marina 01970 611422
Amble Marina 01665 712168
Arbroath Harbour 01241 872166
Ardfern Yacht Centre Ltd 01852 500247
Ardglass Marina 028 44842332
Arklow Marina +353 87 258 8078
Ballycastle Marina 028 2076 8525
Banff Harbour Marina 01261 815544
Bangor Marina 028 91 453297
Beaucette Marina 01481 245000
Bembridge Harbour Authority 01983 872828

MARINA GUIDE 2018

Berthon Lymington Marina	01590 647405
Birdham Pool Marina	01243 512310
Blackwater Marina	01621 740264
Boston Gateway Marina	07480 525230
Bradwell Marina	01621 776235
Bray Marina	01628 623654
Brentford Dock Marina	020 8232 8941
Bridgemarsh Marine	01621 740414
Brighton Marina	01273 819919
Bristol Marina	0117 921 3198
Brixham Marina	01803 882929
Bucklers Hard Marina	01590 616200
Burnham Yacht Harbour Marina Ltd	01621 782150
BWML Glasson Basin	01524 751491
BWML Limehouse Marina	020 7308 9930
Cahersiveen Marina	+353 66 947 2777
Caley Marina	01463 236539
Campbeltown Marina	07798 524821
Cardiff Marina	02920 396078
Carlingford Marina	+353 42 9373072
Carrickfergus Marina	028 9336 6666
Castlepark Marina	+353 21 477 4959
Chatham Maritime Marina	01634 899200
Chelsea Harbour Marina	07770 542783
Chichester Marina	01243 512731
Clyde Marina Ltd	01294 607077
Cobbs Quay Marina	01202 674299
Coleraine Harbour Town Centre Marina	028 7034 2012
Coleraine Marina	028 703 44768
Conwy Quays Marina	01492 593000
Cork Harbour Marina	+353 87 3669009
Cowes Yacht Haven	01983 299975
Craobh Marina	01852 500222
Crinan Boatyard	01546 830232
Crosshaven Boatyard Marina	+353 21 483 1161
Dart Marina Yacht Harbour	01803 837161
Darthaven Marina	01803 752242
Dartside Quay	01803 845445
Deganwy Quays Marina	01492 576888
Dingle Marina	+353 (0)87 925 4115
Douglas Marina	01624 686627
Dover Marina	01304 241663
Dun Laoghaire Marina	+353 1 202 0040
Dunstaffnage Marina Ltd	01631 566555
East Cowes Marina	01983 293983
Emsworth Yacht Harbour	01243 377727
Endeavour Quay	02392 584200
Essex Marina	01702 258531
Falmouth Haven Marina	01326 310991
Falmouth Marina	01326 316620
Fambridge Yacht Haven	01621 740370
Fenit Harbour & Marina	+353 66 7136231
Fleetwood Haven Marina	01253 879062
Fox's Marina & Boatyard	01473 689111
Foyle Port Marina	02871 860555
Gallions Point Marina	0207 476 7054
Galway Harbour Marina	+353 91 561874
Gillingham Marina	01634 280022
Gosport Marina	023 9252 4811
Hafan Pwllheli	01758 701219
Hamble Point Marina	02380 452464
Harbour of Rye	01797 225225
Hartlepool Marina	01429 865744
Haslar Marina	023 9260 1201
Heybridge Basin	07712 079764
Holy Loch Marina	01369 701800
Holyhead Marina	01407 764242
Howth Marina	+353 1839 2777
Hull Marina	01482 609960
Hythe Marina Village	02380 207073
Inverness Marina	01463 220501
Ipswich Haven Marina	01473 236644
Island Harbour Marina	01983 539994
James Watt Dock Marina	01475 729838
Kemps Quay	023 8063 2323
Kilmore Quay Marina	+353 5391 29955
Kilrush Marina	+353 65 9052072
Kinsale Yacht Club Marina	+353 21 477 2196
Kip Marina	01475 521485
Kirkcudbright Marina	01557 331135
Kirkwall Marina	01856 871313
Lady Bee Marina	01273 593801
Lake Yard Marina	01202 674531
Largs Yacht Haven	01475 675333
Lawrence Cove Marina	+353 27 75044
Littlehampton Marina	01903 713553
Liverpool Marina Bar & Grill	0151 707 6777
Lossiemouth Marina	01343 813066
Lowestoft Cruising Club	07810 522515
Lowestoft Haven Marina	01502 580300
Lymington Harbour Commission	01590 672014
Lymington Yacht Haven	01590 677071
Malahide Marina	+353 1 845 4129
Mallaig Marina	07824 331031
Maryport Harbour and Marina	01900 814431
Mayflower International Marina	01752 556633
Melfort Pier & Harbour	01852 200333
Mercury Yacht Harbour	023 8045 5994
Meridian Quay Marina	01472 268424
Milford Marina	01646 696312
Mylor Yacht Harbour	01326 372121
Nairn Marina	01667 456008
Neptune Marina Ltd	01473 215204
Newhaven Marina	01273 513881
Neyland Yacht Haven	01646 601601
Northney Marina	02392 466321
Noss Marina	01803 839087
Oban Marina & Yacht Services Ltd	01631 565333
Ocean Village Marina	023 8022 9385
Padstow Harbour	01841 532239
Parkstone Yacht Club Haven	01202 738824
Peel Marina	01624 842338
Penarth Quays Marina	02920 705021
Penton Hook	01932 568681
Peterhead Bay Marina	01779 477868
Plymouth Yacht Haven	01752 404231
Poole Quay Boat Haven	01202 649488
Port Bannatyne Marina	01700 503116
Port Edgar Marina	0131 331 3330

MARINA SUPPLIES AND SERVICES GUIDE

Port Ellen Marina	07464 151200
Port Hamble Marina	023 8045 2741
Port of Poole Marina	01202 649488
Port Pendennis Marina	01326 211211
Port Solent Marina	02392 210765
Port Werburgh	01634 252107
Portaferry Marina	07703 209780
Portavadie Marina	01700 811075
Portishead Quays Marina	01275 841941
Portland Marina	0345 430 2012
Preston Marina	01772 733595
Quay Marinas Rhu	01436 820238
Queen Anne's Battery	01752 671142
Ridge Wharf Yacht Centre	01929 552650
Royal Clarence Marina	02392 523523
Royal Cork Yacht Club Marina	+353 21 483 1023
Royal Harbour Marina Ramsgate	01843 572100
Royal Harwich Yacht Club Marina	01473 780319
Royal Norfolk and Suffolk Yacht Club	01502 566726
Royal Northumberland Yacht Club	01670 353636
Royal Quays Marina	0191 272 8282
Ryde Leisure Harbour	01983 613879
Salterns Marina Ltd	01202 709971
Salve Engineering Marina	+353 21 483 1145
Sandpoint Marina (Dumbarton)	01389 762396
Saxon Wharf	023 8033 94900
Seaport Marina	01463 725500
Seaton's Marina	028 703 832086
Shamrock Quay	023 8022 9461
Sharpness Marine	01453 811476
Shepards Wharf Marina	01983 297821
Shotley Marina	01473 788982
South Dock Marina	020 7252 2244
South Ferriby Marina	01652 635620
Southsea Marina	02392 822719
Sovereign Harbour Marina	01323 470099
Sparkes Marina	023 92463572
St Helier Marina	01534 447708
St Katharine Marina Ltd	0207 264 5312
St Peter Port Marinas	01481 720229
St Peter's Marina	0191 265 4472
Stornoway Marina	01851 702688
Stranraer Marina	01776 706565
Stromness Marina	01856 871313
Suffolk Yacht Harbour Ltd	01473 659240
Sunderland Marina	0191 514 4721
Sutton Harbour	01752 204702
Swansea Marina	01792 470310
Swanwick Marina	01489 884081
Tarbert Harbour	01880 820344
The Shipyard	01903 713327
Titchmarsh Marina	01255 672185
Tobermory Harbour Association	01688 302876
Tollesbury Marina	01621 869202
Torquay Marina	01803 200210
Town Quay Marina	02380 234397
Troon Yacht Haven	01292 315553
Universal Marina	01489 574272
Victoria Marina	01481 725987
Walton Yacht Basin	01255 675873
Waterford City Marina	+353 87 238 4944
Weymouth & Portland BC	01305 838423
Weymouth Marina	01305 767576
Whitby Marina	01947 602354
Whitehaven Marina	01946 692435
Whitehills Marina	01261 861291
Wick Marina	01955 602030
WicorMarine Yacht Haven	01329 237112
Windsor Marina	01753 853911
Wisbech Yacht Harbour Office	01945 588059
Woolverstone Marina	01473 780206
Yarmouth Harbour	01983 760321

MARINE ENGINEERS

AAS Marine	Aberystwyth	01970 631090
Allerton Engineering	Lowestoft	01502 537870
APAS Engineering Ltd	Southampton	023 8063 2558
Ardmair Boat Centre	Ullapool	01854 612054
Arisaig Marine	Inverness-shire	01687 450224
Arun Craft	Littlehampton	01903 723667
ASL Auto Services	Boston	01205 761560
Atlantis Marine Power Ltd	Plymouth	01752 208810
Attrill & Sons, H	Bembridge	01983 872319
Auto & Marine Services	Botley	07836 507000
Auto Marine	Southsea	023 9282 5601
Baker, Keith	Brentford	07792 937790
BJ Marine Ltd	Bangor	028 9127 1434
Bristol Boat Ltd	Bristol	01225 872032
Browne, Jimmy	Tralee	+353 87 262 7158
Buccaneer Ltd	Macduff	01261 835199
Buzzard Marine Engineering	Yarmouth	01983 760707
C & B Marine Ltd	Chichester Marina	01243 511273
Caddy, Simon Falmouth Marina	Falmouth	01326 372682
Caledonian Marine	Rhu Marina	01436 821184
Caratek	Hull	07957 922301
Cardigan Outboards	Cardigan	01239 613966
Channel Islands Marine Ltd	Guernsey	01481 716880
Channel Islands Marine Ltd	Jersey	01534 767595
Cook's Diesel Service Ltd	Faversham	01795 538553
Cragie Engineering	Kirkwall	01856 874680
Wartsila	Havant	023 9240 0121
Crinan Boatyard Ltd	Crinan	01546 830232
Cutler Marine Engineering, John	Emsworth	01243 375014
Dale Sailing Co Ltd	Milford Haven	01646 603110
Davis Marine Services	Ramsgate	01843 586172
Denney & Son, EL	Redcar	01642 483507
DH Marine (Shetland) Ltd	Shetland	01595 690618
Emark Marine Ltd	Emsworth	01243 375383
Evans, Lyndon	Brentford	07795 218704

MARINA GUIDE 2018

MARINE ENGINEERS – NAVIGATION EQUIPMENT

Evans Marine Engineering, Tony
Pwllheli 01758 703070

Felton Marine Engineering
Brighton 01273 601779

Felton Marine Engineering
Eastbourne 01323 470211

Ferrypoint Boat Co
Youghal +353 24 94232

Fettes & Rankine Engineering
Aberdeen 01224 573343

Fleming Engineering, J
Stornoway 01851 703488

Floetree Ltd Loch Lomond Marina
Balloch 01389 752069

Fowey Harbour Marine Engineers
Fowey 01726 832806

Fox Marine Services Ltd
Jersey 01534 721312

Freeport Marine Jersey 01534 888100

French Marine Motors Ltd
Colchester 01206 302133

French Marine Motors Ltd
Titchmarsh Marina 01255 850303

GH Douglas Marine Services
Fleetwood Harbour Village Marina,
Fleetwood 01253 877200

Golden Arrow Marine
Southampton 023 8071 0371

Goodchild Marine Services
Great Yarmouth 01493 782301

Goodwick Marine
Fishguard 01348 873955

Gosport Marina 023 9252 4811

Griffins Garage Dingle Marina,
Co Kerry +353 66 91 51178

Hale Marine, Ron
Portsmouth 023 9273 2985

Hamnavoe Engineering
Stromness 01856 850576

Harbour Engineering
Itchenor 01243 513454

Hartlepool Marine Engineering
Hartlepool 01429 867883

Hayles, Harold
Yarmouth 01983 760373

Herm Seaway Marine Ltd
St Peter Port 01481 726829

HNP Engineers (Lerwick Ltd)
Lerwick 01595 692493

Hodges, T
Coleraine 028 7035 6422

Home Marine Emsworth Yacht
Harbour, Emsworth 01243 374125

Hook Marine Ltd Troon 01292 679500

Humphrey, Chris
Teignmouth 01626 772324

Instow Marine Services
Bideford 01271 861081

Jones (Boatbuilders), David
Chester 01244 390363

Keating Marine Engineering Ltd, Bill
Jersey 01534 733977

Kingston Marine Services
Cowes 01983 299385

Kippford Slipway Ltd
Dalbeattie 01556 620249

Lansdale Pannell Marine
Chichester 01243 512374

Lencraft Boats Ltd
Dungarvan +353 58 68220

Llyn Marine Services
Pwllheli 01758 612606

Lynx Engineering
St Helens, Isle of Wight 01983 873711

M&G Marine Services
Mayflower International Marina,
Plymouth 01752 563345

MacDonald & Co Ltd, JN
Glasgow 0141 810 3400

Mackay Marine Services
Aberdeen 01224 575772

Mainbrayce Marine
Alderney 01481 722772

Malakoff and Moore
Lerwick 01595 695544

Mallaig Boat Building and Engineering
Mallaig 01687 462304

Marindus Engineering
Kilmore Quay +353 53 29794

Marine Engineering Looe
Brixham 01803 844777

Marine Engineering Looe
Looe 01503 263009

Marine Engineering Services
Port Dinorwic 01248 671215

Marine General Engineers Beaucette
Marina, Guernsey 01481 245808

Marine Propulsion
Hayling Island 07836 737488

Marine & General Engineers
St. Sampsons Harbour, Guernsey
 01481 245808

Marine-Trak Engineering
Mylor Yacht Harbour
Falmouth 01326 376588

Marine Warehouse
Gosport 023 9258 0420

Marlec Marine
Ramsgate 01843 592176

Martin Outboards
Galgate 01524 751750

Meiher, Denis
Fenit +353 87 958 4744

MES Marine Greenock 01475 744655

MMS Ardrossan 01294 604831

Mobile Marine Engineering Liverpool
Marina, Liverpool 01565 733553

Mount's Bay Engineering
Newlyn 01736 363095

MP Marine Maryport 01900 810299

New World Yacht Care
Helensburgh 01436 820586

North Western Automarine Engineers
Largs 01475 687139

Noss Marine Services Dart Marina,
Dartmouth 01803 833343

Owen Marine, Robert
Porthmadog 01766 513435

Pace, Andy Newhaven 01273 516010

Penzance Dry Dock and Engineering
Co Ltd Penzance 01736 363838

Pirie & Co, John S
Fraserburgh 01346 513314

Portavon Marine
Keynsham 0117 986 1626

Power Afloat, Elkins Boatyard
Christchurch 01202 489555

Powerplus Marine Cowes Yacht Haven,
Cowes 01983 290421

Pro-Marine Queen Anne's Battery
Marina, Plymouth 01752 267984

PT Marine Engineering
Hayling Island 023 9246 9332

R & M Marine
Portsmouth 023 9273 7555

R & S Engineering
Dingle Marina +353 66 915 1189

Reddish Marine
Salcombe 01548 844094

RHP Marine Cowes 01983 290421

River Tees Engineering & Welding Ltd
Middlesbrough 01642 226226

RK Marine Ltd Hamble 01489 583585

RK Marine Ltd
Swanwick 01489 583572

Rossiter Yachts Ltd
Christchurch 01202 483250

MARINA SUPPLIES AND SERVICES GUIDE

Ryan & Roberts Marine Services	
Askeaton	+353 61 392198

Salve Marine Ltd
Crosshaven   +353 21 4831145

Seamark-Nunn & Co
Felixstowe   01394 275327

Seapower Ipswich   01473 780090

Seaward Engineering
Glasgow   0141 632 4910

Seaway Marine
Gosport   023 9260 2722

Shearwater Engineering Services Ltd
Dunoon   01369 706666

Silvers Marina Ltd
Helensburgh   01436 831222

Starey Marine
Salcombe   01548 843655

Tarbert Marine
Arbroath   01241 872879

Thorne Boat Services
Thorne   01405 814197

Tollesbury Marine Engineering
Tollesbury Marina   01621 869919

Tony's Marine Service
Coleraine   028 7035 6422

TOR (Gerald Hales)
Stornoway   01851 871025

Vasey Marine Engineering, Gordon
Fareham   07798 638625

Volspec Ltd
Tollesbury   01621 869756

Wallis, Peter Torquay Marina,
Torquay   01803 844777

WB Marine Chichester   01243 512857

West Coast Marine
Troon   01292 318121

West Marine
Brighton   01273 626656

Weymouth Marina Mechanical Services
Weymouth   01305 779379

Whittington, G Lady Bee Marine,
Shoreham   01273 593801

Whitewater Marine
Malahide   +353 1 816 8473

Wigmore Wright Marine Services
Penarth Marina   029 2070 9983

Wright, M Manaccan   01326 231502

Wyko Industrial Services
Inverness   01463 224747

Ynys Marine
Cardigan   01239 613179

Youngboats
Faversham   01795 536176

1° West Marine Ltd
Portsmouth   023 9283 8335

MASTS, SPARS & RIGGING

JWS Marine Services
Portsmouth   02392 755155

A2 Rigging
Falmouth   01326 312209

Allspars Plymouth   01752 266766

Amble Boat Co Ltd
Morpeth   01665 710267

Arun Canvas & Rigging
Littlehampton   01903 732561

B+ St Peter Port   01481 726071

Buchanan, Keith
St Mary's   01720 422037

Bussell & Co, WL
Weymouth   01305 785633

Carbospars Ltd
Hamble   023 8045 6736

Cable & Rope Works
Bexhill-on-Sea   0101424 220112

Clarke Rigging, Niall
Coleraine   07916 083858

Coates Marine Ltd
Whitby   01947 604486

Dauntless Boatyard Ltd
Canvey Island   01268 793782

Davies Marine Services
Ramsgate   01843 586172

Eurospars Ltd
Plymouth   01752 550550

Exe Leisure
Exeter   01392 879055

Fox's Marine Ipswich Ltd
Ipswich   01473 689111

Freeland Yacht Spars Ltd
Dorchester on Thames 01865 341277

Gordon, AD Portland   01305 821569

Grimsby Rigging Services Ltd
Grimsby   01472 362758

Hamble Custom Rigging Centre
Hamble   023 8045 2000

Harris Rigging Totnes 01803 840160

Heyn Engineering
Belfast   028 9035 0022

Holman Rigging
Chichester   01243 514000

Irish Spars and Rigging
Malahide   +353 86 209 5996

JWS Marine Services
Portsmouth   02392 755155

Kildale Marine Hull   01482 227464

Lowestoft Yacht Services
Lowestoft   01502 585535

Laverty, Billy Galway +353 86 3892614

Leitch, WB
Tarbert, Loch Fyne   01880 820287

Lewis, Harry
Kinsale   +353 87 266 7127

Marine Resource Centre
Oban   01631 720291

Martin Leaning Masts & Rigging
Hayling   023 9237 1157

Mast & Rigging
Crosshaven   +353 21 483 3878

Mast & Rigging Services
Largs   01475 670110

Mast & Rigging Services
Inverkip   01475 522700

MP Marine Maryport   01900 810299

Ocean Rigging
Lymington   01590 676292

Owen Sails Oban   01631 720485

Pro Rig S Ireland   +353 87 298 3333

Ratsey, Stephen
Milford Haven   01646 601561

RigIt Ardrossan   07593 220213

Rig Magic Ipswich   01473 655089

Rig Shop
Southampton   023 8033 8341

Roberts Marine Ltd, S
Liverpool   0151 707 8300

Ronstan
Gosport   023 9252 5377

Salcombe Boatstore
Salcombe   01548 843708

Seldén Mast Ltd
Gosport   01329 504000

Silvers Marina Ltd
Helensburgh   01436 831222

Silverwood Yacht Services Ltd
Portsmouth   023 9232 7067

Spencer Rigging
Cowes   01983 292022

Storrar Marine Store
Newcastle upon Tyne 0191 266 1037

Tedfords Rigging & Rafts
Belfast   028 9032 6763

TJ Rigging Conwy   07780 972411

TS Rigging Malden   01621 874861

Windjammer Marine
Milford Marina   01646 699070

NAVIGATION EQUIPMENT – SAILMAKERS & REPAIRS

Yacht Rigging Services
Plymouth 01752 226609

Yacht Shop, The
Fleetwood 01253 879238

Z Spars UK Hadleigh 01473 822130

NAVIGATION EQUIPMENT – GENERAL

Belson Design Ltd, Nick
Southampton 077 6835 1330

Brown Son & Ferguson Ltd
Glasgow 0141 429 1234

Cooke & Son Ltd, B
Hull 01482 223454

Diverse Yacht Services
Hamble 023 8045 3399

Dolphin Maritime Software Ltd
Lancaster 01524 841946

Dubois Phillips & McCallum Ltd
Liverpool 0151 236 2776

Garmin
Southampton 02380 524000

Geonav UK Ltd
Poole 0870 240 4575

Imray Laurie Norie and Wilson Ltd
St Ives, Cambs 01480 462114

Kelvin Hughes
Southampton 023 8063 4911

Lilley & Gillie Ltd, John
North Shields 0191 257 2217

Marine Chart Services
Wellingborough 01933 441629

Navico UK Romsey 01794 510010

PC Maritime Plymouth 01752 254205

Price & Co, WF Bristol 0117 929 2229

Raymarine Ltd
Portsmouth 023 9269 3611

Royal Institute of Navigation
London 020 7591 3130

Sea Chest Nautical Bookshop
Plymouth 01752 222012

Seath Instruments (1992) Ltd
Lowestoft 01502 573811

Smith (Marine) Ltd, AM
London 020 8529 6988

South Bank Marine Charts Ltd
Grimsby 01472 361137

Southcoasting Navigators
Devon 01626 335626

Stanford Charts
Bristol 0117 929 9966

London 020 7836 1321
Manchester 0870 890 3730

Todd Chart Agency Ltd
County Down 028 9146 6640

UK Hydrographic Office
Taunton 01823 337900

Warsash Nautical Bookshop
Warsash 01489 572384

Yachting Instruments Ltd
Sturminster Newton 01258 817662

PAINT & OSMOSIS

Advanced Blast Cleaning Paint
Tavistock 01822 617192
  07970 407911

Herm Seaway Marine Ltd
St Peter Port 01481 726829

Gillingham Marina 01634 280022

Hempel Paints
Southampton 02380 232000

International Coatings Ltd
Southampton 023 8022 6722

Marineware Ltd
Southampton 023 8033 0208

NLB Marine
Ardrossan 01563 521509

Pro-Boat Ltd
Burnham on Crouch 01621 785455

Rustbuster Ltd
Peterborough 0870 9090093

Smith & Son Ltd, EC
Luton 01582 729721

SP Systems
Isle of Wight 01983 828000

PROPELLERS & STERGEAR/REPAIRS

CJR Propulsion Ltd
Southampton 023 8063 9366

Darglow Engineering Ltd
Wareham 01929 556512

Propeller Revolutions
Poole 01202 671226

Sillette – Sonic Ltd
Sutton 020 8337 7543

Vetus Den Ouden Ltd
Southampton 02380 454507

RADIO COURSES / SCHOOLS

Bisham Abbey Sailing & Navigation School Bisham 01628 474960

East Coast Offshore Yachting – Les Rant Perry 01480 861381

Hamble School of Yachting
Hamble 023 8045 6687

Pembrokeshire Cruising
Neyland 01646 602500

Plymouth Sailing School
Plymouth 01752 493377

Southern Sailing
Swanwick 01489 575511

Start Point Sailing
Kingsbridge 01548 810917

REEFING SYSTEMS

Atlantic Spars Ltd
Brixham 01803 843322

Calibra Marine International Ltd
Southampton 08702 400358

Eurospars Ltd
Plymouth 01752 550550

Holman Rigging
Chichester 01243 514000

Navimo UK Ltd
Hedge End 01489 778850

Sea Teach Ltd
Emsworth 01243 375774

Southern Spar Services
Northam 023 8033 1714

Wragg, Chris
Lymington 01590 677052

Z Spars UK
Hadleigh 01473 822130

REPAIR MATERIALS & ACCESSORIES

Akeron Ltd
Southend on Sea 01702 297101

Howells & Son, KJ
Poole 01202 665724

JB Timber Ltd
North Ferriby 01482 631765

Robbins Timber
Bristol 0117 9633136

Sika Ltd
Welwyn Garden City 01707 394444

Solent Composite Systems
East Cowes 01983 292602

Technix Rubber & Plastics Ltd
Southampton 01489 789944

Tiflex Liskeard 01579 320808

Timage & Co Ltd
Braintree 01376 343087

MARINA SUPPLIES AND SERVICES GUIDE

Trade Grade Products Ltd
Poole   01202 820177
Wessex Resins & Adhesives Ltd
Romsey   01794 521111

ROPE & WIRE

Cable & Rope Works
Bexhill-on-Sea   01424 220112
Euro Rope Ltd
Scunthorpe   01724 280480
Marlow Ropes
Hailsham   01323 444444
Mr Splice Leicester   0800 1697178
Spinlock Ltd Cowes   01983 295555
TJ Rigging Conwy   07780 972411

SAFETY EQUIPMENT

AB Marine Ltd
St Peter Port   01481 722378
Adec Marine Ltd
Croydon   020 8686 9717
Anchorwatch UK
Edinburgh   0131 447 5057
Avon Inflatables
Llanelli   01554 882000
Cosalt International Ltd
Aberdeen   01224 588327
Crewsaver Gosport   01329 820000
Glaslyn Marine Supplies Ltd
Porthmadog   01766 513545
Exposure Lights
Pulborough   01798 839300
Guardian Fire Protection
Manchester   0800 358 7522
Hale Marine, Ron
Portsmouth   023 9273 2985
Herm Seaway Marine Ltd
St Peter Port   01481 722838
IBS Boats South Woodham Ferrers
                     01245 323211/425551
KTS Seasafety Kilkeel   028 41762655
McMurdo Pains Wessex
Portsmouth   023 9262 3900
Met Office Bracknell   0845 300 0300
Nationwide Marine Hire
Warrington   01925 245788
Norwest Marine Ltd
Liverpool   0151 207 2860
Ocean Safety
Southampton   023 8072 0800
Navimo UK Ltd
Romsey   01794 526800
Polymarine Ltd
Conwy   01492 583322

Premium Liferaft Services
Burnham-on-Crouch   0800 243673
Ribeye Dartmouth   01803 832060
South Eastern Marine Services Ltd
Basildon   01268 534427
Suffolk Sailing
Ipswich   01473 604678
Whitstable Marine
Whitstable   01227 262525
Winters Marine Ltd
Salcombe   01548 843580

SAILMAKERS & REPAIRS

Allison-Gray
Dundee   01382 505888
Alsop Sailmakers, John
Salcombe   01548 843702
AM Trimming Windsor   01932 821090
Arun Canvas & Rigging
Littlehampton   01903 732561
Arun Sails Chichester   01243 573185
Bank Sails, Bruce
Southampton   01489 582444
Barrett, Katy
St Peter Port   07781 404299
Batt Sails Bosham   01243 575505
Bissett and Ross
Aberdeen   01224 580659
Boatshed, The
Felinheli, Bangor   01248 679939
Breaksea Sails Barry   01446 730785
Bristol Sails Bristol   0117 922 5080
Buchanan, Keith
St Mary's   01720 422037
C&J Marine Textiles
Chichester   01243 782629
Calibra Sails
Dartmouth   01803 833094
Clarke Rigging, Niall
Coleraine   07916 083858
Coastal Covers
Portsmouth   023 9252 0200
Covercare Fareham   01329 311878
Covers + Stuff
Douglas, Isle of Man   07624 400037
Crawford, Margaret
Kirkwall   01856 875692
Crusader Sails Poole   01202 670580
Crystal Covers
Portsmouth   023 9238 0143
Cullen Sailmakers
Galway   +353 91 771991
Dolphin Sails Harwich   01255 243366
Doyle Sails
Southampton   023 8033 2622

Downer International Sails & Chandlery
Dun Laoghaire   +353 1 280 0231
Duthie Marine Safety, Arthur
Glasgow   0141 429 4553
Dynamic Sails
Emsworth   01243 374495
Flew Sailmakers
Portchester   01329 822676
Fylde Coast Sailmaking Co
Fleetwood   01253 873476
Freeman Sails
Padstow   07771 610053
Garland Sails Bristol   01275 393473
Goacher Sails
Cumbria   01539 488686
Gowen Ocean Sailmakers
West Mersea   01206 384412
Green Sailmakers, Paul
Plymouth   01752 660317
Henderson Sails & Covers
Southsea   023 9229 4700
Hood Sailmakers
Lymington   01590 675011
Hooper, A Plymouth   01752 830411
Hyde Sails
Southampton   0845 543 8945
Jackson Yacht Services
Jersey   01534 743819
Jeckells and Son Ltd (Wroxham)
Wroxham   01603 782223
Jessail Ardrossan   01294 467311
JKA Sailmakers
Pwllheli   01758 613266
Kemp Sails Ltd
Wareham   01929 554308/554378
Kildale Marine
Hull   01482 227464
Lawrence Sailmakers, J
Brightlingsea   01206 302863
Leitch, WB
Tarbert, Loch Fyne   01880 820287
Leith UK
Berwick on Tweed   01289 307264
Le Monnier, Yannick
Galway   +353 87 628 9854
Lodey Sails Newlyn   01736 719359
Lossie Sails
Lossiemouth   07989 956698
Lucas Sails Portchester   023 9237 3699
Malakoff and Moore
Lerwick   01595 695544
McCready and Co Ltd, J
Belfast   028 90232842

SAILMAKERS & REPAIRS – TUITION/SAILING SCHOOLS

McKillop Sails, John
Kingsbridge   01548 852343

McNamara Sails, Michael
Great Yarmouth   01692 584186

McWilliam Sailmaker (Crosshaven)
Crosshaven   +353 21 4831505

Sail Shape
Fowey   01726 833731

Montrose Rope and Sails
Montrose   01674 672657

Mountfield Sails
Hayling Island   023 9246 3720

Mouse Sails Holyhead   01407 763636

Nicholson Hughes Sails
Rosneath   01436 831356

North Sea Sails
Tollesbury   01621 869367

North West Sails
Keighley   01535 652949

Northrop Sails
Ramsgate   01843 851665

O'Mahony Sailmakers
Kinsale   +353 86 326 0018

O'Sullivans Marine Ltd
Tralee   +353 66 7129635

Owen Sails Benderloch 01631 720485

Parker & Kay Sailmakers –
East Ipswich   01473 659878

Parker & Kay Sailmakers –
South Hamble   023 8045 8213

Penrose Sailmakers
Falmouth   01326 312705

Pinnell & Bax
Northampton   01604 592808

Pollard Marine
Port St Mary   01624 835831

Quantum Sails
Ipswich Haven Marina   01473 659878

Quantum-Parker & Kay Sailmakers
Hamble   023 8045 8213

Quay Sails (Poole) Ltd
Poole   01202 681128

Ratsey & Lapthorn
Isle of Wight   01983 294051

Ratsey Sailmakers, Stephen
Milford Haven   01646 601561

Relling One Design
Portland   01305 826555

SO31 Bags
Southampton   023 8045 5106

Rig Shop, The
Southampton   023 8033 8341

Rockall Sails
Chichester   01243 573185

Sail Locker
Woolverstone Marina   01473 780206

Sail Style
Hayling Island   023 9246 3720

Sails & Canvas Exeter 01392 877527

Sail Register Ulceby   01469 589444

Saltern Sail Co
West Cowes   01983 280014

Saltern Sail Company
Yarmouth   01983 760120

Sanders Sails
Lymington   01590 673981

Saturn Sails Largs   01475 689933

Scott & Co, Graham
St Peter Port   01481 259380

Shore Sailmakers
Swanwick   01489 589450

SKB Sails Falmouth   01326 372107

Sketrick Sailmakers Ltd
Killinchy   028 9754 1400

Solo Sails Penzance   01736 366004

Storrar Marine Store
Newcastle upon Tyne   0191 266 1037

Suffolk Sails
Woodbridge   01394 386323

Sunset Sails Sligo   +353 71 62792

Torquay Marina Sails and Canvas
Exeter   01392 877527

Trident UK Gateshead 0191 490 1736

UK McWilliam Cowes   01983 281100

Underwood Sails
Queen Anne's Battery
Plymouth   01752 229661

W Sails Leigh-on-Sea   01702 714550

Warren Hall
Beaucette, Guernsey   07781 444280

Watson Sails Dublin   +353 1 846 2206

WB Leitch and Son
Tarbert   01880 820287

Westaway Sails
Plymouth Yacht Haven   01752 892560

Wilkinson Sails
Burnham-on-Crouch   01621 786770

Wilkinson Sails
Teynham   01795 521503

Yacht Shop, The
Fleetwood   01253 879238

SOLAR POWER

Ampair Ringwood   01425 480780

Barden UK Ltd Fareham 01489 570770

Marlec Engineering Co Ltd
Corby   01536 201588

SPRAYHOODS & DODGERS

A & B Textiles
Gillingham   01634 579686

Allison–Gray Dundee   01382 505888

Arton, Charles
Milford-on-Sea   01590 644682

Arun Canvas and Rigging Ltd
Littlehampton   01903 732561

Boatshed, The
Felinheli, Bangor   01248 679939

Buchanan, Keith
St Mary's   01720 422037

C & J Marine Textiles
Chichester   01243 785485

Covercare Fareham   01329 311878

Covercraft
Southampton   023 8033 8286

Crystal Covers
Portsmouth   023 9238 0143

Jeckells and Son Ltd
Wroxham   01603 782223

Jessail Ardrossan   01294 467311

Lomond Boat Covers
Alexandria   01389 602734

Lucas Sails Portchester 023 9237 3699

Poole Canvas Co Ltd
Poole   01202 677477

Sail Register
Ulceby   01469 589444

Saunderrsfoot Auto Marine
Saundersfoot   01834 812115

Trident UK Gateshead 0191 490 1736

SURVEYORS AND NAVAL ARCHITECTS

Amble Boat Company Ltd
Amble   01665 710267

Ark Surveys East Anglia/South Coast
               01621 857065/01794 521957

Atkin & Associates
Lymington   01590 688633

MARINA SUPPLIES AND SERVICES GUIDE

Barbican Yacht Agency Ltd Plymouth	01752 228855
Battick, Lee St Helier	01534 611143
Booth Marine Surveys, Graham Birchington-on-Sea	01843 843793
Byrde & Associates Kimmeridge	01929 480064
Bureau Maritime Ltd Maldon	01621 859181
Byrde & Associates Kimmeridge	01929 480064
Cannell & Associates, David M Wivenhoe	01206 823337
Cardiff Commercial Boat Operators Ltd Cardiff	029 2037 7872
Clarke Designs LLP, Owen Dartmouth	01803 770495
Cox, David Penryn	01326 340808
Davies, Peter N Wivenhoe	01206 823289
Down Marine Co Ltd Belfast	028 90480247
Evans, Martin Kirby le Soken	07887 724055
Goodall, JL Whitby	01947 604791
Green, James Plymouth	01752 660516
Greening Naval Architect Ltd, David Salcombe	01548 842000
Hansing & Associates North Wales/Midlands	01248 671291
JP Services – Marine Safety & Training Chichester	01243 537552
MacGregor, WA Felixstowe	01394 676034
Mahoney & Co, KPO Co Cork	+353 21 477 6150
Marinte Surveys UK Emsworth	07798 554535
Marintec Lymington	01590 683414
Norwood Marine Margate	01843 835711
Quay Consultants Ltd West Wittering	01243 673056
Scott Marine Surveyors & Consultants Conwy	01492 573001
S Roberts Marine Ltd Liverpool	0151 707 8300
Staton-Bevan, Tony Lymington	01590 645755/ 07850 315744
Thomas, Stephen Southampton	023 8048 6273
Towler, Perrin Lymington	01590 718087
Victoria Yacht Surveys Cornwall	0800 083 2113
Ward & McKenzie Woodbridge	01394 383222
Ward & McKenzie (North East) Pocklington	01759 304322
YDSA Yacht Designers & Surveyors Association Bordon	0845 0900162

TAPE TECHNOLOGY

CC Marine Services (Rubbaweld) Ltd London	020 7402 4009
Trade Grade Products Ltd Poole	01202 820177
UK Epoxy Resins Burscough	01704 892364
3M United Kingdom plc Bracknell	01344 858315

TRANSPORT/YACHT DELIVERIES

Boat Shifters	07733 344018/01326 210548
Convoi Exceptionnel Ltd Hamble	023 8045 3045
Debbage Yachting Ipswich	01473 601169
East Coast Offshore Yachting	01480 861381
Forrest Marine Exeter	08452 308335
Hainsworth's UK and Continental Bingley	01274 565925
Houghton Boat Transport Tewkesbury	07831 486710
MCL Transboat	08455 201900
Moonfleet Sailing Poole	01202 682269
Performance Yachting Plymouth	01752 565023
Peters & May Ltd Southampton	023 8048 0480
Reeder School of Seamanship, Mike Lymington	01590 674560
Seafix Boat Transfer North Wales	01766 514507
Sealand Boat Deliveries Ltd Liverpool	01254 705225
Shearwater Sailing Southampton	01962 775213
Southcoasting Navigators Devon	01626 335626
West Country Boat Transport	01566 785651
Wolff, David	07659 550131

TUITION/SAILING SCHOOLS

Association of Scottish Yacht Charterers Argyll	07787 363562 01852 200258
Bisham Abbey Sailing & Navigation School Bisham	01628 474960
Blue Baker Yachts Ipswich	01473 780008
Britannia Sailing (East Coast) Ipswich	01473 787019
British Offshore Sailing School Hamble	023 8045 7733
Coastal Sea School Weymouth	0870 321 3271
Dart Harbour Sea School Dartmouth	01803 839339
Dartmouth Sailing Dartmouth	01803 833399
Drake Sailing School Plymouth	01635 253009
East Anglian Sea School Ipswich	01473 659992
East Coast Offshore Yachting – Les Rant Perry	01480 861381
Gibraltar Sailing Centre Gibraltar	+350 78554
Glenans Irish Sailing School Baltimore	+353 28 20154
Hamble School of Yachting Hamble	023 8045 6687
Haslar Sea School Gosport	023 9252 0099
Hobo Yachting Southampton	023 8033 4574
Hoylake Sailing School Wirral	0151 632 4664
Ibiza Sailing School	07092 235 853
International Yachtmaster Academy Southampton	0800 515439
Island Sea School Port Dinorwic	01248 352330
JP Services – Marine Safety & Training Chichester	01243 537552

MARINA GUIDE 2018

NOT ON COMPARISON WEBSITES!

The Specialists

See how much you can save in an instant

craftinsure.com

- Cruising yachts
- Motor cruisers
- Narrowboats
- RIBs
- Speedboats
- Racing dinghies
- Dayboats and keelboats
- Small craft
- Sailboards

Top Quality Boat Insurance for complete peace of mind

The UK's first online boat insurance provider.

Created by boating people for those who love their boats!

- Quick and easy online quotations and cover
- 24 hour claims help line and simple online claims tracking
- Monthly payments for premiums over £100 at NO EXTRA COST!
- £5,000,000 Third Party liability cover
- Multi-boat insurance discounts – insure two or more boats for less
- Underwritten by Navigators & General
  a trading name of Zurich Insurance plc

Read what our customers have to say about us:

"Very impressed with the ease of purchasing and the excellent customerservice!" – BJ

"Your company provides excellent value and service. Claims service is fast and efficient. Would recommend to anyone" – PB

"Unbelievably fast, hassle free, no jargon. In a word, it's TERRIFIC" – AH

"The most efficient insurance company I have used. – IC

"I must say that I found your website the easiest I have ever used" – BB

www.craftinsure.com
or call: 03452 607888

Authorised and regulated by the Financial Conduct Authority

MARINA SUPPLIES AND SERVICES GUIDE

Lymington Cruising School
Lymington 01590 677478

Marine Leisure Association (MLA)
Southampton 023 8029 3822

Menorca Cruising School
  01995 679240

Moonfleet Sailing
Poole 01202 682269

National Marine Correspondence School Macclesfield 01625 262365

Pembrokeshire Cruising
Neyland 01646 602500

Performance Yachting & Chandlery
Plymouth 01752 565023

Plain Sailing
Dartmouth 01803 853843

Plymouth Sailing School
Plymouth 01752 493377

Port Edgar Marina & Sailing School
Port Edgar 0131 331 3330

Portsmouth Outdoor Centre
Portsmouth 023 9266 3873

Portugal Sail & Power 01473 833001

Safe Water Training Sea School Ltd
Wirral 0151 630 0466

Sail East
Felixstowe 01255 502887

Sail East
River Crouch 07860 271954

Sail East
River Medway 07932 157027

Sail East Harwich 01473 689344

Sally Water Training
East Cowes 01983 299033

Sea-N-Shore
Salcombe 01548 842276

Seafever
East Grinstead 01342 316293

Solaris Mediterranean Sea School
  01925 642909

Solent School of Yachting
Southampton 023 8045 7733

Southcoasting Navigators
Devon 01626 335626

Southern Sailing
Southampton 01489 575511

Start Point Sailing
Dartmouth 01548 810917

Sunsail
Port Solent/Largs 0870 770 6314

Team Sailing Gosport 023 9252 4370

Workman Marine School
Portishead 01275 845844

Wride School of Sailing, Bob
North Ferriby 01482 635623

WATERSIDE ACCOMMODATION & RESTAURANTS

Abbey, The Penzance 01736 366906
Al Porto Hull Marina 01482 238889
Arun View Inn, The
Littlehampton 01903 722335
Baywatch on the Beach
Bembridge 01983 873259
Beaucette Marina Restaurant
Guernsey 01481 247066
Bella Napoli
Brighton Marina 01273 818577
Bembridge Coast Hotel
Bembridge 01983 873931
Budock Vean Hotel
Porth Navas Creek 01326 252100
Café Mozart Cowes 01983 293681
Caffé Uno Port Solent 023 9237 5227
Chandlers Bar & Bistro
Queen Anne's Battery Marina
Plymouth 01752 257772
Chiquito Port Solent 02392 205070
Cruzzo Malahide Marina
Co Dublin +353 1 845 0599
Cullins Yard Bistro
Dover 01304 211666
Custom House, The
Poole 01202 676767
Dart Marina River Lounge
Dartmouth 01803 832580
Deer Leap, The
Exmouth 01395 265030
Doghouse Swanwick Marina,
Hamble 01489 571602
Dolphin Restaurant
Gorey 01534 853370
Doune Knoydart 01687 462667
El Puertos
Penarth Marina 029 2070 5551
Falmouth Marina Marine Bar and Restaurant
Falmouth 01326 313481
Ferry Boat Inn West Wick Marina
Nr Chelmsford 01621 740208
Ferry Inn, The (restaurant)
Pembroke Dock 01646 682947
First and Last, The Braye,
Alderney 01481 823162
Fisherman's Wharf
Sandwich 01304 613636
Folly Inn Cowes 01983 297171
Gaffs Restaurant
Fenit, County Kerry +353 66 71 36666

Godleys Hotel Fenit
County Kerry +353 66 71 36108
Harbour Lights Restaurant
Walton on the Naze 01255 851887
Haven Bar and Bistro, The
Lymington Yacht Haven 01590 679971
Haven Hotel Poole 08453 371550
HMS Ganges Restaurant
Mylor Yacht Harbour 01326 374320
Jolly Sailor, The
Bursledon 023 8040 5557
Kames Hotel Argyll 01700 811489
Ketch Rigger, The Hamble Point
Marina Hamble 023 8045 5601
Kings Arms Stoborough 01929 552705
Kota Restaurant
Porthleven 01326 562407
La Cala Lady Bee Marina
Shoreham 01273 597422
Le Nautique
St Peter Port 01481 721714
Lighter Inn, The
Topsham 01392 875439
Mariners Bistro Sparkes Marina,
Hayling Island 023 9246 9459
Mary Mouse II Haslar Marina,
Gosport 023 9252 5200
Martha's Vineyard
Milford Haven 01646 697083
Master Builder's House Hotel
Buckler's Hard 01590 616253
Millstream Hotel
Bosham 01243 573234
Montagu Arms Hotel
Beaulieu 01590 612324
Oyster Quay Mercury Yacht Harbour,
Hamble 023 8045 7220
Paris Hotel Coverack 01326 280258
Pebble Beach, The
Gosport 023 9251 0789
Petit Champ Sark 01481 832046
Philip Leisure Group
Dartmouth 01803 833351
Priory Bay Hotel
Seaview, Isle of Wight 01983 613146
Quayside Hotel Brixham 01803 855751
Queen's Hotel Kirkwall 01856 872200
Sails Dartmouth 01803 839281
Shell Bay Seafood Restaurant
Poole Harbour 01929 450363
Simply Italian Sovereign Harbour,
Eastbourne 01323 470911
Spinnaker, The
Chichester Marina 01243 511032
Spit Sand Fort
The Solent 01329 242077
Steamboat Inn
Lossiemouth 01343 812066

MARINA GUIDE 2018 123

WATERSIDE ACCOMMODATION & RESTAURANTS – YACHT CLUBS

Tayvallich Inn, The
Argyll   01546 870282
Villa Adriana Newhaven Marina
Newhaven   01273 513976
Warehouse Brasserie, The
Poole   01202 677238
36 on the Quay
Emsworth   01243 375592

WEATHER INFORMATION

Met Office Exeter   0870 900 0100

WOOD FITTINGS

Howells & Son, KJ
Poole   01202 665724
Onward Trading Co Ltd
Southampton   01489 885250
Robbins Timber
Bristol   0117 963 3136
Sheraton Marine Cabinet
Witney   01993 868275

YACHT BROKERS

ABC Powermarine
Beaumaris   01248 811413
ABYA Association of Brokers & Yacht
Agents Bordon   0845 0900162
Adur Boat Sales
Southwick   01273 596680
Ancasta International Boat Sales
Southampton   023 8045 0000
Anglia Yacht Brokerage
Bury St Edmunds   01359 271747
Ardmair Boat Centre
Ullapool   01854 612054
Barbican Yacht Agency, The
Plymouth   01752 228855
Bates Wharf Marine Sales Ltd
                      01932 571141
BJ Marine Bangor   028 9127 1434
Boatworks + Ltd
St Peter Port   01481 726071
Caley Marina Inverness 01463 236539
Calibra Marine International Ltd
Southampton   08702 400358
Camper & Nicholsons International
London   020 7009 1950
Clarke & Carter Interyacht Ltd
Ipswich/Burnham on Crouch
            01473 659681/01621 785600
Coastal Leisure Ltd
Southampton   023 8033 2222
Dale Sailing Brokerage
Neyland   01646 603105
Deacons
Southampton   023 8040 2253
Exe Leisure Topsham   001392 879055
Ferrypoint Boat Co
Youghal   +353 24 94232

Gweek Quay Boatyard
Helston   01326 221657
International Barge
& Yacht Brokers
Southampton   023 8045 5205
Iron Wharf Boatyard
Faversham   01795 537122
Jackson Yacht Services
Jersey   01534 743819
Kings Yacht Agency
Beaulieu   01590 616316
Kippford Slipway Ltd
Dalbeattie   01556 620249
Lencraft Boats Ltd
Dungarvan   +353 58 68220
Liberty Yachts Ltd
Plymouth   01752 227911
Lucas Yachting, Mike
Torquay   01803 212840
Network Yacht Brokers
Dartmouth   01803 834864
Network Yacht Brokers
Plymouth   01752 605377
New Horizon Yacht Agency
Guernsey   01481 726335
Oyster Brokerage Ltd
Ipswich   01473 602263
Pearn and Co, Norman
(Looe Boatyard) Looe 01503 262244
Performance Boat Company
Maidenhead   07768 464717
Peters Chandlery
Chichester   01243 511033
Portavon Marina
Keynsham   0117 986 1626
Prosser Marine Sales Ltd
Glasgow   0141 552 2005
Retreat BY Topsham   01392 874720
SD Marine Ltd
Southampton   023 8045 7278
Sea & Shore Ship Chandler
Dundee   01382 202666
South Pier Shipyard
St Helier   01534 711000
South West Yacht Brokers Group
Plymouth   01752 401421
Sunbird Marine Services
Fareham   01329 842613
Trafalgar Yacht Services
Fareham   01329 823577
Transworld Yachts
Hamble   023 8045 7704
Walton Marine Sales
Brighton   01273 670707
Portishead   01275 840132
Walton Marine Sales
Wroxham   01603 781178

Watson Marine, Charles
Hamble   023 8045 6505
Western Marine
Dublin   +353 1280 0321
Woodrolfe Brokerage
Maldon   01621 868494
Youngboats Faversham 01795 536176

YACHT CHARTERS & HOLIDAYS

Ardmair Boat Centre
Ullapool   01854 612054
Association of Scottish Yacht
Charterers Argyll   01880 820012
Blue Baker Yachts
Ipswich   01473 780111/780008
Camper & Nicholsons International
London   020 7009 1950
Coastal Leisure Ltd
Southampton   023 8033 2222
Crusader Yachting
Turkey   01732 867321
Dartmouth Sailing
Dartmouth   01803 833399
Dartmouth Yacht Charters
Kingswear   01803 752935
Doune Marine Mallaig 01687 462667
Four Seasons Yacht Charter
Gosport   023 9251 1789
Golden Black Sailing
Cornwall   01209 715757
Hamble Point Yacht Charters
Hamble   023 8045 7110
Haslar Marina & Victory Yacht Charters
Gosport   023 9252 0099
Indulgence Charters
Wendover   01296 696006
Liberty Yachts West Country, Greece,
Mallorca & Italy   01752 227911
Nautilus Yachting
Mediterranean & Caribbean
                      01732 867445
On Deck Sailing
Southampton   023 8063 9997
Patriot Charters & Sail School
Milford Haven   01437 741202
West Country Yachts
Plymouth   01752 606999
Falmouth   01326 212320
Puffin Yachts
Port Solent   01483 420728
Sailing Holidays Ltd
Mediterranean   020 8459 8787
Sailing Holidays in Ireland
Kinsale   +353 21 477 2927

MARINA SUPPLIES AND SERVICES GUIDE

Setsail Holidays
Greece, Turkey,
Croatia, Majorca   01787 310445
Shannon Sailing Ltd
Tipperary   +353 67 24499
Sleat Marine Services
Isle of Skye   01471 844216
Smart Yachts
Mediterranean   01425 614804
South West Marine Training
Dartmouth   01803 853843
Sovereign Sailingl
Kinsale   +353 87 6172555
Sunsail
Worldwide   0870 770 0102
Templecraft Yacht Charters
Lewes   01273 812333
TJ Sailing Gosport   07803 499691
Top Yacht Sailing Ltd
Havant   02392 347655
Victory Yacht Charters
Gosport   023 9252 0099
West Wales Yacht Charter
Pwllheli   07748 634869
39 North (Mediterranean)
Kingskerwell   07071 393939

YACHT CLUBS

Aberaeron YC
Aberdovey   01545 570077
Aberdeen and Stonehaven SC
Nr Inverurie   01569 764006
Aberdour BC   01383 860029
Abersoch Power BC
Abersoch   01758 712027
Aberystwyth BC
Aberystwyth   01970 624575
Aldeburgh YC   01728 452562
Alderney SC   01481 822959
Alexandra YC
Southend-on-Sea   01702 340363
Arklow SC   +353 402 33100
Arun YC Littlehampton   01903 716016
Axe YC Axemouth   01297 20043
Ayr Yacht and CC   01292 476034
Ballyholme YC Bangor   028 91271467
Baltimore SC   +353 28 20426
Banff SC   01464 820308
Bantry Bay SC   +353 27 51724
Barry YC   01446 735511
Beaulieu River SC
Brockenhurst   01590 616273
Bembridge SC
Isle of Wight   01983 872237
Benfleet YC
Canvey Island   01268 792278
**Blackpool and
Fleetwood YC**   01253 884205
Blackwater SC Maldon   01621 853923
Blundellsands SC   0151 929 2101
Bosham SC Chichester   01243 572341
Brading Haven YC
Isle of Wight   01983 872289
Bradwell CC   01621 892970
Bradwell Quay YC
Wickford   01268 890173
Brancaster Staithe SC   01485 210249
Brandy Hole YC
Hullbridge   01702 230320
Brightlingsea SC   01206 303275
Brighton Marina YC
Peacehaven   01273 818711
Bristol Avon SC   01225 873472
Bristol Channel YC
Swansea   01792 366000
Bristol Corinthian YC
Axbridge   01934 732033
Brixham YC   01803 853332
**Burnham Overy
Staithe SC**   01328 730961
Burnham-on-Crouch SC
    01621 782812
Burnham-on-Sea SC
Bridgwater   01278 792911
Burry Port YC   01554 833635
Cabot CC   01275 855207
Caernarfon SC (Menai Strait)
Caernarfon   01286 672861
Campbeltown SC   01586 552488
Island YC Canvey Island   01702 510360
Cardiff YC   029 2046 3697
Cardiff Bay YC   029 20226575
Carlingford Lough YC
Rostrevor   028 4173 8604
Carrickfergus SC
Whitehead   028 93 351402
Castle Cove SC
Weymouth   01305 783708
Castlegate Marine Club
Stockton on Tees   01642 583299
Chanonry SC Fortrose   01463 221415
Chichester Cruiser and Racing Club
    01483 770391
Chichester YC   01243 512918
Christchurch SC   01202 483150
Clyde CC Glasgow   0141 221 2774
Co Antrim YC
Carrickfergus   028 9337 2322
Cobnor Activities Centre Trust
    01243 572791
Coleraine YC   028 703 44503
Colne YC Brightlingsea   01206 302594
Conwy YC Deganwy   01492 583690
Coquet YC   01665 710367
Corrib Rowing & YC
Galway City   +353 91 564560
Cowes Combined Clubs
    01983 295744
Cowes Corinthian YC
Isle of Wight   01983 296333
Cowes Yachting   01983 280770
Cramond BC   0131 336 1356
Creeksea SC
Burnham-on-Crouch   01245 320578
Crookhaven SC   +353 87 2379997
Crouch YC
Burnham-on-Crouch   01621 782252
Dale YC   01646 636362
Dartmouth YC   01803 832305
Deben YC Woodbridge   01394 384440
Dell Quay SC Chichester   01243 514639
Dingle SC   +353 66 51984
Douglas Bay YC   01624 673965
Dovey YC
Aberdovey   01213 600008
Dun Laoghaire MYC   +353 1 288 938
Dunbar SC
Cockburnspath   01368 86287
East Antrim BC   028 28 277204
East Belfast YC   028 9065 6283
East Cowes SC   01983 531687
East Dorset SC Poole   01202 706111
East Lothian YC   01620 892698
Eastney Cruising Association
Portsmouth   023 92734103
Eling SC   023 80863987
Emsworth SC   01243 372850
Emsworth Slipper SC   01243 378881
Essex YC Southend   01702 478404
Exe SC (River Exe)
Exmouth   01395 264607
Eyott SC Mayland   01245 320703
Fairlie YC   01294 213940
Falmouth Town SC   01326 373915
Falmouth Watersports Association
Falmouth   01326 211223

YACHT CLUBS

Fareham Sailing & Motor BC
Fareham 01329 280738
Felixstowe Ferry SC 01394 283785
Findhorn YC Findhorn 01309 690247
Fishguard Bay YC
Lower Fishguard 01348 872866
Flushing SC Falmouth 01326 374043
Folkestone Yacht and Motor BC
Folkestone 01303 251574
Forth Corinthian YC
Haddington 0131 552 5939
Forth YCs Association
Edinburgh 0131 552 3006
Fowey Gallants SC 01726 832335
Foynes YC Foynes +353 69 91201
Galway Bay SC +353 91 794527
Glasson SC Lancaster 01524 751089
Glenans Irish Sailing School
 +353 1 6611481
Glenans Irish SC (Westport)
 +353 98 26046
Gosport CC Gosport 02392 586838
Gravesend SC 07538 326623
Greenwich YC London 020 8858 7339
Grimsby and Cleethorpes YC
Grimsby 01472 356678
Guernsey YC
St Peter Port 01481 725342
Hamble River SC
Southampton 023 80452070
Hampton Pier YC
Herne Bay 01227 364749
Hardway SC Gosport 023 9258 1875
Hartlepool YC 01429 233423
Harwich Town SC 01255 503200
Hastings and St Leonards YC
Hastings 01424 420656
Haven Ports YC
Woodbridge 01473 659658
Hayling Ferry SC; Locks SC
Hayling Island 023 80829833
Hayling Island SC 023 92463768
Helensburgh SC Rhu 01436 672778
Helensburgh 01436 821234
Helford River SC
Helston 01326 231006
Herne Bay SC 01227 375650
Highcliffe SC
Christchurch 01425 274874
Holyhead SC 01407 762526
Holywood YC 028 90423355
Hoo Ness YC Sidcup 01634 250052
Hornet SC Gosport 023 9258 0403
Howth YC +353 1 832 2141

Hoylake SC Wirral 0151 632 2616
Hullbridge YC 01702 231797
Humber Yawl Club 01482 667224
Hundred of Hoo SC 01634 250102
Hurlingham YC London 020 8788 5547
Hurst Castle SC 01590 645589
Hythe SC Southampton 02380 846563
Hythe & Saltwood SC 01303 265178
Ilfracombe YC 01271 863969
Iniscealtra SC
Limerick +353 61 338347
Invergordon BC 01349 893772
Irish CC +353 214870031
Island CC Salcombe 01548 531176
Island SC Isle of Wight 01983 296621
Island YC
Canvey Island 01268 510360
Isle of Bute SC
Rothesay 01700 502819
Isle of Man YC
Port St Mary 01624 832088
Itchenor SC Chichester 01243 512400
Keyhaven YC 01590 642165
Killyleagh YC 028 4482 8250
Kircubbin SC 028 4273 8422
Kirkcudbright SC 01557 331727
Langstone SC Havant 023 9248 4577
Largs SC Largs 01475 670000
Larne Rowing & SC 028 2827 4573
Lawrenny YC 01646 651212
Leigh-on-Sea SC 01702 476788
Lerwick BC 01595 696954
Lilliput SC Poole 01202 740319
Littlehampton Yacht Club
Littlehampton 01903 713990
Loch Ryan SC Stranraer 01776 706322
Lochaber YC
Fort William 01397 772361
Locks SC Portsmouth 023 9282 9833
Looe SC 01503 262559
Lossiemouth CC
Fochabers 01348 812121
Lough Swilly YC Fahn +353 74 22377
Lowestoft CC 07810 522515
Lyme Regis Power BC 01297 443788
Lyme Regis SC 01297 442373
Lymington Town SC 0159 674514
Lympstone SC Exeter 01395 278792
Madoc YC Porthmadog 01766 512976
Malahide YC +353 1 845 3372

Maldon Little Ship Club
 01621 854139
Manx Sailing & CC
Ramsey 01624 813494
Marchwood YC 023 80666141
Margate YC 01843 292602
Marina BC Pwllheli 01758 612271
Maryport YC 01228 560865
Mayflower SC Plymouth 01752 662526
Mayo SC (Rosmoney)
Rosmoney +353 98 27772
Medway YC Rochester 01634 718399
Menai Bridge BC
Beaumaris 01248 810583
Mengham Rythe SC
Hayling Island 023 92463337
Merioneth YC
Barmouth 01341 280000
Monkstone Cruising and SC
Swansea 01792 812229
Montrose SC Montrose 01674 672554
Mumbles YC Swansea 01792 369321
Mylor YC Falmouth 01326 374391
Nairn SC 01667 453897
National YC
Dun Laoghaire +353 1 280 5725
Netley SC Netley 023 80454272
New Quay YC
Aberdovey 01545 560516
Newhaven & Seaford SC
Seaford 01323 890077
Newport and Uskmouth SC
Cardiff 01633 271417
Newtownards SC 028 9181 3426
Neyland YC 01646 600267
North Devon YC
Bideford 01271 861390
North Fambridge Yacht Centre
 01621 740370
North Haven YC Poole 01202 708830
North of England Yachting Association
Kirkwall 01856 872331
North Sunderland Marine Club
Sunderland 01665 721231
North Wales CC
Conwy 01492 593481
North West Venturers YC (Beaumaris)
Beaumaris 0161 2921943
Oban SC Ledaig by Oban
 01631 563999
Orford SC Woodbridge 01394 450997
Orkney SC Kirkwall 01856 872331

MARINA SUPPLIES AND SERVICES GUIDE

Orwell YC	Ipswich	01473 602288
Oulton Broad Yacht Station		01502 574946
Ouse Amateur SC	Kings Lynn	01553 772239
Paignton SC	Paignton	01803 525817
Parkstone YC	Poole	01202 743610
Peel Sailing and CC	Peel	01624 842390
Pembroke Haven YC		01646 684403
Pembrokeshire YC	Milford Haven	01646 692799
Penarth YC		029 20708196
Pentland Firth YC	Thurso	01847 891803
Penzance YC		01736 364989
Peterhead SC	Ellon	01779 75527
Pin Mill SC	Woodbridge	01394 780271
Plym YC	Plymouth	01752 404991
Poolbeg YC		+353 1 660 4681
Poole YC		01202 672687
Porlock Weir SC	Watchet	01643 862702
Port Edgar YC	Penicuik	0131 657 2854
Port Navas YC	Falmouth	01326 340065
Port of Falmouth Sailing Association	Falmouth	01326 372927
Portchester SC	Portchester	023 9237 6375
Porthcawl Harbour BC	Swansea	01656 655935
Porthmadog SC	Porthmadog	01766 513546
Portrush YC	Portrush	028 7082 3932
Portsmouth SC		02392 820596
Prestwick SC	Prestwick	01292 671117
Pwllheli SC	Pwllheli	01758 613343
Queenborough YC	Queenborough	01795 663955
Quoile YC	Downpatrick	028 44 612266
R Towy BC	Tenby	01267 241755
RAFYC		023 80452208
Redclyffe YC	Poole	01929 557227
Restronguet SC	Falmouth	01326 374536
Ribble CC	Lytham St Anne's	01253 739983
River Wyre YC		01253 811948
RNSA (Plymouth)		01752 55123/83
Rochester CC		01634 841350
Rock Sailing and Water Ski Club	Wadebridge	01208 862431
Royal Dart YC	Dartmouth	01803 752496
Royal Motor YC	Poole	01202 707227
Royal Anglesey YC (Beaumaris)	Anglesey	01248 810295
Royal Burnham YC	Burnham-on-Crouch	01621 782044
Royal Channel Islands YC (Jersey)	St Aubin	01534 745783
Royal Cinque Ports YC	Dover	01304 206262
Royal Corinthian YC (Burnham-on-Crouch)	Burnham-on-Crouch	01621 782105
Royal Corinthian YC (Cowes)	Cowes	01983 293581
Royal Cork YC	Crosshaven	+353 214 831023
Royal Cornwall YC (RCYC)	Falmouth	01326 312126
Royal Dorset YC	Weymouth	01305 786258
Royal Forth YC	Edinburgh	0131 552 3006
Royal Fowey YC	Fowey	01726 833573
Royal Gourock YC		01475 632983
Royal Highland YC	Nairn	01667 493855
Royal Irish YC	Dun Laoghaire	+353 1 280 9452
Royal London YC	Isle of Wight	019 83299727
Royal Lymington YC		01590 672677
Royal Mersey YC	Birkenhead	0151 645 3204
Royal Motor YC	Poole	01202 707227
Royal Naval Club and Royal Albert YC	Portsmouth	023 9282 5924
Royal Naval Sailing Association	Gosport	023 9252 1100
Royal Norfolk & Suffolk YC	Lowestoft	01502 566726
Royal North of Ireland YC		028 90 428041
Royal Northern and Clyde YC	Rhu	01436 820322
Royal Northumberland YC	Blyth	01670 353636
Royal Plymouth Corinthian YC	Plymouth	01752 664327
Royal Scottish Motor YC		0141 881 1024
Royal Solent YC	Yarmouth	01983 760256
Royal Southampton YC	Southampton	023 8022 3352
Royal Southern YC	Southampton	023 8045 0300
Royal St George YC	Dun Laoghaire	+353 1 280 1811
Royal Tay YC	Dundee	01382 477133
Royal Temple YC	Ramsgate	01843 591766
Royal Torbay YC	Torquay	01803 292006
Royal Ulster YC	Bangor	028 91 270568
Royal Victoria YC	Fishbourne	01983 882325
Royal Welsh YC (Caernarfon)	Caernarfon	01286 672599
Royal Welsh YC	Aernarfon	01286 672599
Royal Western YC	Plymouth	01752 226299
Royal Yacht Squadron	Isle of Wight	01983 292191
Royal Yorkshire YC	Bridlington	01262 672041
Rye Harbour SC		01797 223136
Salcombe YC		01548 842593
Saltash SC		01752 845988
Scalloway BC	Lerwick	01595 880409
Scarborough YC		01723 373821
Schull SC		+353 28 37352
Scillonian Sailing and BC	St Mary's	01720 277229
Seasalter SC	Whitstable	07773 189943
Seaview YC	Isle of Wight	01983 613268
Shoreham SC	Henfield	01273 453078
Skerries SC	Carlingdford Lough	+353 1 849 1233
Slaughden SC	Duxford	01728 689036
Sligo YC	Sligo	+353 71 77168
Solva Boat Owners Association	Fishguard	01437 721538
Solway YC	Kirkdudbright	01556 620312
South Caernavonshire YC	Abersoch	01758 712338
South Cork SC		+353 28 36383

YACHT CLUBS – YACHT VALETING

South Devon Sailing School	
Newton Abbot	01626 52352
South Gare Marine Club - Sail Section	
Middlesbrough	01642 505630
South Shields SC	0191 456 5821
South Woodham Ferrers YC	
Chelmsford	01245 325391
Southampton SC	023 8044 6575
Southwold SC	01986 784225
Sovereign Harbour YC	
Eastbourne	01323 470888
St Helier YC	01534 721307/32229
St Mawes SC	01326 270686
Starcross Fishing & CC (River Exe)	
Starcross	01626 891996
Starcross YC Exeter	01626 890470
Stoke SC Ipswich	01473 624989
Stornoway SC	01851 705412
Stour SC	01206 393924
Strangford Lough YC	
Newtownards	028 97 541202
Strangford SC	
Downpatrick	028 4488 1404
Strood YC Aylesford	01634 718261
Sunderland YC	0191 567 5133
Sunsail Portsmouth	023 92222224
Sussex YC	
Shoreham-by-Sea	01273 464868
Swanage SC	01929 422987
Swansea Yacht & Sub-Aqua Club	
Swansea	01792 469096
Tamar River SC	
Plymouth	01752 362741
Tarbert Lochfyne YC	01880 820376
Tay Corinthian BC	
Dundee	01382 553534
Tay YCs Association	01738 621860
Tees & Hartlepool YC	01429 233423
Tees SC	
Aycliffe Village	01429 265400
Teifi BC - Cardigan Bay	
Fishguard	01239 613846
Teign Corinthian YC	
Teignmouth	01626 777699
Tenby SC	01834 842762
Tenby YC	01834 842762
Thames Estuary YC	01702 345967
Thorney Island SC	01243 371731
Thorpe Bay YC	01702 587563
Thurrock YC Grays	01375 373720
Tollesbury CC	01621 869561
Topsham SC	01392 877524
Torpoint Mosquito SC -	
Plymouth	01752 812508
Tralee SC	+353 66 7136119
Troon CC	01292 311190
Troon YC	01292 315315
Tudor SC Portsmouth	023 92662002
Tynemouth SC	
Newcastle upon Tyne	0191 2572167
Up River YC	
Hullbridge	01702 231654
Upnor SC	01634 718043
Vanguard SC	
Workington	01228 674238
Wakering YC Rochford	01702 530926
Waldringfield SC	
Woodbridge	01394 283347
Walls Regatta Club	
Lerwick	01595 809273
Walton & Frinton YC	
Walton-on-the-Naze	01255 675526
Warrenpoint BC	028 4175 2137
Warsash SC Soton	01489 583575
Watchet Boat Owner Association	
Watchet	01984 633736
Waterford Harbour SC	
Dunmore East	+353 51 383389
Watermouth YC	
Watchet	01271 865048
Wear Boating Association	
	0191 567 5313
Wells SC	
Wells-next-the-sea	01328 711190
West Kirby SC	0151 625 5579
West Mersea YC	
Colchester	01206 382947
Western Isles YC	01688 302371
Western YC	
Kilrush	+353 87 2262885
Weston Bay YC	
Portishead	07867 966429
Weston CC Soton	02380 466790
Weston SC Soton	02380 452527
Wexford HBC	+353 53 22039
Weymouth SC	01305 785481
Whitby YC	07786 289393
Whitstable YC	01227 272942
Wicklow SC	+353 404 67526
Witham SC Boston	01205 363598
Wivenhoe SC	
Colchester	01206 822132
Woodbridge CC	01394 386737
Wormit BC	01382 553878
Yarmouth SC	01983 760270
Yealm YC	
Newton Ferrers	01752 872291
Youghal Sailing Club	+353 24 92447

YACHT DESIGNERS

Cannell & Associates, David M	
Wivenhoe	01206 823337
Clarke Designs LLP, Owen	
Dartmouth	01803 770495
Giles Naval Architects, Laurent	
Lymington	01590 641777
Harvey Design, Ray	
Barton on Sea	01425 613492
Jones Yacht Design, Stephen	
Warsash	01489 576439
Wharram Designs, James	
Truro	01872 864792
Wolstenholme Yacht Design	
Coltishall	01603 737024

YACHT MANAGEMENT

Barbican Yacht Agency Ltd	
Plymouth	01752 228855
Coastal Leisure Ltd	
Southampton	023 8033 2222
O'Sullivan Boat Management	
Dun Laoghaire	+353 86 829 6625
Swanwick Yacht Surveyors	
Swanwick	01489 564822
Amble Boat Company Ltd	
Amble	01665 710267

YACHT VALETING

Autogleam	
Lymington	0800 074 4672
Blackwell, Craig	
Co Meath	+353 87 677 9605
Bright 'N' Clean	
South Coast	07789 494430
Clean It All	
Nr Brixham	01803 844564
Kip Marina Inverkip	01475 521485
Mainstay Yacht Maintenance	
Dartmouth	01803 839076
Mobile Yacht Maintenance	
	07900 148806
Shipshape Hayling Is	023 9232 4500